Rock in the Musical Theatre

Rock in the Musical Theatre

A Guide for Singers

Joseph Church

OXFORD
UNIVERSITY PRESS

Oxford University Press is a department of the University of Oxford. It furthers the University's objective of excellence in research, scholarship, and education by publishing worldwide. Oxford is a registered trade mark of Oxford University Press in the UK and certain other countries.

Published in the United States of America by Oxford University Press
198 Madison Avenue, New York, NY 10016, United States of America.

CIP data is on file at the Library of Congress
ISBN 978-0-19-094347-9 (pbk.)
ISBN 978-0-19-094346-2 (hbk.)

Contents

Foreword

"Can you sing something from your audition book, preferably a pop/rock song?"

As a music director, I have asked this question countless times when screening performers. I've also been known to say things like "I'd prefer to hear something not from a Broadway show."

I make this request of actors because pop and rock are the genres that are closest to my heart, and probably as a result, they're the styles most closely associated with the projects I work on. Even if the score for a musical favors some specific offshoot of rock music, such as hip-hop, salsa, etc., to me, rock 'n' roll is the springboard most modern popular music comes from. Rock 'n' roll, and the many genres it has given birth to over seventy years, is also the language of most new Broadway musicals, so I often ask actors to sing things from the Top 40 charts rather than show tunes in order to test if they are fluent in a pop/rock vernacular.

Rock and pop styles are hard to fake in a song. If your performance doesn't have those subtle nuances pertinent to each genre—those scoops, those straight tones, and especially those rhythms and grooves—it's a dead giveaway that you're not well-versed in performing in the idiom. Having listened to pop and rock and all their extensions all my life, it bothers me when someone sings a style inauthentically. This is especially true in a theatrical context. If a performance is not stylistically right, I have a hard time being transported to that heightened place where I can forget where I am and just go on a journey with the storyteller in front of me. I contend that the same goes for casual listeners who are not musically trained; they will not be fully "elevated" because something seems out of place, even if they can't pinpoint what it is.

Why do pop and rock appeal to us so much? And why have they made their way into the theatre? My theory is that they inherently contain elements of tension and release that provide musical and dramatic satisfaction. You can see it in the composition: the typical form of a rock song sets up a verse (tension and build), which may lead to a pre-chorus (pulling even tighter), which will eventually land on a chorus (release, drop, and land). You can especially hear it in the vocalism: as the melody builds through the form and arrives at a peak where the singer stretches to the upper limits of his or her range, you can feel that tension, and you can savor it. A breathy tone could make you feel as if you're floating away on a cloud, while a touch of well-placed vibrato can intensify an emotion, or just convince me that a singer is confident with his or her technique. A song might have bold syncopations (friction! non-conformity!) or it might have square-on-the-beat rhythms (stability! reinforcement!). Either way, when written and performed well, it will just simply feel good and *right* to both the listener and the performer. It's important for singers to know more than just a thing or two about how to interpret style and how to maximize as actors and musicians all the native conflict and resolution in rock music.

It makes me so happy that Joseph Church has written this book. It feels like a gift to have a printed guide penned by a musician that has his level of Broadway experience *and* pedagogy. Joe was my first mentor when I got to New York City, and our connection was forged by our mutual loves for pop and rock, from the Beatles to Stevie Wonder to the Who to Billy Joel.

"Joe Church knows his stuff; he's the real deal." I've been saying that since I met him twenty-one years ago, and I will continue to say it to anyone who'll listen.

This book sheds light on techniques that are not commonly talked about in higher education, at least not by a connoisseur of Joe's expertise. His text will explain things that are not usually explained, and it will codify and put to words things that might seem intangible and ephemeral. Thankfully for us, the book is thorough in its descriptions, and it's written with a deep passion about its topic. With this textbook, Joe is merging his love of music and of theater and of teaching, all within a subject that could frankly use more words written about it.

I'm delighted to think that with the knowledge he's imparting, Joe will help singer-actors imbue their performances with more authenticity, more musicality, and more skill. These are the keys to honesty and truth in the telling stories they're sharing on stage, and truth in performance is what makes for the transcendent experience we as listeners hope for when we experience musical theatre.

Alex Lacamoire

Author's Note and Acknowledgments

Outside the St. James Theater in New York City in 1994, two women "of a certain age," avid theatregoers, chat excitedly before a Wednesday matinee. They know little about the musical they are about to see, having been brought in from out of state on a "Broadway Afternoon" tour with a busload of similarly ebullient but slightly confused older patrons. But the pair are impressed by the bright bumblebee yellow of the show's logo on the marquee and a familiar first name in its title. One says to the other, "Oh, I do hope Tommy Tune is in this. I love him."

This was a tale told to me at the time by the drummer for that show (I was the music director), who had overheard it on his way to work that day. The show, as the reader may have figured out, was *Tommy—The Who's Tommy*, that is—a musical far from the all-singing, all-dancing extravaganza that the audience might have expected to see that afternoon. *The Who's Tommy* was, in fact, an all-singing, all-dancing musical, just not in the way many people had until then associated with the Broadway stage. *Tommy* and the other rock and pop shows and songs we will look at in the coming chapters were part of a natural progression of stage musicals from the traditional to the modernistic, a trend shared with all art forms through the second half of the last century. Musical theatre, conservative to a fault, has lagged behind, but here in 2019, it is catching up quickly.

When I was young, I had little interest in musical theatre, even though I grew up in New York City. No, I dreamed of being a rock star. Almost everyone in my age group did at some point in their lives, and kids still do. Grownups, too. Though it may sound like a platitude, rock truly was the revolutionary music of a generation, my generation, and it was something entirely new. It was part of the sweeping changes in culture, society, and politics that characterized the second half of the 1900s. I was a kid with a social conscience, living in an apartment overlooking Washington Sqaure Park, and with a passion for and some skill with music, so I was in the right place at the right time.

On weekends my musician friends and I would rent a cheap studio and do our best to jam on songs like "Whipping Post," "Free Bird," "Revolution," and "Whole Lotta Love," very badly, I'm sure. During the same period, I acted in and accompanied and wrote music for plays and musicals at school, and did my very first professional theatrical music direction job, gathering my rock band friends to go to the high school across the park and serve as the band for Paul Sills's *Story Theatre*—perhaps the very first "jukebox" rock musical. Nothing really changed for me in college or graduate school, where I studied classical music, played and studied the musicology of rock with my friends, and did shows as a music director, composer, pianist, and arranger. I have continued all of these pursuits professionally for many years.

The point of this biography? When rock music began to inundate the musical theatre, I was poised to jump in. And I got lucky, finding an old friend in the Broadway musical *Tommy*, a record album I had grown up with and whose songs I learned to play at the piano as a youngster. (Working on the show with Pete Townshend was close enough to the rock star dream come true for me.) I have worked on many rock musicals before and since then, original and jukebox musicals both, and as a music director, composer, and orchestrator I have had the opportunity to dissect rock music and its profligate styles even further. I have also observed how things work (and don't work) on the musical theatre stage, and behind the scenes.

Now that the majority of the music we hear on Broadway and beyond has a beat, and I mean a rock beat, not a jaunty 2-beat, it's time for this book. That the gap between worlds seems almost completely closed here in the 2018–19 theatre season is reflected in the buzz of the industry, as well as in ticket sales. What are arguably among the "hippest" shows ever written for Broadway—*The Book of Mormon, Hamilton*, and *Dear Evan Hansen*—dominate today's ticket sales and have fully engaged the tastes of millennials (as have less critically heralded musicals). *Hamilton*'s cast album even reached #1 on the rap and pop album charts, the first cast album to attain such blockbuster success as a recording.

Examining this new theatre music in detail and from a scholarly perspective is a venture into mostly uncharted territory. It is my daily activity as a professional and a professor, but writing it down is a different matter. I hope that in doing so I may at least shed new light on the subject, and help the reader gain a deeper understanding. I will not propose any sort of method; indeed, adherence to any single system of rehearsing or performing in the musical theatre is ill-advised. It was prior to the stylistic shift, as well, but is especially unwise given the current eclecticism of musical theatre material, and of rock music. Performing musical theatre will very often entail adapting to the unfamiliar, and no single approach could ever suffice in making all of its possible manifestations operate effectively.

My voice alone is not enough to sing this new song. I could not have written this book without the assistance and input of many learned colleagues from the academic and professional worlds. Discussions with Michael Cerveris, Chilina Kennedy, Lauren Nicole Chapman, and Tony Vincent, among others, all singers known for their rock theatre roles, completely altered how I viewed the subject matter, and provided the working performer's point of view. Interviews and conversations with noted music directors, especially Henry Aronson, Kenny Seymour, and Alex Lacamoire, and academicians, in particular Ana Flavia Zuim and Phil Galdston of New York University, Sariva Goetz from Emerson College, and Mark Allan Davis from San Francisco State University, were invaluably informative. Research assistants Benjamin Weiss and Alex Shelbourne worked tirelessly to gather and fact-check information, and I am in their debt. My friend and colleague Matthew J. Pool earns special thanks for seeing me to the finish with his masterful editing, formatting, and indexing. Norm Hirschy at Oxford University Press has stood by my side now through two books, and I am profoundly grateful for his support, encouragement, kindness, and expertise.

Above all, I thank the students and professionals whom I coached in preparation for this study and have worked with me through the years as a coach, professor, and music director. They have proved to me time after time that teaching is indeed learning.

Introduction

It hasn't been easy for rock music, a phenomenon that epitomizes and embodies rebellion, to find a home in the traditionalist world of musical theatre, especially on Broadway. Those in charge of the commercial theatre industry throughout the twentieth century—producers, theatre owners, investors, and so on—were not necessarily resistant to progressiveness and experimentation, they were just making sure that the mostly conservative tastes of their paying audience were catered to.

Up until now, that is. It seems we have reached a point when the theatre ticket-buying audience's individual and collective memories of the styles and sounds that used to define theatre songs have waned. New expectations and new tastes have replaced them, a result of the passage of time and the changing of the generational guard. Writers and producers have learned that the best way to speak to a modern audience is in a modern vocabulary and syntax. Though a full integration is likely never to occur—the musical theatre takes great pride in its past—the wide variety of genres we refer to as "rock" or "pop" are now the norm in theatre music.

One irrefutable reason for musical theatre's historical conservatism has been its demographics. The median age for a theatre ticket buyer hovers consistently in the late forties to mid-fifties, year after year. Expensive Broadway tickets are purchased most often by those who have sufficient funds to spend on themselves and their families, and they, therefore, are the target customers. (Theatre attendees seem now to be skewing to a younger age group,[1] but the figures on who is paying for the seats are not yet in.)

In addition, Broadway ticket buyers and producers are predominantly Caucasian. By contrast, much of the inception of and maturation of rock and pop styles can be traced to African, African American, Afro-Cuban, and various other Caribbean and Latin American sources and influences, and much of what we call rock music takes a decidedly anti–white establishment stance.

---

1. https://www.nytimes.com/2018/10/19/theater/broadway-league-theater-audience-demographics.html.

The musical tastes of theatregoers in the late twentieth century leaned toward the music of the mid-twentieth century, that is, music that predated rock. By the turn of the millennium, however, the baby boomers had become the ticket buyers, and they had grown up on various forms and shades of rock, pop, r&b, funk, soul, disco, and, later, rap and hip-hop. The tide was turning, although Broadway producers continued to mount and successfully market revivals from the "Golden Age" (1943–1970), and champion original shows with an old-fashioned musical palette.

The first signs of the stylistic shift in musical theatre appeared while the Golden Age musical was still in full force. Presaging what was to come, a spate of late 1960s "rock" musicals made headlines and turned heads with their original, counterculture tones of voice. Commercial rock music very slowly staked its claim to the musical theatre in the years to follow, and harder-edged rock music and urban styles crept in toward the end of the last century. It seems they are here to stay. In our current era of consumerism, the theatre is no longer a dinosaur, but an integral thread of popular culture and popular music, and a fertile source of income. An entirely new, musical theatre–loving generation has emerged, and the industry has responded.

Training programs for performance in the musical theatre have only recently begun to address the particular physical and intellectual demands of contemporary popular musical styles. Most performers are educated according to plans based in classical Western music, which only partly attend to the features and peculiarities of rock. Traditional approaches to rhythmic interpretation and reading notated music, for example, must be examined in a new light, as must acting and musical values that are based in rock culture outside of music.

The shift toward modernism in musical theatre's style and outlook is now reflected more and more in the way musical theatre is studied and taught. Rock music itself has also become the focus of new scholarly study and research, and many secondary school and university music programs now offer coursework in its history, theory, and aesthetics.

My intent in this book is to assist performers in handling this stylistic and aesthetic transformation, in history, theory, and practice. (I assume from the reader a basic knowledge of the history, practices, and technique of musical theatre, as well as at least a rudimentary understanding of music and singing.) As a professor, music director, and composer whose curriculum vitae favors progressive and pop-oriented musical theatre, and as someone whose life and career have roughly spanned the era about which I am writing, I hope to offer both advice and perspective.

The book contains annotated history, comparative analysis, theory, guidelines, and examples of instruction. Of course, in any performing art such as musical theatre, the best way to learn is by doing, and skill improves with experience.

Part I reports on the background of contemporary popular music and of rock music in the contemporary theatre. Also in this section is a discussion of what defines rock music, both alone and in comparison with theatre music. Application of the aesthetic and musical values of rock to musical theatre through technique and practice is the topic of Part II. As actors, musicians, and singers, what are the tools and methods that you can use to effectively assimilate modern characters and new musical styles into your performances? Are traditional approaches of acting and vocal production still useful? Lastly, in Part III, we'll continue to answer these questions through chronicles of coaching sessions and music direction situations.

Throughout the text I will offer many examples of songs from both the commercial rock and theatre rock arenas as illustrations. Many of these songs should be worthy additions to singers' performance repertoires and audition books, and certainly to their listening playlists. It should be an enjoyable exercise for musical theatre singers and their coaches to seek out further examples that correspond and relate to these songs. The appendix, a list of songs from the commercial rock world that might be of interest to musical theatre singers, recaps a partial listing of the songs mentioned in the text. I leave it to the reader to listen to and research all of these titles; doing so will contribute significantly to your education in this field, and it's fun, too.

By necessity, I will largely bypass one primary element of musical theatre, which is dance. Physical movement is a fundamental force in rock music, as well. It is formalized in the musical theatre as musical staging and choreography, which are as essential to storytelling as are songs. The physicality of rock is likewise crucial to successful performance in a rock theatre setting, but dancing to rock is not the same as dancing to jazz or classical music. Unfortunately, I have neither the knowledge nor the space to delve into movement as part of the discussion, important as it is. I may allude to it periodically, but will for the most part leave the topic to those better informed than I.

In my conversations with experts in the field in preparation for writing this book, I found that the lines of inquiry I had originally thought relevant were turning in an unexpected direction, one that revealed the true substance of my topic. My purpose changed from "how to rock out convincingly on stage" to "how to maintain the authenticity of rock while performing believably in a theatrical setting." Giving a convincing performance on stage, one that is *believable* to an audience (I will return to that italicized term countless times), one that an audience can identify and sympathize with, is the overriding goal; this can be true of music and theatre both, but it is central to musical theatre. Rock songs add additional obstacles to believability because their aesthetics and mechanics are so distinctive. The path through these obstacles is found in understanding and practice.

With apologies for casting stones, I have also learned a great deal from observing unconvincing rock performances, and assessing what was wrong. In the musical theatre, when everything is right, every audience member's awareness should cease, and his or her intellectual and emotional engagement should take over. However redundant it may sound, believable performances on stage allow audiences to more readily suspend their disbelief. It is my purpose to help the reader to achieve this most crucial end as a performer.

For performers (and for vocal instructors, coaches, and music directors), awareness and acknowledgment of the change in style is not enough, and much more than an imitative approach is required. Every participant in rock-based modern musical theatre is responsible for learning the nature and origins of rock, its history, its growth, and its enlarged, revisionist sociocultural scope. One would certainly not play Beethoven, or sing Sondheim, without knowing the world of the composer and his music. What's more, the rock material singers will encounter on the contemporary stage will be highly inclusive, representing worldwide influences and drawing from a deep pool of historical, intellectual, social, and aesthetic sources. Musical theatre music, despite its customary musical moderation, has always been open-minded, but now, with the inclusion of rock, it welcomes to its fold a class of music that was already quite adventurous, unselfconscious, and, in spite of its relatively short history, quite mature.

If any branch of rock music and its offshoots is unfamiliar to you, immerse yourself in it before you attempt to perform it. Immersion begins with listening to rock music, learning about rock history and its purveyors (not just artists, but songwriters, producers, record labels, and so on), and attending a lot of rock concerts. Hopefully this will be an enjoyable undertaking—and don't forget your earplugs.

Before moving forward, let's specify how I will use the terms "popular music," "rock 'n' roll," "rock," and "pop."

In this book, "popular music" will refer to the entirety of the commercial song literature intended for a mass market, beginning rather early in the twentieth century, and continuing through today. Songs written expressly for the theatre are excluded from this definition; they are intended to work as part of a show, and if they occasionally enter the mass popular music market, it is not usually by design (see chapter 1).

"Rock" metaphorically implies a hard, loud, steadfast sound, and indeed it was the harder, louder sound of "rock 'n' roll" that, early in the 1950s, instigated the entire rock movement. Thus, the term I will use in this book to refer to virtually all of the popular music written from that time onward will be "rock," unless, empirically, a song simply does not rock in any way. ("Strangers in the Night," a #1 hit from 1966, is not, for example, a rock song.) "Pop" in this book will denote a lighter shade of rock. (The term "popular music" is often abbreviated to "pop," but I find that a confusing shorthand.)

The vast majority of what I am calling "rock" is in some way influenced by rock 'n' roll. Original rock 'n' roll was an amalgam of, among other styles, country, blues, swing, and Afro-Caribbean music, as well as the mainstream popular songs that immediately preceded it. Rock 'n' roll began redirecting the popular music charts in the late 1950s, and many of its seminal qualities have persisted in various styles of popular music since then. Quite early in its lifetime, rock 'n' roll began to share its rhythm, attitude, and energy with more classically constructed melodies and harmonies, sophisticated lyrics, and aesthetic expeditions. Today, a panoply of popular music styles that rock 'n' roll initiated falls under the general classification of "rock."

It is important to note the inherent racism in the terminology, and in the history; rock 'n' roll is largely of non-white origins—rock 'n' roll's closest equivalent is the genre known in the 1950s as "rhythm and blues" (later abbreviated to r&b), recordings of which were "race records," marketed to non-whites. Its sound was patently co-opted by white artists and producers to widen its commercial potential. I hope that in exposing the bias I might be absolved of my use of the word "rock" to indicate all rock-related styles, including those that have been culturally misappropriated.

Lastly, a word about the word "aesthetic." You might be wondering what something as philosophical as an "aesthetic" is doing in a guidebook for theatre performers. The answer is vital to this book: comprehension of the aesthetic, or more accurately the different aesthetics, of rock, is crucial to the effective performance of rock songs. What "aesthetic" means, for the purpose of this study, is "a state of artistic being." We define and study each song (or any work of art) in at least three interconnected ways: first, as something existing on its own, unaffected by how we perceive it; second, as it exists in the context of a larger artistic and historical continuum; and third, as we view it critically, as analysts and practitioners. Once you have grasped the nature of a song on all of these levels, you are able to enact it and manipulate it with far greater ease, and with full justification. You'll find that philosophy, in the case of rock songs, converts readily to procedure.

To anyone who wants to know more about rock in the theatre, how it got there, how it works, and how to do it, this book is for you. I hope you find it informative and helpful, and, may I add, rock on!

History, Aesthetics, and Literature

Background and Rock Aesthetics

Background

The line between popular music and theatre music has always been blurry, and up until the second half of the twentieth century, was freely crossed. Many of the great standard popular songs of the first half of the twentieth century first appeared in musicals. Beginning in the 1960s, however, while musical theatre was still clinging tightly to its orthodoxy, popular music began to branch out into a wide variety of new genres and sub-genres, all sharing a common progenitor: "rock 'n' roll."

The divergence was quite pronounced. It took several years for musical theatre writers and producers to advance the sound and style of this musical revolution to the theatre stage, but gradually, they did. Until the 1980s, rock had gained only a very tenuous foothold in the Broadway theatre. By 1965, on the other hand, rock had overtaken the music world. Elvis Presley had already captivated music and film audiences alike, soul music was mainstream, and the forces of the British Invasion were storming the American popular music gates. That same year, the biggest hits on Broadway were *Hello, Dolly!*, *Fiddler on the Roof*, and *Man of La Mancha*.

In the present climate, the line is blurring once again, but now in new ways, including a tidal wave of "jukebox" musicals (shows built around the catalogue of a musical artist or artists) and pop music artists and writers creating (and sometimes starring in) musicals.

A generation of performers who are far removed from rock's origins, yet are the direct product of rock's cultural prevalence, must now examine what lies beneath rock music: the revolutionary points of view and emotions that gave rise to it, the musical trends and practices that came to define it, and how it in turn helped to define a new society and a new musical standard for the theatre.

The distinguishing features of popular songs of the first half of the twentieth century were the supremacy of melody and clearly declaimed lyrics, and the relationship between music and lyrics. The songs of Cole Porter, Lerner and Loewe, Rodgers and Hammerstein, and Stephen Sondheim, for example, all were musical-dramatic constructions with clever, attractive melodies that deepened the meaning of carefully chosen, often highly articulate lyrics. Unlike opera and art song of earlier centuries, in which composers freely manipulated text according to musical needs, the more populist approach of these newer songs put the words up front, and made them conversational and easily understandable. What had been high art was joining with folk art. (The instrumental and accompanimental content of these songs was important, as well, but usually it was eclipsed by the song itself and its vocal performance. Instrumental virtuosity during this era found an outlet in non-vocal music, primarily jazz. Later, the virtuosic elements of jazz, as well as arrangements and orchestrations masterful by any musical standards, made their way back into popular songs.)

Musicals, too, are a brand of folk art, at times elevated to more rarefied status. But musicals have their own special set of rules—not unbreakable, but common to most successful shows throughout the repertoire. Of paramount concern in creating a musical are, first, a believable, compelling, well-crafted story (or stories); and second, effective and immediate communication of that story. Added to this recipe is a variable measure of entertainment value. To some extent music operates in a musical as a design element, one that has the ability to be either very inconspicuous or very much in the forefront. The melodic and lyrical clarity of pre-rock era popular melodies and lyrics, and their arrangements (vocal, dance, and orchestral), suited the musical theatre stage perfectly.

Rock 'n' roll, what would shortly become rock, the epitome of modern folk art, coalesced in its earliest forms in the mid-1950s, perhaps earlier. Rock 'n' roll strikingly valued rhythm, and often self-expression, over melody or lyrics. The tune and the words were still important, but rock 'n' roll relaxed the rules that melodies must be classically shaped and words immediately intelligible. Within a decade or two of its arrival, rock music in its many burgeoning forms had unseated the "Great American Songbook" as the dynasty in power in popular music.

What first took the world by surprise was how the new music seemed deliberately contrary. It favored loud over soft, danger over safety, roughness over refinement, impudence over respectability, and vulgarity over urbanity. Rock 'n' roll's pronounced rhythms were frank expressions of bawdy fun and raw antipathy, and its sometimes salacious or hostile lyrics ranged from silly to suggestive to graphic. The primacy of rhythm and its visceral intent has filtered into the many genres of rock that have matured over the years and now coexist, even in its softer sides. Rock has proven staunchly true to its creed over time, revising itself to restore these qualities in reaction to any periodic diminishment of its overall outlook. As examples, new wave and punk followed soft rock, rap and hip-hop followed disco, and gangster rap followed rap.

In the present day, more than ever, musical theatre writers are heavily influenced by the rock songs that they grew up with, and that *their* parents grew up with—the cultural memory is now two generations deep. Some theatre songwriters try to create "crossover" songs that would be commercially viable outside their shows, in effect, restoring the bond between theatre music and popular music. ("Crossover" is a term borrowed from the popular music industry, where it is used to describe songs appearing on multiple sales charts.) At the same time, in jukebox musicals, songs that found commercial success on the pop charts are being absorbed into theatrical productions. Some of the writers of those songs are now writing for the musical theatre, or displaying their catalogues in a theatrical setting.

It is interesting, but not surprising, that despite the desire and skill of their writers, rock and pop theatre songs have seldom seen light on the popular music charts. There have been a very few exceptions: "I'll Never Fall in Love Again," "I Say a Little Prayer," "Day by Day," "Aquarius/Let the Sun Shine In," "Ease On Down the Road," Barbra Streisand's recording of "Memory," and Susan Boyle's cover of "I Dreamed a Dream." Yet no one song from *Hamilton* has been a "single" despite the full cast album's phenomenal success. The songs from the immensely popular *Grease* (1971)—a throwback musical, but a rock 'n' roll–based one—did not cross over until they were heard in the Hollywood film version of the show, and the huge success of Pasek and Paul's score and cast recording for *Dear Evan Hansen* was eclipsed by the runaway sales of their album sales for the songs in the film *The Greatest Showman*. Of course, theatre is still something of a cottage industry by comparison to popular music and cinema, and the music and film industries spend far more money on their products and their distribution.

Aside from the financial reasoning, this is because in the theatre, story, and sometimes choreographic or visual elements, will always take precedence over music. Nonetheless, rock music in the theatre and the themes and approaches that the rock aesthetic carries with it demand from performers a considerably modified and updated response to all of the prime directives of musical theatre: believability, clarity, and entertainment.

The delineation between popular songs and theatre songs lies in their mechanisms and in their content. (Specific and thorough comparisons are the topic of chapter 2.) Note, for instance, the simplicity of the lyrics in the theatre/rock crossover songs listed above. They are atypical of theatre songs, the great majority of which are textually more complex, or multilayered. This is not to say that popular songs are not lyrically sophisticated—many are, and became more so as rock evolved, but they do not necessarily carry the burden of character development and large-scale dramatic context (again, there are exceptions; many rock songs tell great stories). Rock songs that are deliberately simple and universal, however, are incapable of detailed musical storytelling in a dramatic or comedic setting. Obvious illustrations are repetitive refrains and nonsense syllables, or limited harmonic content. On the other hand, some theatre songs are quite simple. Of course, many are not, but always, their level of complexity rests on the needs of the story and the show, and not on musical choices or purely to please an audience.[1]

If as a musical theatre performer you pay too much attention to stylistic authenticity in musical theatre rock songs, you risk sacrificing effectiveness of storytelling. Inversely, working too hard to meet steadfast musical theatre standards of character and clarity might threaten the stylistic validity of a rock song. Along the same lines, some of the performance practices of rock are not by nature effective storytelling tools.

There is nothing wrong with a musical moment in the theatre that has only minimal dramatic value, nor is there anything wrong with a theatre song letting go of its rock identity long enough to make a story point. As evidence, over time, the gradient between rock and theatre music, both its creation and performance, has become very evenly and widely populated.

The solution for theatre singers almost always involves some sort of compromise (though there is room for the extremes, as well). Though I fear oversimplifying, the main problem lies in reconciling the informality, generality, and stylistic needs of rock songs with the meticulousness of the score of a musical. The key to believable performance lies in striking the appropriate stylistic and technical balance, on a case-by-case basis. As in all musicals, the balance is determined by the origin and purpose of the song and show, the setting in which it is sung, the character singing it, its contextual dramatic intent, and you, the singer who is singing it.

History of Rock in the Theatre

To find rock songs in the musical theatre, we can look back as early as Charles Strouse and Lee Adams's *Bye Bye Birdie* (1959), or some Burt Bacharach–Hal David and Lionel Bart songs of the early 1960s. As smart and catchy and "groovy" as these may have been, they were awkward attempts at rock. Rather, they sounded like the work of worldly, musically crafty adults trying to imitate the youthful exuberance and musical naïveté of rock 'n' roll, and that, in fact, was exactly what they were.

Later in the 1960s and throughout the 1970s, composers such as Liz Swados, Galt MacDermot, Charlie Smalls, and Marvin Hamlisch, among others, began to push outward at the boundaries of rock music in the theatre. The musical *Hair*, billed as "A Tribal Love-Rock Musical," debuted Off-Broadway at the Public Theatre in 1967. Its score, though quite theatrical, paraded the many colors of rock that were being heard in the mid-1960s: acid rock, Brit-pop, soul, white soul, folk, and others. Its patently counterculture attitude and allegiance to the values of the younger generation, as well its score, make *Hair* a landmark in the history of rock on the Broadway stage.

---

1. This is where many book musicals with jukebox scores tend to go wrong. The choice of song precedes the dramatic need, which may be fine for entertainment purposes, but not for storytelling.

In the 1970s, the biggest game-changers were Andrew Lloyd Webber, Stephen Schwartz, and, joining them a bit later, Alan Menken. Webber was the first. Shortly after the debut of *Hair*, he and lyricist Tim Rice introduced their *Jesus Christ Superstar*—a title no less self-confident than *Hair*'s subtitle—but this time, the music's dedication to the rock genre was full-on. The score was first released as a "concept" album, a popular format for rock artists exploring more grandiose formats. The songs in *Superstar* were shaped as rock songs, not theatre songs, songs that the drama (the Passion of Christ) is sung to, like a classical oratorio. Undisguised musical hooks and catchy grooves were as crucial as lyrical specifics and exploration of character through song.

Around the same time, a young Stephen Schwartz was setting his sights on a hippie-generation audience in shows such as *Godspell* (hot on the heels of the religious rock musical craze initiated by *Superstar*) and *Pippin*. Audiences of the 1960s and 1970s also enjoyed the shock value of musicals that featured onstage sexuality or nudity. In addition to *Hair, Oh! Calcutta!* and *Let My People Come* were surprise hits. Though Webber became more classically oriented as his career continued, these and other early rock shows, and to a lesser extent Webber and Rice's *Joseph and the Amazing Technicolor Dreamcoat* (an innocent nod to psychedelia in a biblical story), inspired a generation of writers. Just not that generation. The full effect was not realized until decades later.

The musical theatre dust bowl of the 1980s and 1990s might be explained by the growing gap between popular musical tastes and the Broadway age demographic. The often-empty Broadway boards in those years featured Sondheim, the more conservative Webber (including *Phantom of the Opera*, a classical-pop crossover score, and *Starlight Express*, a pretty hard rocker but a very forgettable musical), "mega-musicals" such as *Les Miserables* and the more rocking *Miss Saigon*, some lingering jazz and legit shows, as well as revival after revival from the archives. A small contingent of excellent rock-based musicals saved these decades from the stylistic abyss: *Dreamgirls; Little Shop of Horrors; Big River; Tommy; Bring In 'da Noise, Bring In 'da Funk; Rent;* and *Hedwig and the Angry Inch* (some of these were successful enough Off-Broadway to list them among the Broadway pantheon). *Big River* was among the first shows to employ a theatre outsider and pop artist (Roger Miller) as its songwriter, an idea that excited producer-director Des McAnuff to no end.

The revolution, or rather evolution, resumed with the entrance of Disney, and other large corporate production entities, onto the theatrical stage. The first of Disney's movie transfers was Alan Menken and Howard Ashman's *Beauty and the Beast* in 1994 (a mostly classical score, but with a pop tinge), followed by *The Lion King* in 1997 (a hybrid pop-rock–South African–cinema score), and later, to somewhat less acclaim and profit, several other familiar titles imported from Buena Vista and Dreamworks and other Hollywood players (*The Little Mermaid, Tarzan, Shrek*, etc.). These works began as legendary stories on film, usually animated (very artfully), and quite formulaically told. A good portion of their songs, and some entire scores, are pop and rock songs, yet they remain theatrical in their vivid mirroring of the settings and moods of their stories, and the characters acting them out on stage.

These films made up the video literature that much of America's youth of the time hungrily consumed from an early age. Their reincarnations as Broadway musicals funneled that same youthful audience to the theatre—for which their baby boom parents, now atop the demographic hump, bought the tickets. As the children grew up, their affinity for the theatre persisted, and their tastes ran to Elton John, Phil Collins, Menken, Schwartz, and other pop-savvy writers. *High School Musical* and later *Glee* intermingled television and the stage, and further cemented corporately financed musical theatre into its echo-boom demographic. On- and Off-Broadway, we heard more and more catchy pop songs, and on television singing contests like *American Idol*, we began to hear "show tunes."

By 2000, most new musicals were affirming the stylistic shift. The rhythmic, melodic, and formal influences of rock music were nearly pervasive, even in less rock-native scores. The musical trend had turned into a principle, but the antiestablishment nature of the stories told on stage took a bit longer to catch up.

Over time, a movement toward themes with more original and serious contexts emerged, especially youth-oriented ones—themes of alienation, mental illness, social conscience, and sexual identity, for example—going along with the shift in music, perhaps driving it further, but more likely riding the tide of popular culture and its fascination with things risky, scandalous, sensational, outrageous, and most important, novel. Ideas such as these are the stuff of rock 'n' roll. Rock's proud antagonism and individualism began to overtake the dramatic content of musicals, as it did its music. The new wave has now flooded the landscape, and rock culture, or at least a credible version of it, is now Broadway culture, as well.

Also around the turn of the millennium, producers increasingly began to assemble the catalogues of popular music writers and artists into jukebox musicals. Revues were not a new form, nor was the concentration around a songwriter's collected works as a theme, but rock was a new direction, and a new audience to tap, with revised values and new ways of experiencing entertainment. (So far, many attempts have been prone to failure: *The Times They Are A-Changin'*, *All Shook Up*, *Escape from Margaritaville*, *Head over Heels*, and several others underperformed at the box office, and garnered little critical support.)

Seeing the potential for a creative outlet and source of income, and in spite of Broadway's well-known financial risk factor, popular songwriters themselves began to flock to the theatre: Dolly Parton (*9 to 5*), Cyndi Lauper (*Kinky Boots* and, in progress, *Working Girl*), Bono and the Edge (*Spiderman: Turn Off the Dark*), Bryan Adams and Jim Vallance (*Pretty Woman*), and even pop hitmaker Max Martin (*& Juliet*). Despite some failures along the way, overall, the movement is succeeding. The counterculture is now fully assimilated, and commercialized. It is no longer "counter-," but conventional.

In the face of the stylistic change, musical theatre has rightfully refused to relinquish its unique demands.[2] With the intent of reaching a wide audience at the same time as fulfilling its primary theatrical mission, a good portion of post-2000 theatre music has staked a claim to a musical middle ground between authentic pop/rock and its own story-specific voice. Many musicals hover at the edge of rock, without going all the way: works such as Jason Robert Brown's *The Last Five Years* and *Songs for a New World*, Jeanine Tesori and Lisa Kron's *Fun Home*, and Larry O'Keefe and Nell Benjamin's *Bat Boy*, among others. One might also designate a genre of "MOR (middle-of-the-road) theatre pop." This is a musically and stylistically unadventurous pop-rock sound that employs theatrical techniques (such as introductory verses, tempo and meter shifts, deliberately conversation-like lyrics, and so on), but is otherwise familiar and without much character of its own, and without a strong relationship to the subject matter. It has been used in all sorts of dramatic settings, and is commonplace in many original amateur, school, camp, and church musicals, and has occasionally found its way to Broadway. Yet when thoughtfully handled and placed in an appropriate setting, even this contemporary pop pastiche can be communicative, as in the riotous *Avenue Q*. At the other stylistic extreme are a few shows that plunge headlong into hard rock styles and prize originality in their sound: *Bloody, Bloody Andrew Jackson*; *Spring Awakening*; and *Be More Chill* among them.

History confirms that theatre music is able neither to entirely shed its identity nor to abandon its restrictions. Instead, it has co-opted significant aspects of rock and pop to add to its vocabulary, and otherwise reworked the new musical language to suit its own needs. Rock music has always manipulated its tone of voice to please its audiences, and to sell records. Theatre music, which by nature is also malleable and commercial, has benefited greatly from such manipulations. There are still some theatre professionals resistant to the change in style, and some who seem to believe that rock cannot, by nature, succeed on the theatre stage.[3] Even they seem unable to stem the tide.

Rock Aesthetics

Simple as the music may seem on its surface, rock's aesthetic underpinnings are quite complex. Rock music exists, that is to say, it comes into being, in three ways, interactive with one another. There are two forms of performance, live and recorded, and there is oral tradition. To some extent, live performance is what is captured on a recording, although modern recording techniques now allow almost any musical inaccuracy of any kind to be eliminated, and very few of today's studio-recorded performances would qualify as "live." Some aestheticians consider the essence of rock to be in its recorded form, which may be more accurate with regard to recordings made before digital technology was available,

---

2. https://www.americantheatre.org/2016/03/18/rap-broadways-new-jazz/.

3. For example, https://www.hollywoodreporter.com/review/black-suits-theater-review-654528.

but their opinion also discounts live performance as a significant segment of the rock industry's appeal and profitability.

Rock songs tend to be identified with their performers rather than their authors. The modern popular music landscape has long been dominated by megastars who set the taste for and the performance practices of popular music. Still, rock songs can be sung by anyone, at a concert, around a campfire, or in one's bedroom or classroom. They can be recorded and replayed, or they can be taught to someone else, who can then recreate them. They can be stored in a human or electronic memory bank and saved for later. Rock is the essence of populist art.

Rock music is not by nature written down, and therefore is not always precisely codified. Recording or formal orchestration not only codifies certain performances but makes certain recordings definitive of the song itself. Today's musical theatre performers learn songs by hearing them performed live, watching YouTube videos, or listening to them on a handheld device, as often as they do by reading sheet music. These are revised forms of oral tradition.

Rock was both a product and a determinant of modern history, and of the on-coming information age. It resonated with the children of the baby boom, and again with their children, awakening a strong sense of freedom and primitivism, long dormant in the refined musical output of the classical and early popular eras. The notion of "music for a younger generation" is nothing new. Since the onset of modern Western music, that is, music created as intellectual exercise or entertainment (around 1700), most musical revolts have been instigated by younger writers. Such is the typical progression of ideas and art. The rock 'n' roll uprising, though, was exceptionally disruptive, for three primary reasons.

First was *technology*. Beginning in the mid-twentieth century, it became far easier to disseminate music to a wide audience, first through various recorded media and later via the Internet. Nowadays, a song or artist can enjoy literally overnight success. Technology also defined the original sonic palette of rock music, and turned up its volume. Rock was sung into microphones, and its instruments were amplified. Later, synthesizers, sampling, and looping became permanently ensconced in the timbres of rock.

Second was the extremism of the *cultural and societal shifts* that coincided with and propelled the musical rebellion. Many baby boomers grew up advocating political and social viewpoints diametrically opposed to those of the "establishment," which included their parents and government. Their generation produced a musical style and a lyrical approach that symbolized their antipathy. Rock became the standard-bearer for the forces of the "revolution."[4] Songs, more than any other art form, were able to reach and incite an entire population. What's more, their lyrics, at their best, were folk art at its finest; many

---

4. One might interpret this as the modern, intellectually based counterpart of an army marching with its drummers in front to frighten the enemy, a practice since primitive times.

critics lauded them as a new brand of poetry.[5] The aesthetics of rock extend beyond any assessment of it as an entity of feeling and thought, beyond its musical substance, and into its political overtones and its influence on other art forms, and into its rampant and enduring commercial appeal.

The insurgence, however, was most apparent in the *sound*. Rock was loud, energized, electric, explicit, and it was drum- and bass- and guitar-heavy. Folk music was quieter, but just as blunt and brusque. Early rock 'n' roll also assimilated and prominently featured its Afro-Caribbean and Latin roots, which to many listeners of the time were quite foreign or even objectionable sounds. The words, when at all intelligible or meaningful, seemed to have a lot to do with dancing and sex and breaking the rules. This was a noteworthy departure from the melodic, diatonic, gently rhythmic songs popular since 1900, with their genteel subject matter, clever, clearly enunciated lyrics, and amenable musical tone.

The spirit behind rock 'n' roll was inherently audacious and unrestrained. It originated as a challenge to the ordinary and to authority. It did not camouflage its attempts to summon and stimulate feelings that were primitive, prurient, illicit, uncontrolled, and unfamiliar, nor did it hide its intent to evince in the listener insurrection, individualism, and raw animalism. Or so said its opponents, anyway—and its adherents and practitioners were more than happy to agree. The image of a rock musician as an attractive outsider, a free thinker, a cool character, a rebel, even an outlaw, led to the notion of the "rock star" or "pop star" as a cultural and commercial idol, and instituted an apparently inextinguishable bounty.

At first, the new music was also decidedly masculine, although early rock 'n' roll had several female purveyors (songs by Big Mama Thornton are frequently cited as being among the earliest examples of rock 'n' roll), and there have been successful female rock performers and writers all along. In the commercial rock scene overall, however, women took longer than men to make their entrance, possibly because of rock's intrinsic machismo and objectification of women (more prevalent and blatant now than ever in modern pop and hip-hop).

Partly because rock music so swiftly overtook other styles as the focus of a young generation, and partly as a consequence of its longevity, it has multiplied over time into what are now countless variants, genres, and sub-genres, all with additional aesthetics. All are to some extent the offspring of earlier musical traditions. Rock is intrinsically derivative of itself, carefully balancing conformity and expectation with originality and experimentation, so as not to lose its audience, always keeping them engaged.[6] In all but the very tamest of its offshoots, the spirit of defiance and resistance is still evident.

5.   Theodore Gracyk excludes lyrics in his well-known assessment of the aesthetics of rock; I cannot see how they are separable from the music. Nor could critic Richard Goldstein, in his now-forgotten landmark anthology, *The Poetry of Rock* (New York: Bantam Books, 1969).

6.   Richard Meltzer, in his underground classic *The Aesthetics of Rock* (New York: Da Capo Press, 1970), delights in pointing out similarities, obvious and not, among diverse groups of rock songs.

Furthermore, all rock songs somehow reveal their strong roots in blues, country, Latin, and African American music. These antecedents came brimming with passion, and often encumbered with pain. Musically, they lend to rock their blues scales and other modalities, their improvisational tendencies, their constancy of rhythm, and many other musical and textual qualities (see chapters 2 and 4).

Ultimately, the rock aesthetic might best be expressed in terms of an outlook, and best explained by example. It shares too much with all other types of song to warrant complete aesthetic separation. The rock aesthetic is manifest in attitude, demeanor, and points of view, and in the brash, populist musical and lyrical declarations of its songs.

From its beginnings, rock has usually been outspoken, noncompliant, or defiant, in songs such as "Jailhouse Rock," "Hound Dog," "Summertime Blues," and "Good Golly, Miss Molly." Even the Beatles' "Birthday" is a counterattack on the usual jolly songs of celebration. And yes, the grown-ups were right. Rock 'n' roll music was, quite often, all about s-e-x. Big Joe Turner's early rock 'n' roll classic "Shake, Rattle, and Roll" contains the suggestive "I'm a one-eyed cat peepin' in a seafood store," Marvin Gaye sang of "Sexual Healing," and the Captain and Tenille implored, "Do That to Me One More Time," while the Beatles simply asked, "Why Don't We Do It in the Road?"

Of course, many rock songs deal with the same timeworn subjects in the same timeworn ways that songs always have. Love and amorous relationships have been the most common themes among songs in all styles since Schubert churned out Lieder to Romantic poetry. Like art song, it also elevates heartbreak ("Wicked Game," "Until You Come Back to Me," "Without You I'm Nothing," etc.) and despair ("When a Man Loves a Woman," "I Wanna Know What Love Is," "Ain't Too Proud to Beg"). Yet the joy of love as expressed in rock songs is often more innocent and less cynical than the double-edged love songs of the Great American Songbook. This too, was a form of rebellion, an indication of the return to less complicated and institutionalized ways of loving, epitomized in the "free love" movement of the late 1960s, and exemplified in songs such as "Faithfully," "Cherish," "I Got You Babe," and many others.

Rock also pulls no political punches, and even from a softer stance delivers jabs. There are songs that are quietly determined, sometimes understated and sometimes direct: "Ohio," "For What It's Worth," "Mercy Mercy Me," "Rich Man's War," "One of Us," and "Silent All These Years" are fine examples. Tempo, volume, and aggressiveness step up in "Killing in the Name," "Fight the Power," "War," "Won't Get Fooled Again," and many others. Rock is not always contrary, yet brings a strong sense of individualism and resistance to all of its subject matter. In protest, it ranges from the idealism of "Get Together," "Imagine," and "A Change Is Gonna Come," to the resignation of "Holler If Ya Hear Me," "Born in the U.S.A.," and "Dance with the Devil." Storytelling with a similarly delinquent or edgy point of view characterizes songs such as "Mother's Little Helper," "Hurricane," "The Ballad of Billy the Kid," "Folsom Prison Blues," "Space Oddity," and "Stan."

When rock songs turn to milder and subtler sentiments, their tone usually softens accordingly, and they are likely to be more popular with older and more conservative audiences (these songs are usually designated as "pop" rather than "rock"). Songwriters and artists of this variety include Barry Manilow, Neil Diamond, the Carpenters, John Denver, Elvis Presley (his ballads, at least), many of the Brill Building contingent, among them Carole King, Gerry Coffin, Barry Mann, and Cynthia Weil, and their counterparts in the 1970s, Diane Warren, Carole Bayer Sager, Peter Allen, Marvin Hamlisch, and others. These songs were first dubbed "Adult Contemporary," and later, updated (to include rhythm & blues) to "Urban Adult Contemporary." The names on the above list represent some of the most skilled and successful writers and artists of their era, and though their songs are more conservative than others, they are no less inspired by the rock aesthetic than are harder rockers. Their output merely reflects the writers' individual personalities and talents, the trends of their times and surroundings, and the paths of their careers. Also no less musically adept, and no less a part of the rock multitude, are musicians creating various forms of electronic rock and dance music, from ABBA in the 1970s, to Depeche Mode in the 1980s, to EDM in the 1990s, to Radiohead in the 2000s, and to Daft Punk in the 2010s.

In most rock songs music and lyrics correspond in tone, or in some way are suited to one another. The consistency is apparent in low-key jewels such as "Both Sides Now," "Sweet Baby James," or "Like a Rolling Stone," as well as in higher-energy exclamations such as "Smells Like Teen Spirit," "Black Dog," or "Back in Black." Sometimes, though, gentle feelings expressed in a lyric turn to their music to convey a subtextual posture or attitude, as in "Just the Two of Us," "Fall to Pieces," or "Alone." Conversely, some very edgy lyrics are accompanied by very light music, as in "Physical," "Superstar," or "What a Fool Believes."

Rock artists like to push against musical boundaries even within simple statements, such as the Beach Boys' "God Only Knows," a masterpiece of arrangement and form; the Beatles' "Strawberry Fields Forever" and "A Day in the Life," the Who's "Baba O'Riley," "Roundabout," by Yes, and more recently, much of the output of Kendrick Lamar and J. Cole. Others of these excursions result in grandiose structures like "Nights in White Satin," "MacArthur Park," "New York City Serenade," "Bohemian Rhapsody," and "2112."

In addition, the rock aesthetic, and the rock industry, comfortably house and incorporate music of other cultures. Latin artists such as Santana, Ricky Martin, and Jennifer Lopez and reggae stars such as Bob Marley and Jimmy Cliff have reached the top of the rock charts, and K-pop (Korean dance music) is a multi-million-dollar success story. Hip-hop freely quotes anything that strikes its fancy and suits the lyric. Ska, made popular by the Police, the Pretenders, and others, was a style that blended reggae and rock. Sting and Paul Simon have brought Celtic, South African, and Brazilian music to the forefront of their songs. George Harrison's musical career was rejuvenated after his dalliance in Indian music and religion. Sweden, as well, has had a global influence on pop music for decades, from ABBA to Max Martin (né Martin Sandberg).

Rock music is today an eclectic mix of approaches, forms, and attitudes, descendants of the original, subversive style and worldview. Its aesthetic is now a collection of aesthetics, all subdivisions of and variations on rock's original countercultural essence and rhythm-based sound.

Rock's open-mindedness is a perfect fit in modern drama, so it is no wonder that rock is at the heart of today's musical theatre. In addition to their musical eclecticism, musicals quite often highlight characters who are somehow distinctive, or seek distinction, who swim against the tide, or whose relationships are a source of conflict by virtue of being unacceptable or unlikely. Iconic characters such as Billy Bigelow and Julie Jordan snub their noses at authority, and sacrifice their jobs for a romance that has not yet happened. Nellie Forbush and Emile de Becque, Tuptim and Lun Tha, Sky Masterson and Sarah Brown, and Harold Hill and Marian Paroo all pursue forbidden passions. Iconic characters of the musical theatre have always worked through obstacles posed by established norms to achieve objectives that highlight their individualism. That's what rockers do, too; that's why they're rocking. Bucking romantic, political, and societal norms has always made for excellent drama, and is also at the heart of the rock aesthetic.

The runaway success of *Hamilton* is evidence that full-on commitment to a rock-based aesthetic is not only possible, but can be brilliantly theatrical, and commercial. It's been evident in other recent Broadway shows, like *Once* and *Natasha and Pierre and the Great Comet of 1812*. *Hamilton*'s cast of characters is made up of the theatrical equivalent of rock stars. So are *Rent*'s, and *Wicked*'s, and *The Lion King*'s, and those of several other shows. Again, however, it is important to state that merely acting like a rock star while playing a part is not enough ("Hey, look, Ma, I'm rocking!"). The key is in conscientiously attending to the rock aesthetic while simultaneously accomplishing one's theatrical goals. It's a matter of balance, and each song and each performer are different.

The innovative musicals of the past, from *Carousel* to *Guys and Dolls* to *Fiddler* to *Company*, and many less exceptional ones as well, will undoubtedly endure in the repertoire. Upcoming generations of theatregoers will likewise adopt material that belongs exclusively to their era. Rock musicals already loom large in today's public eye, shows such as *Waitress, Dear Evan Hansen, School of Rock, Beautiful, Hamilton,* and *Wicked*; some of them are already staples of the repertoire: *Next to Normal, Spring Awakening, Rock of Ages, Mamma Mia!, Hairspray*, and more.

Modern-day theatre performers take heed: more than likely, a role that you play will entail upholding a rock aesthetic within the specific circumstances of a production or song. Jukebox musicals may soon be as commonplace as book musicals. You'll need to understand what influenced the songwriters as they wrote their songs, and the cultural and political climate from which the songs, the story, and the writers emanate. You'll want to explore, as you always do, the relationship of music and the lyrics, but from a rock-based and rock-informed perspective, and know the musical literature that inspired the style and content. Your explorations might leave you with many questions, such as: what makes a song a rock song, and what sort of rock language does the song speak? Will my vocal production be different when singing rock? Is improvisation permitted, and if so, where do I start? We will look for answers in the chapters to come.

2

Popular Song vs. Theatre Song

To begin comparing theatre songs and popular songs, let's just list the qualities of *song*, any song.

Songs, by definition, are sung. Just about everyone sings, and for an endless variety of reasons.

Songs are an ancient phenomenon, an inherently human phenomenon, and a nearly universal phenomenon. They are part of our psychology. In many ways they are an extension of speech and physicality. Music on its own is quasi-linguistic and abstract; adding text to it and forming it into a song brings it much closer to organized language and realism.

People create songs. Sometimes they do it deliberately, to express something, and sometimes they do it unconsciously, like humming. Songs range from very spontaneous to carefully, artfully crafted.

A song has a melody of some sort, and most songs have an accompaniment to that melody. Most melodies have words, which take many forms. Some are like conversation, some are poetic, and some are mere nonsense.

Melody merges with a lyric either through the setting words of to music, or by assigning words to an existing melody. Quite often, lyrics and melody are created simultaneously. Many songs are able to survive with their melodies or even accompaniments isolated. Once a song is well known, its lyric is, in a sense, optional, or implicit.

Songs have limited forms and limited durations; some are very simple, some quite involved, but none goes on for too long. (There are some exceptions.)

Each song is a unique entity, with a unique identity, regardless of its origin or genre, and even when it is derivative of another song.

Songs can be shared freely and performed in any number of ways, both in their original versions, and in ways their originators might not have thought of. The most reliable gauge of the effectiveness and success of a song is holding a permanent or long-term place in the repertoire, or in the collective consciousness.

Not so much a quality, but an axiom, and something crucial in both theatre songs and popular songs: the most effective songs are those that seem most natural, most believable, as composed, and when sung. The best songs seem as if they had written themselves.

Contemporary Popular Songs

What, then, makes a song a popular song?

A popular song is a song for sale, one that music consumers consume. Beyond its definitive song-ness, that is its essence. Fortunately, human beings are innately creative and communicative, and making popular songs is an outlet for artistry as well as a way of making money. Other than live performance, sheet music represented the first mass means of profitable distribution for popular songs, early in the 1900s. Recordings became the preferred medium shortly thereafter (wax discs through 78s, 45s, LPs, cassettes, 8-tracks, CDs, and all the rest). Now, most songs have been digitized and are up there in the Cloud, for all consumers to enjoy at minimal cost (and much to the detriment of songwriters' annual incomes).

From the outset, composers and lyricists felt right at home in the new frontier of popular song. This was partly in response to years of serious classicism. A song could be a compact and diverting treatment of any number of easily mined thematic resources. Love, laughter, heartbreak, tales of pretty girls and handsome men, nature, society, familiar turns of phrase, newly coined phrases, jokes, fads—all were fair game as ideas for song-making and song-selling. Everyone got in the act, from serious composers to amateurs. Irving Berlin, the most prolific and successful songwriter of his time, was barely musically literate. (This does not mean songs are easy to write; in fact, they are quite tricky, largely due to their simplicity and concision.)

Performers and audiences were no less enamored of the new songs, first snapping up vocal folios, and later, recordings and subscriptions to music streams. Simultaneously, vocalists specializing in the delivery of those songs grew into huge stars, generating even more songs from writers. Radio and television were the perfect media to bring these now very *popular* works to an increasingly wide range of listeners. Recorded music gradually became more technologically sophisticated and affordable. New styles of music were always the product of and the darlings of younger generations, but never were those phenomena more pronounced than during the baby boom, when millions of young adults eagerly awaited adding the next hit single or album to their record libraries.

The emergence of rock 'n' roll marked a singular turning point. Though to twenty-first-century ears, the recordings made in the 1950s may sound entirely outdated, there were two revolutionary elements that set these songs apart. First, the musicians that accompanied these songs used drum kits and amplified instruments, and therefore the microphone levels on the vocalists had to increase to be heard over the band. Second, the melodies of many of these songs interacted with the unremitting rhythmic pulse. The vocalist was a participant in creating the rhythm of the song, or its "groove." These innovations will prove central to singing rock material on the musical theatre stage.

The newly fortified, energized, more rhythmic sound palette had a potent appeal to adolescents, teens, and young adults, especially when hopped up on hormones or intoxicants. They, and soon their parents, too, danced the night away to transistor radios, jukeboxes, and 45s on their record players. Lyrics were simplistic at first, but gradually took on more meaning and import, and in the 1960s connected further with the political and social consciousness of an outspoken younger generation. People were listening harder to the words and thinking of them as poetry, political statements, or as a source of comfort and empathy, and they would treasure lyrics as their own expressions of feeling. FM radio and the LP format provided a new forum for "progressive rock" or "album cuts," songs not aimed at the top 40.

Whether as a corollary or as a result, songwriters started to look beyond simple musical and lyrical ideas, and enthusiastically explored all avenues open to them. The mainstays of rock 'n' roll remained, things such as rhythmic and harmonic patterns, blues-based improvisation, call-and-response, stylized vocal arrangements, and many others. But now rock welcomed in new ideas: jazzy riffing and soloing, metrical irregularities, unusual chord progressions, soundscapes, and other unusual elements. Many writers sought out inspiration in classical music, avant-garde music, psychedelic music, and non-Western music.

Rap and hip-hop represent the current zenith of rhythmic melodic design. These styles have fully crossed over into the mainstream, and now rule the rock domain. Rap and hip-hop songs are better understood as constructions of beats, rhythmic motives, and word patterns than as melodically based songs. Often their melodies (such as they are; much of rap "melody" is spoken), harmonies, and forms defy traditional analysis. That assessment, however, does not preclude rap and hip-hop works from being rock songs, as they still fall well within our definition. Obviously they are of tremendous cultural import, in many of the same ways rock 'n' roll was in its time.

In truth, almost all popular songs borrow in some way from other popular songs, as part of a historical continuum. Because they are commercial by nature, some degree of familiarity is an advantage. The practice of categorizing popular songs into genres and sub-genres provides familiarity by organizing people's tastes, and offers a route to venturing safely outside of them. In light of its derivative nature, a chronicle of rock's growth is a nearly impenetrable matrix of influences (see Sidebar 1).

SIDEBAR 1   Timeline of Popular Music Styles

1950	Rhythm & Blues (Race)	Tin Pan Alley	Country and Western
1955		Rock 'n' Roll	
1960	Dance music Folk Soul		Vocal groups and soloists
	The British Invasion	Motown	Surf music
1965	The Nashville Sound	Bubblegum	Hard Rock and Guitar Gods
	Pop Rock	Latin influences	Psychedelic/Acid Rock
1970	Singer-songwriters	Adult Contemporary/Soft Rock and Soft Soul	
	Country Pop	Oldies	Progressive/Concept Rock
1975	Glam Rock (Glitter)	Reggae/Ska	Progressive Country and Folk-Rock
	Salsa Disco New Wave	Punk Rock/Hardcore	Funk Rap
1980	Techno Rock and Pop	Artist-based Pop, Rock, and R&B	Power Pop
1990 – present	Hip-hop	Grunge and Garage Rock	Heavy Metal
	Dance-pop/Beats	Alternative, Indie, and Emo Rock	Retro

Rock has had quite a robust lifespan (despite taking all those drugs), and the new Millennial generation has further lifted sales off the charts. If, as many critics aver, there has been some recent stagnation and overpopulation in popular music since around 2000, and stylistic innovation has been sparse, it has not deterred songwriters from creating; indeed it seems to have motivated more people to write more songs. What's more, almost every rock style ever born is still alive and well somewhere. It seems there will never be a shortage of rock songs.

What are the particular qualities, then, of what I am calling *rock* songs, beyond the general list of the qualities of a song? Here are six primary elements shared by virtually all of them:

1. **Hooks.** A "hook" is a catchy phrase of music, lyrics, and usually a combination of the two, that is particularly memorable to the listener, and by which a song can be immediately identified. Often the title of a song is its hook, and often the hook is a summary statement of some kind, but hooks can occur anywhere, and are sometimes just instrumental. Many songs have multiple hooks, sometimes hierarchically organized. Some songs might be seen as no more than a series of hooks (as examples, "More Than a Feeling," "Toxic," "We Found Love," or "Get Lucky").

2. **Grooves.** "Groove" refers to the palpable effect of a rhythmic pattern, or patterns, in conjunction with a "feel," which encompasses style, pace, intensity, and mood. Every rock song has a groove—even ballads and a cappella songs. Songs with strong r&b or funk influences are said to have a "deep groove" or "deep pocket" (much of the output of Earth, Wind, and Fire; Stevie Wonder; and Steely Dan, for example). There are soft grooves, sweet grooves, agitated grooves, mellow grooves, all kinds of grooves; being a metaphor itself, "groove" is rife for metaphorical explication. Groove is what we move to; it's what gets under our skin and into our blood. As noted, groove is an essential part of rock melodies, not just accompaniments.

3. **Simple song forms.** Rock songs are generally between three and five minutes long, a custom originating in radio programming formats and the amount of music storable on recordable media. But this limited duration is also convenient for the small stories and ideas that songs have to relate, and for audiences' attention spans. In fact, such brevity dates back to Classical and Romantic-era art song. So does simple formality, which popular song has also inherited. Typically falling into just a few song forms (see Sidebar 2), songs are broken into sections that progress smoothly from one into another, usually working up to some sort of climax (often the hook), sometimes with a contrasting section in the middle (a "bridge" or "release"). Sections themselves also tend to be modest in size and complexity; sometimes they are just one or two phrases. Rock songs usually have some sort of refrain or chorus (again, usually the hook) that recurs more frequently than other sections. Some rock songs also have extended instrumental introductions, interludes, and codas. There are myriad variations and permutations, but a very short list of forms is the basis for the entire literature.

4. **Improvisation.** The genres from which rock music evolved were already somewhat improvisational in nature, particularly in their vocal and percussive elements. Most rock songs were not meant to be written down, and are passed on, as noted, by oral tradition. Sometimes it is hard to know in rock songs where composition ends and improvisation begins.[1] In the rock spectrum, there are songs that involve vocal improvisation, and those that do not, and a lot in between. For example, in songs in which the melody carries the groove or meter, the melody cannot be altered without

---

1. Whether or not a song was written down when originally composed, today's performers can find sheet music for almost every popular song, with the understanding that its notation may be somewhat arbitrary, or resort to certain notational conveniences.

losing the beat. When a groove is fully realized in the accompaniment, vocal improvisation may be more allowable. Certain styles accommodate improvisation more than others, and some styles demand it. In some songs, improvisation is part of the melody, and simply cannot be notated. Each singer will handle improvisation differently. To some extent, there is an improvisatory element in every rock song. It can be abused, and performances can fall victim to excessively ornate vocal improvisation.

5. **Memorable lyrics and music.** Beyond just its hook, the entirety of a popular song is memorable. This relates to its size, its form, its groove, and its "singability." After hearing a popular song a few times, an interested listener appropriates a song to him- or herself; he or she files it in a mental and emotional cabinet with other songs, curates the archives, and selectively revisits his or her favorites. Lyrics that say a lot with a minimum of verbiage, or become part of the language ("It's been a hard day's night . . .," "Take this job and shove it . . .," "Comfortably numb . . .," "I'm a soul man . . ."), transcend memory and take on lives of their own. They are as permanent as sculpture, or a Christmas carol. So, sometimes, are iconic instrumental phrases, such as the bass line of "These Boots Are Made for Walking," the drum fill in "Wipeout," or the trumpet solo in "Penny Lane." It is no wonder that so many hit songs involve call-and-response, because call-and-response is an opportunity for audiences to get into the act: by singing back to the singer, they commit the song to memory—they rehearse. Predictability and derivation also factor into memorability; most pop and rock songs are relatable to other songs, so as not to exceed listeners' mental hard drive capacities.

6. **Universality.** This term encompasses the notions of accessibility (meaning easy to grasp) and commerciality (meaning easy to sell), and is indicative of a song's appeal to a broad range of listeners. Universality is intangible but recognizable. It is a reverse metric; only the reaction of an audience to a song will determine if it is truly universal. Sometimes universality enters through the back door. Punk rock and hip-hop are among the highly successful rock genres that started out deliberately audience-unfriendly, but for their target listeners, the acrimony was appealing. Starting as countercultural fringe artists, punk and hip-hop writers and performers first achieved great popularity within their niches, then capitalized on their offbeat cachet to conquer the mainstream. Indeed, a "cool" factor has always driven the rock industry, and drives the notion of universality as well. Clever marketers in today's environment can fashion a semblance of universality through little more than intensive promotion and high-quality production values.

Theatre Songs

What qualities, then, define theatre songs, not yet by comparison to popular songs, but on their own? Keep in mind the fundamental purpose of musical theatre: to clearly communicate to an audience a believable story in an engaging manner.

As a starting point, because it's relevant to rock in the theatre, let's compare "presentational" and "representational" musical theatre performance. "Presentational" performance acknowledges the presence of the audience, at times playing directly to the audience. It is purposefully demonstrative, often ostentatious. "Representational" performance, by contrast, fabricates a semblance of reality, which audiences view from the other side of an invisible "fourth wall." Presentational performance is found within theatre-like settings such as cabarets, revues, competitions, and spectacles, and can also can exist within the bounds of representational performance (as an example, in "backstage" musicals, or when a concert performance takes place as part of a story). Presentational performance has, for better or worse, influenced the techniques and performance practices of modern musical theatre.

The main problem of achieving believability in musical theatre is easy enough to see but difficult to resolve. It lies in the fundamental conflict between the representational nature of drama and the abstract essence of music. There is an inherent artificiality in singing something that one could just as easily speak. Luckily, there is some common ground. To begin with, in truth, "representational" performance doesn't represent. Rather, it approximates: it can exaggerate or downplay actions and events, and sometimes it condenses or fast-forwards them. Rather than represent, drama *re-presents*, in an artificial environment, events that are based on reality (or reality-based fantasy). Stage conversation, for example, isn't truly like real conversation, but it's near enough that a listener can choose to believe it to be so. (The term "conversational" is often used to describe effectively natural-sounding theatre lyrics.)

Adding music (or choreography, for that matter) to storytelling on stage throws off the audience's "suspension of disbelief," because music is abstract, able to represent only by imitation (horns honking, birds singing, and such). Any reference, meaning, or emotion that music displays exists only on its own terms, and is subject entirely to the experience of the listener. Reconciling the quasi-realistic, or referential, nature of drama with the conceptual nature of music is among the prime directives of musical theatre writers, directors, and performers.

When music and lyrics and all the other elements of theatre align, theatre song transcends its contradictions. It becomes a nearly organic thing, a living, breathing, exciting, emotional *being* unto itself, one with an extraordinary range of possibilities. It can be a soaring aria that sings of days gone by or a brighter future, a heated conversation over love, fame, or revolution, or a satirical take on a sensitive issue that can only be laughed at in song.

As we did with popular songs, let's dissect theatre songs to uncover their essential anatomical parts:

1. **Believability.** Theatre songs are performed *believably*. I reiterate this because without believability, musical theatre is pure exercise, insignificant, even uncomfortable. It is not necessary to achieve "absolute" believability; songs are still on some level

abstract, allowing for personalization, and they are not always sung by someone who resembles the character singing. Audiences are able to find all sorts of ways to suspend disbelief despite obvious cause for doubt, with poor writing and inappropriate casting the usual culprits. Furthermore, theatre can only ever achieve a semblance of reality, not reality itself. The closer it gets to reality, however, the better: the more a play resembles truth in action, the more the audience chuckles, weeps, cheers, and even sings along.

2. **Immediacy.** Theatre audiences usually view a musical only once, and therefore they must apprehend everything they see and hear the first time. For both writers and performers, immediacy is the goal, and their responsibility. Dramatic and comedic threads can be complex, or subtle, which makes the need for clear, instantaneous communication all the more urgent, and difficult. Immediacy is also a function of accessibility. Many audiences have rebuffed Stephen Sondheim's songs, for example, because they consider his music inaccessible and his lyrics too elaborate, and some of the most sophisticated of today's musical theatre writers (Adam Guettel, Michael John LaChiusa, Ricky Ian Gordon) rarely crack the commercial glass ceiling. Though immediate comprehensibility is essential, the notions of universality and familiarity I listed as aspects of popular song are not as important in the theatre. Broadway audiences are prepared to encounter things unusual, and even esoteric (though some obviously still prefer the recognizable); that's one of the justifications for the high price. Intelligent audiences will accept, indeed they crave, all sorts of theatrical experiences, unexpected as they might be—just look at the diversity of material in the 2010s. There are many ways to tell a story with music, but regardless of musical or theatrical approach, immediacy is always of foremost concern.

3. **Character.** Actors on theatre stages are in character, and when they sing, they sing in character. Even in revues and concerts, musical theatre performers usually adopt a character; in these settings the characters they adopt may be themselves. Singer/actors in a theatrical setting are the dramatis personae, literally, the people of the drama. Both performers and songwriters must understand characters' motivations, their intentions, their dramatic progressions, their relationships, and so on, and how singing will communicate them. Many musical theatre songs are expressly created to reveal or highlight aspects of character. Character becomes apparent through objective, physicality, style, and dramatic context. Many crucial songs that comprise traditional musical theatre structures, such as "I am" songs, "I want" songs, or "eleven o'clock numbers," are character-based statements.[2]

4. **Irony, duality, and surprise.** Most characters on stage, like the dramatic situations they inhabit, are elaborate and rarely superficial. In a musical, actors mirror human behavior and emotion, and stories reflect actual situations. Conflict and subtext generate

---

2. There are several available guides on types of theatre songs; see the Additional Reading list.

drama and comedy, and stories and characters take unexpected turns. Theatre music is a part of this process on a large scale, and within their formal boundaries, songs can reveal many levels of meaning of a small idea. Theatre songs favor the extraordinary over the predictable, because life is not predictable, and even the simplest of them often have strong subtextual emotion or feature a tiny but pivotal twist (in either lyrics or music, or both).

5. **Extended or variegated forms.** Due to the complexity inherent in drama and character, theatre song forms tend to mutate to fit their situations. It is difficult to express conflicting feelings in a small, predetermined shape. Musical theatre takes traditional forms and varies them, breaks them apart, or enlarges them to fit the needs of a given moment. Theatre songs are often long and episodic, and may have plenty of sonic contrast. They may also be expanded to accommodate movement or storytelling. Still, within these variations and extensions, and leaving room for entertainment value, economy is of the essence. Music already bloats the duration of a stage play by lingering on certain moments within it, so a song must make its point succinctly. Great lyrics can speak volumes with a minimum of words, and great melodies can carry a tremendous dramatic load.

6. **Stylistic malleability.** As our brief history of musical theatre demonstrates, there really is no such genre as "show tunes." Whatever theatregoers of the past may have deemed to be generic show music is now archaic, and has always been vague. The bouncy two-beats of vaudeville and Tin Pan Alley, the melodic and orchestral warmth of the classic musical dramas, and the brassy jazz and Americana of Golden Age musical comedy seem old-fashioned today, though they do occasionally find their way into contemporary popular music, and of course reappear in revivals. Broadway theatre music in 2018 included: EDM, hip-hop, folk-rock, pop-rock, Celtic pop, hard rock, doo-wop, jazz, swing, salsa, reggae, Klezmer, and South African chants. What is definitive of theatre songs is that their style (or styles) is responsive to the story, or by virtue of being somehow in conflict with the story, takes on its own significance (as in *Jesus Christ Superstar* or *Hamilton*). In most cases, each show exhibits some sort of uniqueness in its musical approach, even if it is just a variation on a theme or an existing musical tradition. (Richard Rodgers and Alan Menken, for example, always sound like Rodgers and Menken, yet they ingeniously and convincingly tinge their work with stylistic elements specific to each drama and milieu for which they are composing.)

7. **Specificity.** Usually—not always—theatre songs treat specific topics rather than general notions. This makes them hard to comprehend or perform without the context of the show to support them. Some transcend their context, which explains the occasional crossover, but still these songs were devised to function at a specific place within a score that accompanies a play. This also makes more difficult the job of a musical theatre composer trying to create a "liftable" song—one that will be performed outside the show, and perhaps make it onto the pop charts.

Comparison of Rock Songs and Theatre Songs

Now that we've seen each kind of song in isolation, let's look into their similarities and differences.

Purpose

Whereas both music theatre and popular music are commercial art forms meant to engage and entertain the listener, theatre songs carry the added burdens of believable storytelling and immediately articulate communication. Lyrics in most popular songs are less specific, more universal, not necessarily character-driven, and more limited in scope than theatre lyrics. One can write a rock song for no particular reason but to sing or dance or tell someone they love them, or to express any old feeling, but effective musical theatre songs are written (or placed, as in a revue or jukebox show) with a specific motivation and something to say, even when their words are simple.

On stage, the quest for believability reigns supreme, and writers, directors, and performers fight their way through the musical-dramatic paradox to achieve it. *Purpose* is a large part of this quest: someone can only sing in a musical when there is no better way to tell the story, thus warranting musical intervention. It is not worth musicalizing an idea that does not deserve to be sung; it would be a major pitfall on the path to suspension of disbelief. When actors on stage sing what a listener consciously or even subliminally questions should be sung as opposed to spoken, the listener cannot invest in the story—he or she is too aware of watching people on a stage sing a story about something. Nonetheless, there are such songs, and it is left to performers to imbue them with purpose.

Rock songs have emotional or meaningful purpose, as well, but instead of elucidating an aspect of plot or identity in a story (they do that occasionally, too), in their effort to reach as wide an audience as possible, their lyrical content is more general. It may be hard to pinpoint the specific meaning of a rock song (especially upon first hearing), and it may mean entirely different things to different listeners (the same song that reminds one fan of falling in love may remind another of a breakup, for example). But in theatre, most songs are not subject to diverse interpretations by listeners; rather, they are directed and performed in order to present a replica of actual ideas and emotions that everyone watching will "get" right away, and in a similar way.

Form

Theatre song forms are more likely to be multipartite and unpredictable than those of popular songs, because they tend to display a wider range of feelings or move a story forward. Popular songs don't as often deal with conflicting or complex emotion, because they strive for accessibility and universality. Everyone shares emotions, but does not necessarily share specific emotional states. A theatre song can start happily and end sadly, or the other way around, but most popular songs stick to a single mood. When someone listens to a popular song on the radio or on a recording, he or she can turn it off; but a theatre audience is captive. The theatre audience's experience, as much as a performer's, is liable to be immersive and in flux. This is not necessarily true in a popular song, which is repeatedly heard and can be readily experienced even when in the background.

Verse-chorus songs (see Sidebar 2) are far more common in rock than in the theatre, as they contain repeated lyrical material. Choruses are an exclusively musical formal element (there are refrains in poetry, but rarely choruses). In the theatre, where content determines form, that is, where songs are shaped so that they communicate immediately, concisely, and believably, a verse-chorus song will only work if there is material that bears believable repetition. A theatre audience must attain a deeper level of suspension of disbelief to be comfortable with the notion of words heard many times over, a pattern that is not representative of conversation. In a popular song, these repetitions are precisely what invites listeners to remember the song and sing along. Most theatre songs have refrains and hooks, as pop songs do—they, too, like most songs, focus on one encapsulated idea that is expressed in a central melodic/lyric idea—but the hooks are more often contained within AABA, ABAB, ABACA, and related forms. The more that musical theatre embraced rock over times, the more verse-chorus songs appeared in musical theatre scores.

The asymmetrical, irregular song forms in shows such as Lin-Manuel Miranda's *Hamilton* and *In the Heights* are among the many vivid illustrations of the expandability of rock styles for theatrical purpose, and such forms are widespread through the repertoire, past and present. Many theatrical production numbers, opening and closing numbers, and group anthems expand verse-chorus form into larger-scale forms, and rarely is any simple form in any type of theatre song left intact; there is almost always some formal mutation.

Format

Formats, too, tend to be simpler in the rock and pop world. For the most part, and especially since the advent of video music and music streaming, popular songs stand alone and not in groups, as in a theatre score. They are, to varying degrees, stories unto themselves. The duration of a group of songs packaged as one "album" was, from 1960 until about 2000, dictated by the capacity of its medium: an LP or cassette, and later a CD. "Double albums" (that is, two LPs packaged together, equaling ninety-plus minutes of music) were a risky proposition for record companies; they were expensive to produce and harder to sell, due to audiences' short attention spans and teenaged-sized wallets. Only artists with secure followings and something "artistic" to say were permitted this format (among them Pink Floyd, Bruce Springsteen, and later OutKast), and some used it with dramatic purpose. A few pop and rock musicians have come close to full-fledged dramatic works in their "concept albums," a few of which, like *Tommy, Jesus Christ Superstar, Chess, Aida*, and *American Idiot*, have been staged as musicals.

Contemporary musical theatre, on the other hand, has a little of everything, in terms of format: through-sung folk and rock operas, book musicals, dance musicals, revues, plays with songs, and so on. In recent years, there has been a spate of pop-rock theatrical "song cycles," a term borrowed from art song to denote a carefully programmed, emotionally or dramatically related sequence of songs. (The attraction to theatre writers makes sense, in that a short format and looser connection among the musical numbers exempts them from highly specific plot necessities, and because the writers themselves grew up on concept albums and imaginative, outward-reaching popular music. It is also an easier and less expensive format to produce.)

Like their song forms, the larger-scale structures of all effective musical theatre works are determined by their content, and most are unique. *Natasha, Pierre, and the Great Comet of 1912* can only be what it is (an anachronistic spectacle surrounding a very slight story), and so too, can *Rock of Ages* (a send-up that prizes its musical authenticity) or *Godspell* (a mélange of pop-rock and experimental theatre). The creators of these shows made musical choices to suit their storytelling and its style, and as a consequence, the shows became defined by their music. Direct story adaptations, such as movie transfers, are more likely to employ familiar storytelling templates and a pop musical pastiche. The stage versions of Disney's *Frozen* and *Newsies, Pretty Woman, Legally Blonde*, and *The Wedding Singer*, among others, are carefully but formulaically constructed book musicals consisting of alternating scenes, songs, movement, and stagecraft.

Music and Lyrics and Their Connection

Believability on stage is also accomplished through careful text setting. If an audience is to give credence to the notion that someone is singing, as opposed to speaking, a song must be a plausible alternative to speech. Part of this rests on dramatic and compositional craft, and part is in marrying text to music. Performers look to the marriage of text and music to achieve believability, in rehearsal when analyzing a song, and in performance, as a means of effective communication of ideas and feelings.

Some lyrics, as printed on the page, appear awkward, overblown, or like platitudes, but when sung, are perfectly acceptable. Melodies on their own may be quite ordinary, but when words are added, they come to life. In theatre music, in order to facilitate communication, most text is sung with the same rhythms and contour (the ups and downs of pitch in a melody) with which it would be spoken, although the pace at which certain words and phrases are delivered is deliberately manipulated for expression. Seldom are syllabic or melodic stresses in the wrong place in the words attached to a theatre melody; if they were, the audience would question the lyric's truthfulness. This is not the case in rock songs, which (increasingly, and especially in rap and hip-hop) handle text setting and melody with liberty, sometimes with invention, and sometimes with carelessness, freely synchronizing weak syllables with strong beats and giving unimportant words melodic emphasis. This tendency has, over time, bled somewhat into theatre. It presents a challenge for an actor trying to make sense of a jointly textual and musical phrase, because imprecise scansion is a detriment to believably sung conversation.

Rock music also traffics freely in near-rhyme, whereas musical theatre lyricists avoid it, again, hopeful of not distracting the listener, whose attention might be drawn to the near-rhyme instead of to the lyric and the dramatic moment. In musical theatre, even rock musical theatre, perfect (and intelligent) rhyming is a great asset, at least when the character singing is smart enough to engage in it. Alexander Hamilton shows off his skills with words in *Hamilton*; by contrast, Rocky Balboa, in *Rocky the Musical*, sticks to a carefully chosen vernacular. Use of a stylized vernacular is a common performance practice in rock song—how often do you hear the word "ain't" in a rock lyric?—but in theatre song, songwriters elucidate character using their approach to and use of language, always in search of believability.

Another impediment to realism is poetic structure. Rock songs, like metered poetry, often present a rhythm in the first line, then repeat that rhythm in the next line, and perhaps several more times. People do not speak in poetry, in parallel phrases, or poetic meter. Therefore, theatre songs commonly break up patterns of phrase lengths, and sometimes break out of meter entirely, both the written meter of the piece (4/4, 3/4, etc.) and the poetic meter within a phrase, in order to believably make their point.

Vocal Arrangements

Rock music is sung by vocal ensembles as well as solo singers, and many solo vocalists are recorded with backup singers. Doo-wop music and male and female vocal groups prevailed in the early 1960s, and almost no singer of that early era sang alone, especially those whose voices were unique, such as Elvis Presley or Frankie Valli, who needed additional support (Elvis sometimes had a choir, and Frankie Valli always had his Four Seasons). Double-tracking lead vocal lines is a time-honored rock recording practice. The basis for this sort of vocal arranging is sonic and musical more than textual, although arrangers did, of course, account for lyrical content and mood in their writing. Many of these vocal arrangements were created ad hoc, but others were quite consciously manipulated (the Beach Boys are a prime example).

In theatre, by comparison, vocals lines are distributed according to the needs of storytelling. When there are musically formulated vocal arrangements, they originate naturalistically from the setting or story. Because the act of storytelling includes the setting of time and place, vocal arrangements are usually fashioned with an eye to the correct musical genre, location, and period, to assist in setting the scene. In theatre music, a group singing a single melody is very commonplace, but not for the same reason that rock vocals are doubled; rather, it is a way to economically communicate the shared feeling or intent of several people at the same time. Theatre singing may be in harmony, but unison group singing is more frequent ("Five hundred twenty-five thousand six hundred minutes . . ."). This approach is not as often heard in popular music, and distributing solo lines among different singers is quite rare.

Theatre vocal arranging retains from opera the notion of overlaying melodies from different voices, and even from different songs, particularly at climactic points in a story, such as production numbers and opening numbers or finales. This practice persists in rock musical numbers, such as "Skid Row," from *Little Shop of Horrors*, "On My Way," from *Violet*, and "Blackout," from *In the Heights*. On the theatre stage, backup vocals, the kind that listeners recognize from their favorite rock records, only come into play where the musical genre expressly calls for it, as in *Beautiful, A Bronx Tale*, or, as in *Little Shop*, as a dramatic convention (a Greek chorus, and appropriate to the context, a "girl group"). Over time, certain theatre scores have superfluously assumed some rock vocal arranging practices, and modern audiences accept them more readily because their ears are now acclimated to them as a customary element of all popular music.[3]

Vocalism and Improvisation

On stage, clear declamation of melodized text is mandatory. This is because stories must be told with immediate accessibility. Now tell me the words to "Jumpin' Jack Flash." Or "Rock the Casbah," "Burning Down the House," or especially "Louie, Louie." If you know them, it's because you've listened to them dozens of times, or looked them up. You can't do either of those things in the theatre (turn off that smartphone!). Much as we may love the vocal oddities of a Mick Jagger or Eddie Vedder, in a musical we need to hear the words.

Word-blurring is innate to rock tradition, and so is screaming a melody like Axl Rose or James Brown. A theatre singer who clearly declaims a lyric on stage and eschews his or her throat as a means of articulation is doing right by the rules of vocal production, but as a result may lose some of the "grit" or "edge" that helps establish the rock aesthetic. Good theatre-rock songwriting can mitigate some of the effect by making musical and textual choices that engender these qualities in a melody while protecting the singer (you'll see several examples of this in the coaching sessions in Part III). Singers must evaluate the conflict, and strike a balance in preparation and performance.

Vocal improvisation as an essential element of rock poses another problem on the theatre stage. If improvising consumes any time or attention whatsoever without contributing to the storytelling, then the bylaws of musical theatre say it has no purpose. It does not move a story forward, and it is certainly not conversational. As with other rock values, over time, it has insinuated itself into theatre music in such a way that it can

---

3. If you as a musical theatre student or singer have an opportunity to work as a backup vocalist, either in a concert/recording or stage setting, I highly recommend it as both a learning tool (for singing rhythmically and understanding rock melodies and harmonies) and as a fulfilling musical experience. In some ways, it's the rock version of singing in the choir.

at very least assist in storytelling through style and milieu, and, when handled just right, can actually contribute to character definition (as in "Waving through a Window" and other songs from *Dear Evan Hansen*). Moreover, audiences have begun to accept vocal embellishment, thanks to *American Idol* and its kin, as something that has a place in every musical setting. When improvisation crosses over into meaningless flamboyance or self-indulgence, however, it can easily bring down believability, a theatrical taboo even in a presentational setting.

Song themes in rock and the theatre

Let's now demonstrate these comparisons in context, using as examples songs with related themes, a few each from the popular and theatre worlds. Many of the song examples referred to below appear in the Appendix, and readers are encouraged to listen as they read this section.

Songs of Iniquity

Outlaws and villains have a strong presence in rock music. A nefarious character of some sort as the subject of a song, or its lead singer, is archetypal. The Rolling Stones sang of a "Street Fighting Man" and had "Sympathy for the Devil," Gregg Allman sang about a "Midnight Rider," AC/DC about a "Live Wire," and N.W.A about a "Gangsta Gangsta." Female performers soon got in on being sinister, as well; among others, Patti Smith, Sister Souljah, and L'il Kim all made significant marks in the music industry with their distaff malevolence.

Yet the storytelling element in such songs is often vague. Their evocative lyrics often tell less about the character singing the song than about the artist with whom the song is identified (rap, in particular, loves to reference itself and its performers). The musical tone agrees with the mood of the texts, thereby deepening the songs' identity and accessibility, but not contributing to their specificity.

Rock songs in the musical theatre assigned to bad guys and gals are scarce. In keeping with the axiom that theatre music adapts to character and scene, and in light of the traditionalism of musical theatre, many villains' songs sound formulaically villainous, as if they were borrowed from monster movies, using minor keys and tangos and chromaticism and other stock tools of the trade, including comedic pastiche, even within rock and pop scores (such as "King Herod's Song," from *Jesus Christ Superstar* or "Poor Unfortunate Souls," from *The Little Mermaid*).

There are, however, a few stage villains that do rock. "Feed Me (Git It)," sung by the man-eating space plant in *Little Shop of Horrors*, has significance on several levels. Aside from being a successful musical scene that propels the plot into heightened conflict, the song is replete with references to time and place, it examines the moral dilemma of the characters' choices, and its Motown-funk vocabulary alludes to the racial divide of its era. Dr. Frank-N-Furter's "Sweet Transvestite" from *The Rocky Horror Show* tells us not only that the singer is in drag, but why. The song introduces secondary characters, and again, also serves to move the plot forward. In Frank Wildhorn and Don Black's "Raise a Little Hell," from their musical *Bonnie and Clyde*, the antiheroic Clyde wrestles with issues of life and death in relation to his actions, and does so over a gradually evolving rhythmic and melodic palette, essentially a long crescendo from beginning to end, underscoring the character's increasing frustration. (Wildhorn is a veteran of both the popular and theatrical music industries, and his theatre songs are clear evidence of this duality.) "Don't Nobody Bring Me No Bad News" from *The Wiz* and *The Lion King*'s "Be Prepared" make strong stylistic statements; as in *Jesus Christ Superstar*, the infusion of a foreign musical flavor into a familiar tale is meaningful in and of itself.

Songs of Encouragement

The intention of many singers, in theatre and rock songs alike, is to encourage, uplift, or motivate. These are relatively simple sentiments, less prone to ambiguity than others, so the gap between theatre and rock is not as great, but still it is there. Encouraging rock lyrics are usually quite general, and many are peppered with a healthy measure of cliché, modish, or recycled phrases. Predictably, the music is equally uplifting and rhythmically motivating. Listen to Britney Spears's "Stronger," Katy Perry's "Roar" or "Firework," or Sara Bareilles's "Brave," effective songs on their own level, no doubt, but written to encompass many situations in which encouragement is relevant. Even Simon and Garfunkel's timeless "Bridge over Troubled Water" is one of Simon's more conventional lyrics, at least on paper, yet transforms so beautifully to melody that listeners don't seem to notice. When rock singers perform such songs, they may generalize their emotion, rather than working to make each emotional beat clear, as a theatre performer would.

Most theatre rock songs whose objective is to encourage also do not venture far from a generalized approach. "Electricity" from *Billy Elliot*, "Cross the Line" from *Bring It On*, "King of the World" from *Songs for a New World*, as well as many a happy tune from the scores of movie transfers, are mostly generic songs tailored slightly to fit a certain character's point of view, with occasional reference to dramatic situation. Because stage action is representative of character and situation, and because theatre songs are sung with intent, this makes sense: one person's encouragement of another is usually genuine, and without ulterior motive; therefore, the songs understandably display less contrast.

Of course, when there is subtext, when encouragement is disingenuous in some way, it is more theatrical. There are songs of deceitful or devious encouragement, such as the seductive "Light My Candle" and "Out Tonight" from *Rent* and "The Word of Your Body" from *Spring Awakening*, "Opportunity" from *13*, and "Sincerely, Me" from *Dear Evan Hansen*. These songs could only survive in a theatrical environment.

The songs from *Rent* are too relevant to character and situation to be a commercial rock song. "The Word of Your Body" is too poetically explicit; rock prefers either the poetic or the explicit, not both, because both is too complicated. The gentle harmonic twists of its accompaniment, apparently motivated by the song's romantically uninhibited, almost graphic stage context, are likewise too unexpected to appear in a rock song. "The Word of Your Body" masterfully captures the tension of youthful sexuality in its restraint and occasional gentle surprise, an approach to musical storytelling far too convoluted for a commercial rock song, but which on stage is powerful and moving, and erotic.

On the much lighter side, there are songs like "Popular," from *Wicked*, which fall squarely into the "pop" category; "Popular" has the flavor of many commercial pop songs with bright, swingy bubblegum feels. Its musical familiarity and bounce provide an unobtrusive background for character-based comedy (this is true of many comedy songs, which feature text over music); it is an exploration of personality and relationships set to pop pastiche that would only be comfortable on a theatre stage, or in a rock novelty song ("Yellow Submarine," for example). Stephen Schwartz, the composer of *Wicked*, and his several collaborators have always shown a knack for creating theatre songs with uplifting light-pop grooves and soaring pop melodies, and with lyrics that might have qualified as commercial rock lyrics had they not so often included mentions of specific names, places, and circumstances, among them, "Corner of the Sky" (*Pippin*), "The Wizard and I" and "Defying Gravity" (*Wicked*), and "Colors of the Wind" (the film *Pocahontas*). One can still hear echoes of "Corner of the Sky" in Andrew Lippa's song "Stranger," from *Big Fish*, forty years later.

Songs of Loss and Loneliness

Where would rock be without loss and loneliness? Indeed, have not such feelings motivated people to sing ever since people began singing? They certainly motivate the blues, and the blues motivated rock. It seems obvious that the most basic human utterances of grief and pain—crying, sighing, wailing, grunts and groans, and such— have metamorphosed over time into melody, given how strongly they resemble music, and anthropologists, sociologists, and psychologists concur.[4] Rock's vocabulary carries on the musical characteristics and soulful vocal inflections of the blues, and its subject matter favors the blues' favorite themes, as well as its spontaneity and freedom. The singer of a blues song has somewhat specific motivations ("My baby left me," "Got no job and no money," "Nobody knows how I feel"), the emotion is deeply felt, and the impetus to sing is genuine; yet the singing reflects a primal emotional state, rather than a complex and situational emotional state. Many gifted singers and musicians have brought greater depth and reputation to the blues genre (among them Leadbelly, Muddy Waters, Etta James, Eric Clapton, Jimi Hendrix, Stevie Ray Vaughan, and

---

4. Steve Mithen, *The Singing Neanderthals* (Cambridge, MA: Harvard University Press, 2006).

more recently the White Stripes), but still the songs they sing and play seldom tell a detailed story. The blues in its original state has made little mark on the theatre, except in terms of its influence on other music, which is significant.

Beginning in the late 1960s, imaginative rock artists began to offer character-based tales redolent of loneliness, and they dipped a toe into the theatrical waters with short musical dramas such as the Beatles' "Eleanor Rigby" and much of the "Sgt. Pepper" album, "Alone Again (Naturally)," and as a product of the space age, "Space Oddity" and "Rocket Man." Many rock songs like these are narrative, and not in the first or second person as a theatre song would more likely be. There are songs of sadness in the catalogues of every major popular music artist.

Popular songs can make us cry because they are sad, but musical theatre can take us even deeper, provoking not only sadness, but levels of sadness, and sadness in combination and contrast with other emotions. In the repository of musical theatre plots, perhaps the most common sort of protagonist is one who is lonely, or misunderstood, or lost, and needs to find his or her way. Therefore, the quantity of material about loneliness is no smaller in the theatre than in rock, but again, theatre songs are mostly driven by specific, real-time statements of character and situation.

There is a wide and full range of rock theatre songs about loss and loneliness between those that are direct, or "on the nose," and those that are more oblique or subtextual. There are the plain narratives of "On My Own" and "I Dreamed a Dream" (*Les Miserables*), "Out Here on My Own" (*Fame*), and "When There's No One" (*Carrie*). In the gradient are songs such as "Lifeboat," from *Heathers*, and "I'm Here," from *The Color Purple*. The latter manages to include many references to the character's time and place, and is delivered in a very convincingly mannered linguistic style, yet succeeds as a pop song, and garnered some attention from pop and r&b listeners. Boy George, in *Taboo*, contributes "Stranger in This World," which adheres closely to its 1980s rock feel, but other than references to "Mother" is mostly nonspecific, albeit a bit poetic. *Spring Awakening*'s "And Then There Were None" takes a generic but stylistically correct approach, and becomes theatrical by interjecting into its form sections of dialogue from the singer's antagonist. Further into theatrical specificity and irony is a song that had a brief life on the pop and country charts (when the movie version was released), "Hard Candy Christmas" from *The Best Little Whorehouse in Texas*. This plaintive but double-edged country-rock ballad is sung by a group of women bemoaning their sudden imminent unemployment by gamely but tenuously imagining bright futures, while revealing difficult memories of the past through a clever title hook.

In terms of duality, rock songs about loneliness and loss may have an anomalous edge over their theatre counterparts. Sadness is rocked in songs like the Police's "So Lonely" and Whitesnake's "Here I Go Again," and even made light of, as in Billy Idol's "Dancing with Myself" or Whitney Houston's "I Wanna Dance (with

Somebody)." Most sad songs on the stage, on the other hand, have music that was written to sound sad, in keeping with the moment. Some theatre rock songs about alienation are transfers from concept albums, such as "See Me/Feel Me" from *Tommy* and "Wake Me Up When September Ends" from *American Idiot*. These songs are highly abstract, yet the characters singing them are very clear, unusual, and colorful. Therefore the vagueness of their lyrics is something of an asset, teasing an audience into wanting to understand the characters better. Despite their superficial generality, these two songs were inspired by specific events in their writers' lives. They are also both very rhythmic, despite slow tempos.

Songs of Self-Discovery

Rock songs that deal with the theme of self-discovery are mostly simplistic, at least on the surface. Suggestion takes precedence over detailed representation in bestselling songs such as Taylor Swift's "A Place in This World," One Republic's "Say (All I Need)," and KT Tunstall's "Suddenly I See." But some artists have reached further. Beyoncé finds some duality in "Pretty Hurts," as do Five for Fighting in "Superman," Talking Heads in "Once in a Lifetime," Sia in "Chandelier," and Britney Spears in "Lucky." The picturesque approach of the Beastie Boys' "All Lifestyles" is characteristic of the colorful details found in many hip-hop songs.

In the musical theatre, self-discovery or self-realization is the essential through-line for most characters in most stories, stories that usually involve feelings of confusion or isolation that transform into feelings of self-awareness and fulfillment—and sometimes tragedy. The point in a story when a character reaches the point of self-discovery is usually unambiguous, or at least less so than moments of conflict. Therefore, as with "Songs of Encouragement," self-discovery songs in the theatre tend to be decisive and without duality.

On stage, self-discovery often results in some form of action or tangible self-actualization, which may explain why its expressions in song form regularly occur as a part of musicalized dramatic scenes and dance numbers. Examples include: "Sensation," from *Tommy*, an interior monologue sung aloud with elaborate vocal counterpoint from the others in the scene; "Wig in a Box," from *Hedwig and the Angry Inch*, a sarcastically editorial yet heartfelt chronicle of the singer's daily routine; and "Gethsemane (I Only Want to Say)," from *Jesus Christ Superstar*, which plays out with the structure and the force of an operatic mad scene.

"Man," from *The Full Monty*, is also a musical scene, and has near-dialogic sections, but culminates in a more generalized statement of determination. "Arlington Hill," a coming-of-age number from *Passing Strange*, wanders farther into musical theatre territory without abandoning its downtown sound by working a hard rock ballad into an extended dramatic scene. "Ring of Keys," from *Fun Home*, blends a conversational reminiscence (a common component of rock and theatre songs both) with a repeated metaphorical title hook. The song's musical and lyrical simplicity are very much in keeping with the innocence of the young singer, and as the song's groove intensifies, so does the character's self-realization. Jason Robert Brown's pop rhythm ballad "Stars and the Moon," from *Songs for a New World*, fashions self-discovery into a three-act, verse/chorus song structure, with the singer's ironic realization of her fatal flaw saved for the eleventh hour, where it corresponds with a subtle yet striking change in the musical form. Narrative songs brought over from record albums might fall into this category, as well, such as "Scenes from an Italian Restaurant" or "Goodnight Saigon" from *Movin' Out*.

Clearly evident in the above comparisons is a large and diverse population of rock songs in the theatre, partitioned by purpose, and by dramatic setting and circumstances. These songs were all influenced by commercial rock music in some way, but function discretely as theatre songs. The non-theatrical rock songs I referred to have all been successful because they, too, had a definite reason to be sung, just as theatre song does, and, in some form or another, had a story to tell. All good songs do, even if the song is just the alphabet, or "Happy Birthday," or just some scat syllables in a jazz improvisation.

Also evident from the comparisons is that most rock theatre songs live in the spectrum between authentic rock and theatre music. This contradicts neither my central thesis that rock now dominates the Broadway stage, nor my earlier observation of the great variety in musical theatre styles, nor does it disqualify any musical style from the theatre. It merely reinforces that musical theatre imposes conditions on what might otherwise be rock songs, remodeling them, by necessity, into theatre songs.

Rock in the theatre was an inevitable development. It is a natural progression of artistic trends, supported by historical precedent. A comprehensive understanding of rock music will give you, the theatre singer, an advantage in this emergent professional environment. When singing rock, you may be speaking a musical language that on the surface seems simple and familiar, but an effective, authentic, *believable* performance will require insight, research, and commitment beyond the obvious, and into the depths of the aesthetics and musical principles that give rock its unique importance.

SIDEBAR 2

Song Forms

Note: This is an overview, presented to familiarize the reader with basic information, and makes no claim to be comprehensive. The terminology used to define song forms varies widely, and can be confusing.

AAA

Other Terms

Strophic song, Ballad

Description

Probably the earliest form of structured song; a simple section that repeats. Each section might have a refrain, usually at the end of each verse, with the same lyric each time (an early form of hook).

Historical Context

Story songs ("ballads") in traditional and country music, folk songs, children's songs, hymns

Variations

Few. Most varied are the number of verses, and the lyrical content of each verse (other than a refrain). Some instrumental breaks.

Examples

This Land Is Your Land, Barbara Allen, Blowin' in the Wind, By the Time I Get to Phoenix, Try to Remember, The Rose

AABA

Other Terms

Sometimes referred to as a list of the names of its sections; see "Description."

Description

The terminology used to describe the form changes with the user, but the basic form consists of four sections of very similar length (usually 8 or 16mm.): two refrains (or "choruses," or "verses"), a release (or "bridge"), and a final refrain. Because the form is short, it is often repeated in its entirety.

Historical Context

The most common form in popular and musical theatre songs through the first half of the 1900s; less common in contemporary pop but still widespread; still very common in musical theatre.

Variations

The A sections frequently differ, especially at their cadences, and the final A is often extended using closing musical material (AA'BA"). Sometimes there is an introductory verse as well, preceding the complete AABA form. Occasionally a second release is added (AABACAABA).

Examples

I Got Rhythm, Over the Rainbow, Send in the Clowns, Yesterday, Ease On Down the Road, Every Breath You Take

Simple ABAB

Other Terms

Sometimes confused with or used interchangeably with "verse/chorus."

Description

Two alternating sections of equal musical and lyrical weight.

Historical Context

None in particular; appears in many songs across genres and time periods.

Variations

Most common is the inclusion of an additional section. With additional sections, it resembles classical rondo form, in which certain sections are hierarchically more important than other, by virtue of their content or the number of times they appear. The final A section may be varied.

Examples

Swanee, Fly Me to the Moon, Superstition (simple ABAB), Moon River, Far from the Home I Love, Desperado (extended ABAB structures)

Verse-Chorus

Other Terms

ABAB, ABCABC (see "Simple ABAB" and below, "Variations")

Description

Alternating sections in which one section takes precedence over the others by virtue of content, identifiability, or number of repetitions. Often a "climb," or "prechorus," falls between the verse and the chorus, usually to build musical and lyrical energy to a climax in the chorus. The complete structure is usually repeated at least once, and choruses (or a single phrase within them) may be repeated several times.

Historical Context

Vaudeville and British Music Hall, comedy and novelty songs, and the majority of the pop/rock literature since 1960. Uncommon in musical theatre until 1970s.

Variations

The sizes of each section vary widely, from one phrase to many. As well as the climb, there may be an additional bridge after the chorus, creating an ABCAB or ABCDABC structure. The number of verses that precede the chorus may vary (AAB, AABC structures), and the chorus may come first, before any verses. Climbs and choruses may be multipartite. Sometimes the boundaries between sections are unclear. Instrumental interludes are also common.

Examples

Oh, Susanna; After the Ball; Up Where We Belong; Hotel California; Umbrella; Gee, Officer Krupke; Suddenly, Seymour

12-Bar Blues

Other Terms

AAB

Description

Typically, three phrases of 4 mm. each based on a simple I7-IV7-I7-V7-I7 harmonic progression. Characterized by melodic embellishments that bend into notes of the scale, especially the tonic triad, called "blue" notes. The forerunner of r&b. Its conventions appear in the harmonic and melodic detail of much of the modern pop literature

Historical Context

Authentic blues, rock, and blues-rock music from 1950 onward. Blues songs in the musical theatre are portrayed as such, and treated with at least some authenticity and/or reverence.

Variations

Mostly harmonic; sometimes the twelve-bar structure will house other chord progressions. Occasionally the form will be truncated or extended, or presented in double-time or half-time. The form may also function as a section within other forms, such as AABA and verse/chorus.

Examples

Minnie the Moocher, The Thrill Is Gone, Love in Vain, Johnny B. Goode, Born under a Bad Sign, Mustang Sally, Green Onions

Throughcomposed Songs

Description

Discrete sections, or one long section, with no repeated material.

Historical Context

Rare in all popular genres; found mostly in Romantic art song.

Variations

Many songs come close, repeating only a minimal percentage of their material, but few are truly throughcomposed, and each throughcomposed song is unique.

Examples

You'll Never Walk Alone, Bohemian Rhapsody, Happiness Is a Warm Gun, Prisoner in Disguise

Compound or Episodic Song Forms

Description

Many of these forms are covered among the variations of the forms listed above. Sometimes the combinations are more elaborate, and sometimes two separate forms are combined into a single song. Some are highly episodic and cover a great deal of musical ground.

Historical Context

"Progressive" rock music, singer-songwriter artists, and the musical theatre.

Examples

Good Vibrations, Strawberry Fields Forever, Prelude/Angry Young Man, Don't Rain on My Parade, 96,000, Movin' Too Fast

Theory and Technique

3

Acting Values in Rock Theatre Songs

In Part II, we will examine how rock's aesthetics and musical language influence the interpretation and execution of rock songs. We'll start with acting, specifically: how to bring your rock-inspired characterization to life, and how to activate the forces that motivate and sustain your performance of a rock song in a theatrical setting. Next is a discussion of the musical elements that distinguish rock style and sound, and the essentials of rock performance practice. After that, we'll look at the vocalism of rock, and what it signifies for musical theatre singers. Lastly, there is a selective list of a variety of commercial rock songs, with descriptions of their operations and some selective performance advice.

The intent here is to learn how to make a rock song believable and effective on stage. This is not a textbook on acting, or musical theatre acting; there are many books and courses, as well as entire curricula, on those subjects.[1] Some espouse a particular method of some sort, but in truth, successful performance, that is, *believable* performance, is achieved in any number of ways, by a great variety of people.

Neither is this a book on rock music theory.[2] No single text could possibly educate the reader on all of rock's widespread musical practices. Rather, we will concentrate on those qualities of rock music that are shared among significant segments of the literature—genres, decades, artists and their catalogues, and so on—and those that are useful to theatre singers. Likewise, only vocal techniques that have to do with singing rock in the theatre will be covered here. There are many courses and texts on the subject

---

1. One excellent text is Joe Deer and Rocco Dal Vera's very thorough reference, *Acting in Musical Theatre: A Comprehensive Text* (London: Routledge, 2015).

2. Rock music theory books are scarce; those I've found are quite elementary. There are, however, many fine blogs and courses available online.

of vocal production, but there can be never be a comprehensive guide to singing on the theatre stage, as each voice, character, and musical is individual and unique.

Acting Songs

The success or failure of all good musical theatre rests on how drama and music (and movement and design) work together to tell a story. The most important part of any story is its characters, and believability is the foremost goal of the actors personifying them. Whenever an actor sings, he or she is embodying character, even if the character is vaguely defined, or, as one might find in presentational performance, the character and the singer are one. Therefore, when singing in a musical, actor-singers are *vehicles* for the storytelling. It's worth a reminder here that the notion of singing a song in the midst of a realistic environment is a tricky proposition, by virtue of the aesthetic disparity between drama and music. Believability is difficult to achieve, and it begins with comprehension of character.

Actors on stage portray characters, but actors are themselves individuals. Whatever aspects of personality that an actor brings to a performance—for example, an emotional life, an accent, a "type," a "vibe," a physical stature, a hair color, or a vocal timbre—are as crucial to believable stage performance as are the materials he or she works with and the techniques he or she employs. A director, teacher, or performer can hypothesize what will make the best possible performance, but ultimately the audience will decide what is believable, and each audience will have a unique process of assessing believability based on its background, desires, and expectations (and perhaps the ticket price). Mere virtuosity may have greater appeal to certain audiences than a convincing characterization, or the other way around. Different actors and performance styles appeal to different segments of the theatregoing public. Actors must cultivate their ability to inhabit others' worlds, and understand how to use their own personae to their advantage, to diverse audiences in an assortment of venues, and even if they are not the ideal portrayers of the characters they are portraying.

The widely proscribed mechanisms of acting a song that most students and professionals learn as part of their training, in school, or on the job are just as applicable to acting rock songs as they are to all theatre song. Rock music does not change these very useful and almost universal processes.

Any song in the theatre functions like a scene, in that it accomplishes some facet of a story by acting it out; that facet can be something as small as expressing a feeling, and can be as large as a century of history. As actors in a scene, musical theatre singers shape their song performances according to *objective, intention,* and *action.*

Every character has objective, an overriding want or need, and an *obstacle* (or obstacles) to achieving it. This is usually the basic *conflict* that generates every story. The kids in *Spring Awakening* are overflowing with sexual urges, but their parents and their repressive community forbid it. Alexander Hamilton wants to show everyone how things ought to be done, but his rivals, his arrogance, and his peccadilloes get in his way. In many a rock bio-jukebox musical, an artist wants to express himself or herself with a sound or style that his or her parents, the recording industry, or society at large have not yet accepted.

Characters have *intention*, an immediate need, which leads them to the heightened states of emotion that call for song at a given moment. (Songs themselves do not have intention; rather, they have purpose, or function, while the characters in the songs have intention.) Intention is the reason a character sings, and the reason he or she sings *now*. In *The Full Monty*, Jerry reaches a point of financial desperation, and persuades his friends to be male strippers by appealing to their masculine pride in "Man." Mufasa sings "They Live in You" from *The Lion King* as a warning couched in a lesson, in immediate response to his son's life-threatening recklessness. In "Baptize Me," from *The Book of Mormon*, two characters look to each other for spiritual fulfillment as a last resort—in opposite ways, as we hear—in the form of a rock ballad, with comedic subtext typical of the raunchy humor found throughout the show.

Intentions are accomplished by way of *actions*; "action" is the basic material of "acting." Simply put, action just means doing something. (Seems so easy, doesn't it?) Actions guide actors through a believable set of behaviors, some internalized, some outward, all in service of their intention, and ultimately, their objective. (The term "action" should be differentiated from "activity," which refers to simply doing something other than working to accomplish the intention, usually a simple or mundane deed, at the same time as acting out/singing a scene.) In a way, even presentational performance is intentional: it presents a song to an audience, in a certain way, for a certain effect. Objective, and to a lesser degree intention, are written into characters, but actions belong largely to the actor.

Of course, the procedure described above is not immutable; it cannot be. For one thing, it also involves other people, including the director, your fellow actors, the music director, and of course the audience. Depending on the material and situation, some acting approaches will be more useful than others. For example, in a rock theatre piece whose songs only allude to the drama (as opposed to telling it in detail and with specific characterization) and whose lyrics are poetic or indirect—a song from *American Idiot* or *Once*, for example—actors must fill in the missing pieces with greater commitment to character and moment. Songs with very general or literal lyrics may call for a correspondingly generalized or literal acting style, but singer-actors will then have to reach within themselves to find emotions and actions that will elevate the song to a state of reality and believability. In some cases, the actor must concoct an underlying meaning or story in order to bring realism to a song that on its own is unconvincing. By contrast, other songs, such as "Moving Too Fast" (*The Last Five Years*) and "Goodnight Saigon" (*Movin' Out*) are profoundly detailed as written. In songs such as these an actor can allow the lyrics and music to carry much of the emotional load, and simply convey what the writers intended, as the vehicle for the music and lyrics. This is also true in songs with narrative lyrics, those in which the singer describes something happening, or that has happened in the past, but some songs like this will need an actor's emotional investment to be more than dully narrative (such as many songs from *Les Miserables*).

Some fundamental acting techniques might seem antithetical to rock performance practice. Perhaps foremost among these is clarity of lyrics. For example, when an actor sings a rock song in a nonnative musical score, such as *Rock of Ages* or *Mamma Mia!*, the words must be audible and the intention of the character clear, even if the original recording artists were not attentive to such matters and the lyric is somewhat vague, or not organized to be quasi-representational. In some cases, when the lyrics of these songs are sung with clarity, their rock-ness seems somehow diluted. If blurring the lyrics, whether haphazardly or deliberately, is an essential musical value of rock (it is, but obviously not nearly always), how can a musical theatre actor singing that song achieve stylistic authenticity and communicate at the same time?

The improvisatory element implicit in many rock songs can also be problematic in musical theatre. If every musical decision in a musical is rooted in the storytelling, if there must be economy in phrasing, and if specific meaning takes precedence over generality, where does that leave improvisation? On the other hand, if you deny the improvisation in a song written with an essential improvisatory element, where does that leave the song?

The answer to all of these questions is that absolute rock authenticity is not always a mandate. Nor, to some extent, are naturalistic theatrical styles of acting. You must examine each song and each show case by case, because the material varies so widely, and because different interpretations might be possible. Determining the importance of upholding authenticity in a performance will be a primary issue in rehearsal, and is also, of course, a prime concern of those who write, produce, coach, or direct a song or a show.

Let's go back to some very basic questions about acting, because their answers will help musical theatre performers begin to unravel these entanglements, and figure out how to act and rock at the same time.

The most fundamental: what is "acting?" Acting is based in the innate animal behavior of play; therefore "play" is a term for a work of theatre. Children pretend and role-play as essential processes in their development. By doing so they apprehend and learn about their environments, test their possibilities, overcome fear, and integrate socially. Actors do much the same, as a vocation, but in order to convincingly play a character, they must project the meaning and significance of their feelings and actions outward to an audience. This they learn to do through training, research, practice, and experience. It is notable that when children "play-act," they are prone to breaking into song (even long before they were raised on Disney musical movies). We needn't dwell on the psychology of stage acting, except that it puts great importance on the need for an actor to fully inhabit a character and to effectively *communicate* that character to others.

We have established that acting on stage involves taking on character. Acting in a musical adds another art form, music, as a layer of characterization. The musical material that a character sings, and the way the actor playing the role sings it, become part of the character.

There is undeniably some form of acting going on in rock music performance, as well as in the theatre, but it is acting of a different sort. Many rock singers don't seem to be acting, in the way that theatre stipulates acting. Rather, they are quite straightforward in their delivery, relying on the content of the material and the uniqueness of their voices and personae to communicate meaning. Nonetheless, every one of them, regardless of their performance styles, puts thought into how a song should be communicated to an audience. On one end, there are the soul- and chest-baring wails of Arthur Brown, the bluster of Dr. Dre, or the strutting of Mick Jagger; on the other, the detached cynicism of Randy Newman, the stark honesty of Fiona Apple, or the boyish cool of Ed Sheeran and John Mayer. Musical theatre actors can look to these performers and their songs (and countless others), and their generalized forms of rock "acting," for inspiration in their own performances.

What makes a successful characterization? For a musical theatre audience to accept and believe, and hopefully connect with, root for, and love a given character, they must, above all, never question that the character is who he or she says he or she is. No matter if the character is Aaron Burr, Spongebob, or Tina Turner, the audience must see Aaron Burr, Spongebob, or Tina Turner. It's perfectly acceptable for them to be aware that an actor is playing the role, but they must not question that actor's complete identification with the part, and they must temporarily invest in the reality that the actor *is* the character (suspension of disbelief). That's the overriding measure of success.

An actor achieves successful characterization through a combination of *understanding, ability, conveyance,* and *rightness.* Singing rock songs and performing rock musicals might entail alterations to any or all of these.

Understanding begins with knowledge of a character. In exhaustive terms, who is this person? Where is she from, what is his historical context? What is her occupation, who are his family and friends, what does she eat? . . . and so on. Every character has a backstory, and a trajectory that has led him or her to the point where his or her story must be told, and a song must be sung.

Understanding therefore extends to the circumstances of the character and story, as well. What is happening around the character at the time that the story is happening? This is a question not only of time and place, which of course are crucial, but of the lives of other characters, and of relevant matters that exist outside of the story, but have implications for the story (a political or moral climate, for example). When you play a character, you as an actor are aware of how the story turns out, but the character you play is not; he or she is living in the moment. Your need at a certain moment is so dire that it translates to song at a specific moment. What are the circumstances of that moment, beyond what your character knows?

Rock music, with its strong attachment to its historical and cultural context, is often heavy with circumstance, and thereby connects well with the social conscience or moral ambiguity of the stories of many rock musicals. When discussing circumstance in rock songs, we revisit rock history and aesthetics. Achieving full understanding of a rock-based character requires familiarity with the social, political, cultural, and artistic history of rock, and with its vast and varied literature. Therein lie many clues to creating a believable character.

Ability, or skill, comes from mastery of technique. For you as a musical theatre performer, ability includes not only expertise in creating character, but also control of your voice and physicality, facility with diction and rhythmic declamation of text, and musical proficiency. A person on stage who is struggling vocally or musically belies the non-reality of the endeavor. Likewise, a person in a rock musical unable to convincingly rock risks implausibility. Any of a number of musical and specifically rock-musical skills may be called upon at any given time; therefore, a wide range of abilities is necessary. Nevertheless, if you are of limited vocal or musical ability, singing a rock song in a show is still not out of your reach—after all, rock was meant for everyone. Obviously you should hone your skills, but rock has a different set of standards for ability: as long as your voice is interesting, your musicianship is competent, you fully understand and embrace the rock aesthetic, and you are a convincing actor, you can rock a song.

In a rock context, although the basic techniques of acting do not significantly change, the language does, the musical syntax and vocabulary do, the vocal inflections do. It's a bit like learning a new language, maybe not as hard as singing in Italian or German, but there are still rules of semantics and grammar that you'll have to get comfortable with. To increase your rock musical ability, memorize lyrics in different styles and recite them as poems, or monologues. Regularly sight-read and analyze songs from all rock eras and genres. Learning how to rap well is an excellent way to master rhythmic intricacy and syncopation, as well as to prepare for the rap songs and musicals that are popping up everywhere. Exercises such as these make for enjoyable practice time, while immersing you in the literature. Improvising in various styles is also very helpful, as is playing a musical instrument and learning to play and accompany in rock styles. (Chapter 5 contains a number of rock-specific vocal and musical exercises.)

Conveyance refers to the effective communication of ideas and emotions to an audience. An actor may truthfully feel an emotion on stage, yet the audience might not perceive it. Unbiased observers, particularly directors, music directors, and coaches, are helpful in working with you to ensure that your emotions on stage are not only genuine, but manifest to others, and that the meaning of the drama (or song) makes sense to all listeners, and not just to you and those in the rehearsal room. They may find that a feeling is not clear enough or not sufficiently explicit. Just as often they will have to hold you back, reminding you, as so many acting students have been reminded, to *have* your feelings, rather than *show* them.

Conveyance in a rock setting is complicated by rock's inclination toward generality, as well as by the specific aesthetic context of each song. Effective conveyance of character arises from commitment to character and from the choices you make in embodying that character. When performing rock songs in the theatre, characterization and choices are informed by rock aesthetics and techniques. Yet you cannot simply put a rock facade on a performance or use a presentational rock-inspired approach to convey sincere and specific emotion, rock-based or not. (Some forms of comedy might be exceptions.) Rather, by experiencing the aesthetic and musical underpinning of rock songs and mastering the techniques that rock artists use to communicate their generalized emotions, you enhance your conveyance of rock-based characters. Each song performance is a balance of truth in acting and truth in style.

Rightness is a highly subjective concept. As noted, whether an actor is believable in a role is up to the audience, and actors and directors can only prepare what they think will be a believable performance. Quite often there are practical matters that disallow rightness, an obvious example being the unavoidable miscasting in amateur and academic theatre. Needless to say, literal physical rightness is not necessary for believability; otherwise there would be no amateur or academic theatre, and there would be no *Hamilton*, or rock adaptations of classic novels. It is completely possible for a character to be "right" in more than one way. To some extent, an actor can fabricate rightness in the face of uncertainty, or, put another way, rightness can come from commitment to character even when an audience's expectations are not met. Nevertheless, meeting an audience's expectations of what a character should look and sound like goes a long way toward believability. The rightest rightness, of course, occurs when high levels of understanding, ability, and conveyance meet with rightness of physicality and personality. That's when we say that someone is "perfect for the role."

Rock music in the theatre presents its own obstacles to rightness, because rock can be a conspicuous, impactful style that is only right under certain terms. Good authorship, however, along with your understanding of and trust in the material as an actor, can break through these barriers with convincing realism or glorious theatricality. Again, I cite *Hamilton*, and in their day, *Jesus Christ Superstar, Pippin, Tommy*, and *Rent*. Within moments, the audience at *Hamilton* knows that the guy in the blue uniform is Aaron Burr, because he is written as Aaron Burr, and says the things that Aaron Burr would say, even though he is rapping. David Woolard's brilliant costuming in *Tommy* surrounded the hero, always dressed in white, with a kaleidoscope of color (and black and white), according to character and scene. Not unexpectedly, most production teams cast their leads, and when possible their ensembles, according to physical and vocal type, as in, at the time of this writing, *Spongebob: The Musical, The Cher Show, Beautiful*, and *Ain't Too Proud: The Life and Times of the Temptations*.

Rightness for roles in a rock musical theatre context has not changed, but it is professionally advantageous to actors to cultivate knowledge of the roles and material in the modern repertoire, and align themselves with these parts as they would for any others. Knowledge of the rock repertoire engenders comfort with rock styles, and comfort will also translate to rightness: any performance perceived as effortless is automatically more convincing.

Acting in Rock Musicals

Your acting process does not have to be overhauled just because rock is involved. It does, however, require you to know why a character you are playing is singing, why he or she is singing in a rock style, and how best to enact and convey that style, as well as your character.

What is it that distinguishes a character as an authentic product of the rock era, and how do you approach or modify your portrayal of that character to attain the necessary authenticity (excluding for the moment musical approaches)? Tara Rubin, one of the theatre and film's premier casting directors, offers this point of view: "When we cast rock musicals we look for actors who have an affinity for the rock sensibility; artists who like to live in the questions and the margins of life, rather than in the center where all the answers might be." Rock is undoubtedly off-center, or was meant to be, and does its best to stay there. It looks for answers on its own terms, as do the characters who live in its world.

For another opinion, let's listen to an expert. Bono, the lead singer of U2, has famously said, "As a rock star, I have two instincts: I want to have fun, and I want to change the world." As is typical of many rock stars, and of many rock songs and performances, his statement is at once wide-eyed and brash. It is also remarkably pithy; it pretty much sums up the outlook from which rock was born, and the conviction it has carried with it throughout its history.

Underlying Bono's terse sentiment are the principles of rock culture discussed earlier, starting with the attributes of rock 'n' roll that first mortified an older generation of listeners, and that made rock music revolutionary beyond the songs themselves. Along with the musical upheaval of rock came new types of characters in novels, television, and film, with updated motivations and modernized modes of behavior. They were reflected not just in content but in linguistic style and physicalization. Films such as *Rebel without a Cause*, *The Wild One*, *The Graduate*, *American Graffiti*, *Quadrophenia*, and *Risky Business* feature such characters, and are required viewing for any aspiring rock actor.

One of the best routes toward becoming a rock-savvy actor or portraying a rock-based character is to observe some of the famous (and infamous) rock personalities whose lives are so widely chronicled, and whose personal journeys are often captured in their musical output. (In his interview that concludes this chapter, Michael Cerveris notes his early perception of his rock idols as theatrical personae, and how he learned most about being a rocker by carefully observing his exemplars and experiencing the lifestyle firsthand, from an early age.) You can watch the performers themselves in dozens of excellent rock concert films and documentaries such as *The Last Waltz*, *The Decline of Western Civilization*, and *Stop Making Sense*.

Dissect, with a critical and technical as well as aesthetic eye, the attributes of each performer you examine, and the musical and personal qualities that make their stories communicative and their performances engaging. Ask yourself, first, if it is feasible or appropriate for you to do things dramatically, musically, and vocally similar to those you are using as models, because certain materials and techniques will simply not suit you. (Of course, on occasion, a song can be performed completely out of the intended character, or with a deliberately opposite acting choice.) If the answer is yes, then identify the essential background and exhaustively rehearse the necessary techniques. With all the material that's out there, a lifetime of such learning is available.

There is an obvious connection between these performers and their audiences. Charisma cannot be learned, but personality can be exploited, and in this effort, rock has helped show the way.

How was Elvis Presley such a successful rock singer and a believable actor at the same time? Aside from the fact that movies were built around his personality, his singing and his acting both emanate seamlessly from his boyish, mildly devilish charm. None of you will ever be Elvis, I'm afraid, but some of you might well be cast as a boyish, mildly devilishly charming character. Elvis's fine musicianship and great sense of groove seem inborn and effortless, as does his one-of-a-kind physicality. Take Elvis's advice: be yourself, be a good musician, keep great time with your voice, and dance like you mean it. The same qualities could be ascribed in the modern era to Beyoncé, who like Elvis has inexhaustible charm and likability, and a strongly identifiable point of view. Just as Elvis did, she has both chops and magnetism. She fully comprehends the music she is singing, how to get it across, and what it means to its listeners. The combination is palpable, and evident in her critical acclaim and mass appeal, as well as her easy transfer to and remarkable presence on screen.

Mick Jagger has acted in films, too, as well as having a decades-long career as a rock icon, but really, he is acting every time he sings, especially in live performance. He commands the stage, and commands each song he sings, with his exaggerated, idiosyncratic self. It's audible in his bluesy, slurred, satchel-mouthed vocalism and visible in the lithe, awkward/graceful way he poses and moves. Like Mick, don't suppress your peculiarities. If you're somehow offbeat, capitalize on your offbeat-ness as a rock hallmark. Alanis Morissette does the same sort of thing, and like Jagger, tells it like it is, to your face. (Her songs were recently adapted into the score of a book musical.) She uses her unlikely mezzo-soprano both as a penetrating tool of conversation and the sound of an alarm. Lady Gaga had no trouble making the transition from song to screen; this is unsurprising, as her songs and videos were already theatre pieces of their own, and she was always known for her unique style of role-playing. Bruce Springsteen, a musical storyteller (and now a Broadway star), uses his everyday, working-class vocalism, with a rocking sense of rhythm, and his amicable but somewhat stern persona, to convey truth in every line, to tacitly encourage the audience to sing along. Similar to Springsteen but with an urban rap vocabulary, is Eminem, another musical artist with a strong screen presence.

Beyond superficial appeal, there is a core to all these performers that burns with an independent spirit, a rebellious nature, or unbridled feeling. These are the aesthetic bases of rock, and they will come through in your acting of rock songs, if you exercise your own rock core, whatever it may be. By analyzing how these great rock performers achieve the acting ideals of understanding, ability, conveyance, and rightness, at least on their rock performance terms, you can borrow from them and apply what you borrow to musical theatre performance. I am not suggesting that you imitate them. I am, however, strongly advocating that you first investigate, then emulate to the extent that is relevant and suitable to you and the characters you play, the qualities that make them so effective, as a means of conveyance and to achieve believability through authenticity.

Furthermore, more exact imitation can come in handy when you are performing in biographical jukebox musicals, an increasingly common musical theatre genre. In these shows, you will be called upon to portray a real singing character, and for the most part, accurate vocal (and physical) portrayals are the best means to truthful storytelling and reaching the audience, who may come in with musical expectations of what the characters should sound like and be like.

Let's now look at rock-based characters from the inside, and more specifically. The following list of essential characteristics is a sampling from the vibrant spectrum of rock-based themes and values that define rock-based characters, and which provide the foundation for acting choices when singing in rock styles in the theatre. We'll see these qualities in action, and meet the sorts of characters they define, during the coaching sessions in Part III.

Alienation, or disenfranchisement. One main stimulus of rock culture and rock music was the dissatisfaction a younger generation felt with the social and political establishment. A large swath of a growing population felt ignored, discriminated against, undervalued, or otherwise at odds with the rest of the world, that is, the world of their elders. At first their reaction played out viscerally, in song, dance, and language, but soon fueled a generation-wide movement toward greater awareness and "mind expansion," social responsibility, inclusion, and the general good. Outside of music, there was growing interest in existentialist and nihilist literature, beat poetry, avant-gardism, the burgeoning field of abnormal psychology, and risqué films like *Breathless* and *Splendor in the Grass.* Young people raised their feelings, and trends such as these, to a philosophical order, which in turn motivated their attitudes and actions, and the musical by-products thereof. Characters who were defined by their alienation later followed on the musical theatre stage; they were somewhat slow in entering the dramatic scene, but now are commonplace. Song examples: "Nowhere Man," the Beatles; "I Started a Joke," the Bee Gees; "Shiver Me Timbers," Tom Waits; "Glory Days," Bruce Springsteen; "One of Us," Joan Osborne; "Walking in My Shoes," Depeche Mode. Character examples: Pippin (*Pippin*), Tommy (*Tommy*), Evan Hansen (*Dear Evan Hansen*), Cady (*Mean Girls*).

Progressivism and rebellion. In reaction to alienation, rock characters want to rethink existing orders and rebel against oppressive systems. In addition to helping to rescue themselves from alienation, these desires and actions are their attempts to improve the general state of humanity and weed out corrupt and outmoded ideas. These are the social and political ideals and idealists of rock culture, and they are evident in a large segment of rock music. Statements in song have ranged from rationally ideological to openly violent. We find several characters similarly proactive in the musical theatre. Song examples: "Blowin' in the Wind," Bob Dylan; "What's Goin' On," Marvin Gaye; "God Save the Queen," the Sex Pistols; "Rock the Casbah," the Clash; "Get Up, Stand Up," Bob Marley and the Wailers; "Killing in the Name," Rage against the Machine. Character examples: Rizzo (*Grease*), Ren (*Footloose*), Matilda (*Matilda*), Gideon Fletcher (*The Last Ship*).

Unbridled celebration; uninhibited sensual pleasure. These are expressions of the joy brought on by liberation from, or sometimes victory over, what a younger generation considered unjust, repressive systems and conventions. They also represent the gradual crossing of long-standing boundaries in sexual behavior, sex education, sexual awareness, and sexual identity. Quite often in song, feelings of ecstasy transform to overt sexuality, already an essential component of rock's musical and lyrical content. Bringing what had been taboo into the open gave license in a mass market to themes of sexual freedom, growth, confusion, and realization. Rarely in the theatre is positivity the only aspect of character; a character who is entirely joyous is devoid of conflict, and conflict makes for stories. The theatre stage, however, is home to many joyous moments, and quite often they are collective, rather than individual, as in production numbers and happy-ending finales. Song examples: "I Got You (I Feel Good)," James Brown; "I'm a Believer," The Monkees; "Let Your Love Flow," the Bellamy Brothers; "Walking on Sunshine," Katrina and the Waves; "La Vida Loca," Ricky Martin. Character examples: Berger (*Hair*), Mama Euralie (*Once on This Island*), Tanya and Rosie (*Mamma Mia!*), Cynthia Weil and Barry Mann (*Beautiful*).

Defense of individualism. Perhaps the most sought-after freedom of the rock generation was that of "being oneself," an ideology that recognized the egalitarian worth of each individual. (*Sesame Street* brought the spirit to children, as did Marlo Thomas with her *Free to Be . . . You and Me* project.) It also spoke to the civil rights issues that plagued much of the rock era. Freedom of choice, freedom of identity, freedom of religion, freedom from prejudice, independence of spirit, and the right to autonomy have remained principles of the highest order in rock. Recently they have been re-energized by a new society whose engines include social media and information sharing, where people want to be noticed, usually for who they are. Themes of individualism count for a huge sector of the musical theatre rock repertoire, as well. Song examples: "My Generation," the Who; "Rocky Mountain High," John Denver; "Elsewhere," Sarah McLachlan; "Papa Don't Preach," Madonna; "The Great Escape," Boys Like Girls; "Independent Women," Destiny's Child. Character examples: Billy (*Billy Elliot*), Angel (*Rent*), Elphaba (*Wicked*), Tick (*Priscilla, Queen of the Desert*).

Self-actualization. Related to all of the above issues is the notion of coming into oneself, of reaching some stage of enlightenment, manifest on a large scale by younger generations making the transition from adolescence to adulthood. Thus it is found at both the individual and societal levels in rock culture, and in several generations of rock history. Here is a typical self-actualization story, in condensed form: a character who has felt disenfranchised becomes empowered, and rebels against an opposing force, personal or communal. Once he or she has prevailed over the obstacle, he or she reaches a new realization of and satisfaction with self. (Sometimes this creates additional problems; it may only be the end of Act 2 in a three-act structure.) This story can be found throughout the repertoire of rock theatre. It is also in keeping with the Eastern religions and philosophies that piqued the interest of many a rock artist. Song examples: "I Can See Clearly Now," Johnny Nash; "Message in a Bottle," the Police; "I Won't Back Down," Tom Petty; "Stronger," Britney Spears; "Put Your Records On," Corinne Bailey Rae; "Masterpiece," Jessie J. Character examples: Tracy Turnblad (*Hairspray*), Elle (*Legally Blonde*), Celie (*The Color Purple*).

Downfall. Rock is also the province of those who fail at overcoming their alienation, or are unable to surmount the insurmountable. Rock songs are replete with tragic figures; indeed the blues might be thought of as a celebration of despair. Suffering has always been a powerful motivator of song—indeed of all music. Rock and theatre songs both draw many musical and lyrical tendencies from undisguised expressions of downheartedness, and the two worlds share a variety of attitudes toward sadness, from the desperate to the self-effacing to the downright funny. Song examples: "When a Man Loves a Woman," Percy Sledge; "She's out of My Life," Michael Jackson; "Losing My Religion," R.E.M.; "Crucify," Tori Amos; "Give Me Back My Hometown," Eric Church; "Saint Veronika," Billy Talent. Character examples: Alexander Hamilton (*Hamilton*), Hedwig (*Hedwig and the Angry Inch*), Huey Calhoun (*Memphis*).

Interview with Michael Cerveris

I can think of no better performer to turn to for some first-hand thoughts on acting in rock musicals than one of the premier actors on the Broadway stage, and one of the most experienced in the field of rock musical theatre, Michael Cerveris. He has brilliantly played at least two iconic rock characters, Tommy in *The Who's Tommy* and Hedwig in *Hedwig and the Angry Inch*, but has appeared in as many straight plays as musicals. Michael is also a dedicated rock musician and a fine guitarist, and has fronted and played in rock bands throughout his life and career.

> JC: For you, what makes a rock musical? You just finished *Fun Home*, for instance. Was that a rock show?
>
> MC: Even though *Fun Home* isn't really a rock musical, it uses pop-rock song forms and has a rock sensibility. Certainly both Jeanine [Tesori] and Lisa [Kron] come from the modern world, and so they understand what it means to exist in a rock culture, and they use a lot of different kinds of music to tell their story, including rock.

I find that most musicals are really quite traditional, but *Tommy* was special. I was frustrated by the fact that *Rent* got the attention at the time for being a groundbreaking rock musical that *Tommy* actually deserved. *Rent* was a fairly conventional musical with entertaining pop-rock music, where there was a lot of rock posturing and singing in a theatrical context. But *Rent* wouldn't have succeeded or even made it to Broadway if it weren't for *Tommy* kicking down the walls first, and much as I enjoyed *Rent*, the music seemed to be straining to call itself rock. I walked out of it thinking, why is it so hard to get the mixture of great theatre and rock music right? No slight to *Rent* at all, it just wasn't what I expected from the buzz.

Then the same week I saw *Rent*, I saw *Hedwig* for the first time. I had been working with John Cameron Mitchell on a new Queen bio-musical; we were playing the bassist and drummer in the band. We were in a rehearsal for "Bohemian Rhapsody" (I remember thinking that if you needed to be taught "Bohemian Rhapsody," you shouldn't even be there), and we were being the bad kids in the back of class. John kept asking me what he should call his new show—was it glam-pop-post-punk-rock? post-punk-glam-rock?—and he invited me to see it. I came out of *Hedwig* and said, here's what I've been looking for, here's the answer. Part of the problem in a musical is always explaining why someone is singing. In this case, Hedwig is in the band, so that problem was solved very easily. But these were great rock songs, and even if I didn't know the show, I'd go and buy the album. For a while after *Tommy*, we were sort of the poster children for rock theatre. I kept getting asked to audition for new stuff, but I passed on most of it because most it felt like paler versions of *Tommy*.

JC: What made *Tommy* so important to you? And why do you think it wasn't a greater success, other than obvious errors in marketing it?

MC: You know, I grew up simultaneously as a rock 'n' roll kid, and a kid doing theatre. I would go to concerts, and think, "This is amazing," and I felt a kind of narrative that was there in the performance. It could be the Ramones, or Bowie, or Peter Gabriel, or Kiss, and you'd see this definite sense of the theatrical in what they did, even though they're not burdened with a narrative. But the enthusiasm you have at a rock show, the excitement and the energy, I thought, if you could put that into theatre, it would be amazing. Even with the more traditional shows, the *Carousel*s and so on, I wondered why we couldn't get audiences as excited about those as they were about rock shows. Then *Tommy* came up, and I was so happy to be participating in trying to put these two things together. It's not that rock had never been on stage before, but more than *Hair* or *Superstar*, which were the kind of shows that got me most into theatre, *Tommy* had a strain of un-adulterated rock that hadn't been seen before, and Des [McAnuff] managed to harness what Pete [Townshend] did into a story and dramaturgy that audiences could connect with. We also treated the music in mostly the same way as the

Who did. One of the places we diverged was in the vocal arrangements, but even those weren't done like a traditional show would have done them. Instead, like the Beach Boys counterpoint you wrote for "Sensation," they were throwbacks to earlier forms of rock 'n' roll, and that's absolutely what Pete is about, too. We had served a rock vision and Pete's vision, but maybe we didn't serve a Broadway audience's expectation. And the ambiguous ending of the show might have left audiences a little unsatisfied.

JC: Does that mean that Broadway really still isn't ready for rock, or is rock an inadequate storyteller? Can Broadway really get a tattoo and wear a leather motorcycle jacket, and still have wide appeal?

MC: It may sound confusing, but I think of Sondheim as a rock 'n' roll composer. By that I don't mean that what he writes sounds anything what you hear on the radio. I mean that in terms of his brazenness, his maverick spirit, and that he's interested pushing the boundaries of theatre music. He hasn't pandered to traditional Broadway audiences' tastes, either. For example, *Company*, *Assassins*, and *Pacific Overtures* are all pretty revolutionary, and he's playing with music and forms that don't aim to satisfy an audience as the conventional wisdom says they should. That's what rock 'n' roll is about. Even if it doesn't have electric guitars, it's unapologetic about what it's trying to say and how it says it. For me, Sondheim's work has more rock spirit than something that mostly just dresses itself up in the trappings of rock. You know, you can take off the leather jacket and wash off the stick-on tattoos the next day. Broadway, with its commercial imperatives, seems a better place for a *safer* sort of rock 'n' roll, and maybe real rock really does belong . . . downtown.

JC: When acting in an authentic rock musical, is it any different for you from your normal way of doing things? Can you pinpoint it? Is it an attitude? A frame of mind?

MC: Like most musical theatre, it's mostly a matter of believing what you're saying, and communicating it honestly, in this case in the rock genre. You have to know what rock 'n' roll is, and commit to your belief in it.

In *Tommy*, I certainly didn't sing those songs in the same way as I would with a band. I sort of instinctively adjust to the place where I'm singing. When playing Tommy on Broadway, my focus was on telling the story. It's a monologue that's happening on pitches, and I'm thinking about the text. When I'm doing a concert, it's more emotional, I'm trying to express a feeling, and in some ways I'm addressing the audience, and feeding off their energy. That's another thing that helps in *Hedwig*, where the audience attending *Hedwig* is Hedwig's audience.

An interesting story—we opened for Boy George and Culture Club at Radio City Music Hall on New Year's Eve, as Hedwig and the Angry Inch the band, not as actors from the show. Most of the people there didn't know what *Hedwig* was, so we were just this weird, transgender-fronted band playing songs that most people hadn't heard, because they were there for this flashback weekend kind of thing. So there were some hecklers there, and you hear them really well at Radio City. If it had been me, as myself, I would have shriveled up and died, but with the mask of Hedwig on, I could come up with responses to anyone, and was able to give it right back, and the audience came around, and we ended up having the time of our lives.

I like to respect what the writer wrote, so in all cases I basically just sing the song. For me, it's the song, not the singer. I don't think you need to add that much to a song. Any song you sing will be different because it's *you* singing it, and almost every time I see someone trying to "interpret" a well-written rock song, I don't find it that satisfying.

JC: You were an actor first, were you not? How did you start singing?

MC: My dad is a classical musician and educator, so I always was around music, but the things that interested me most about music were not really a part of his musical world. In junior high school, I loved singing in the choir, and my music teacher singled me out and asked me to sing a solo. That was the first time I even thought of myself as a singer at all. I taught myself guitar and played in a band—we were very bad but very loud—and I was always frustrated the singers I wanted to sing like sang so much higher than I did, and I couldn't find songs I could sing. Then I discovered Bowie, a baritone, and I could sing some of his things, and that was my entry into rock singing. Then in college, the theatre program at Yale undergraduate wasn't a pre-professional program. We didn't have any speech and voice training or movement training, so I took dance classes through the phys ed program, and I started studying voice in the music department with Blake Stern, who was a German Lieder specialist, but I was really taking lessons because I wanted to do Shakespeare, and classical verse. He told me that he'd train me as he knew how, and assured me that I'd be able to apply his teachings to whatever I wanted to do. So I did Italian art song, and I did recitals, and sang Barber and Bernstein and other modern American music I really loved. When I graduated and came to New York, like everyone else, I thought I should put together a book [of songs for auditions], but I didn't have any rock songs in my book. I sang things like "Luck Be a Lady." I'd go out for a lot of things like the twelfth national tour of *Les Mis*, and would sing "Empty Chairs at Empty Tables," but they'd always end up casting a good singer who could act a little rather than me, an actor who could sing a little. I did mostly plays, and I did get to do Shakespeare, and didn't really think much about musicals.

JC: What got you to the *Tommy* audition, and what did you sing? I remember having just gotten off the plane from New York and arriving at the old Debbie Reynolds studio just in time to catch your audition—Des excitedly hurried me into the room to show me this actor he thought was perfect.

MC: That's awfully nice to hear—and I wish I'd known it at the time! Or maybe not, actually. . . . I did a TV show, playing an English guitar student on *Fame*, which is why I was out in L.A. to audition for *Tommy*. At my *Fame* audition, I had to play the guitar, so I played and sang Bowie's "Young Americans," because it was by Bowie, and I could sing it. It got me that job, so when the *Tommy* audition came around, I thought, again, I wouldn't have a piano player play something for me. I'll just bring my guitar, and that was at a time when not a lot of musical theatre singer-actors played guitar.

JC: Are there technical changes you made to your voice for singing rock, and singing *Tommy*?

MC: I added five or six notes to my range when doing *Tommy*, just through sheer practice and repetition. I sang well enough at first to get the job, I guess, but my voice got stronger and bigger as the show went on, and more durable, too.

I was so very lucky to be in the company of all these great singers, like Jonathan Dokuchitz [Captain Walker on Broadway], who has this effortless sound, and Lee Morgan [The Hawker], who was a perfect model of a rock singer. I had learned something about how to place my voice and how to use the musculature from Blake, but I wondered how Jonathan would *feel* when he made these soaring sounds—and I tried to work it out for myself, listening to him and trying to sponge it up. On the other hand, you had Lee, who sounded like he was going to lose his voice at the end of every verse, but could sing for hours at a time. I would to listen to him in the same way as I did Jonathan, and asked them both questions. I just kept experimenting with what my voice could do, and I just got to practice it so much and for so long, I learned a lot about endurance, the kind of things that no one really teaches you and you have to work out for yourself.

I knew that I didn't want it to sound like I was singing in a musical. I think the only conscious choices I made were if I heard something coming out of my mouth that was not rock and roll, I would stop doing it. We had done all this great dramaturgical work early in rehearsal about the history of rock, and Pete even brought me over to London to hang with him—he said to me, "I can't teach you how to act, but I can teach you how to be a rock star." He never said, "You have to sing it like this," but more by osmosis I picked up some of his swagger and boldness. Those things informed the sound of my voice, because I was thinking and feeling certain things, and when I used my voice when thinking and feeling those things, it came out right. I guess "I'm Free" was a good example. I didn't want to sound like Roger Daltrey (well, I would have *loved* to sound like Daltrey, but that was never going to happen), I just wanted to sound like someone who would be standing before a giant arena singing a rock song.

JC: Were you thinking about the technical process of using diction as a rhythmic impulse and using the voice as an element of groove, which are some of the things I'm trying to teach singers in this book?

MC: Looking back, I suppose I did, but I wasn't a trained enough singer-musician to know that that's what I was doing. But because I work from the text, that's very much a part of what I do, and that's also why I tend never to backphrase. It works well for me not to have a lot of technical training, because I think that led me to develop a really good ear. I learn very fast by ear, and I like working with the composer. By listening I feel as if I can get inside what the writer had inside his head, and I try to capture that, and then, over time, in rehearsal, I eventually make it start to sound like me. But always, it's the consonants that lock me into the feel. I try to be like another instrument in the band.

JC: And as a consequence of your consonants, you would rain down saliva on me as I conducted the show. That outpouring, so to speak, to me was an indication of how you worked the diction into your strong sense of rock performance, and I think it helped your endurance. Did you ever blow yourself out, vocally?

MC: I do think that leading with consonants helps with vocal production and endurance. But it can't all just be technique, there's a certain amount of careful carelessness that comes into performance of any kind—and especially in rock singing. Really, you can't know your limits until you've passed them at least a bit. If everything felt good and truthful, I wouldn't care if my high notes weren't pristine, just that they sounded honest, and that they didn't hurt. I came up in the pre–social media era, and I would go on somehow, no matter how sick or injured, unless I was bleeding profusely, but nowadays I know that actors will call out for fear that a subpar performance will become a public disgrace. I wish it was like being an opera singer, who can leave it all out on the stage because you know you don't have to sing again for five days. You really don't want to hold back, but some part of you is reminding you that it's only Tuesday, so of course you have to make some concessions. At first, because I had never done it before, I tried all sorts of things to keep my voice healthy, but eventually I started to feel like the monastic approach was robbing me of some of my life force and I'd have to let my hair down—this is when I still had hair. It always seemed to catch up with me Friday night, before the four-show weekend, and I'd wake up on Saturday and regret how unprofessional I'd been in the days before, and then, of course, I'd end up having my best show of the week. But I was at least wise enough to know I couldn't be irresponsible all the time and expect it not to catch up with me. So much of singing is psychological, and if you're nervous or too cautious or just too convinced you have to be perfect, then you're more likely to hurt yourself, by not breathing properly or tightening up. Like they say, "perfect is the enemy of good." And, I would add, it ain't rock 'n' roll.

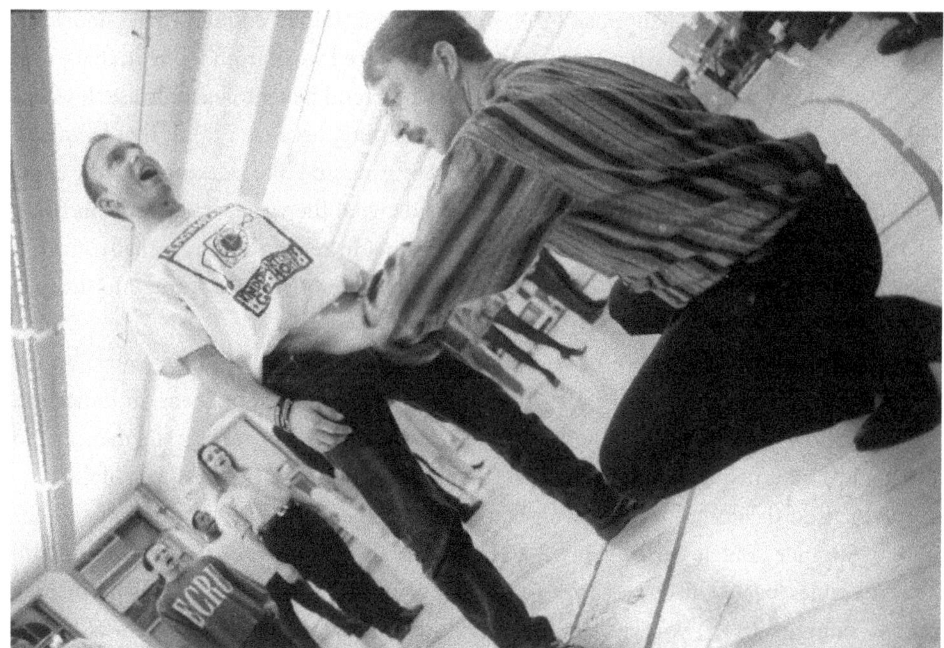

PHOTO 1: The author conducting Michael Cerveris and the cast of Broadway's *Tommy* in rehearsal (photo by Peter Cunningham, reprinted by permission of the photographer)

PHOTO 2: At the *Tommy* original cast recording session, the author with orchestrator Steve Margoshes, record producer Sir George Martin, Michael Cerveris, and Pete Townshend (photo by Peter Cunningham, reprinted by permission of the photographer)

PHOTO 3: Backstage at *Tommy* with Jerry Garcia of the Grateful Dead (photographer unknown, property of the author)

4

Musical Values in Rock Theatre Songs

Performers approach music of all styles, including rock, in pretty much the same way. Singers and instrumentalists everywhere, regardless of their specialties, follow their hearts, their habits, their training, and their tastes throughout their study and professional pursuit of music. They listen, study, learn, adjust, collaborate, rehearse, practice, perform . . . and then do it again, and over and over again. Music is a discipline in which the ongoing accumulation of knowledge and experience feeds one's aptitude and enjoyment. No matter how good you are at making music, you can always get better.

Every musical style carries with it performance practices necessary to making it viable. Ignoring these practices will usually interfere with, if not negate, that style. As an example, Baroque music played without proper ornamentation would be historically incorrect, as would be soul and gospel performances that omitted their indigenous vocal ornamentation. Embracing authenticity to some extent is always important, but especially crucial when performing rock, because rock is so recent and such a strong component of the modern cultural consciousness. A musical layperson probably won't know if the trills and mordents in a Bach suite are being wrongly applied, but they will know if a soul or gospel singer's riffs sound false.

Rock songs open up to theatre singers new dimensions of performance possibilities, and pitfalls. The materials and practices of rock might be unfamiliar to anyone who has been classically trained, and sometimes making the adjustment involves altering a long-held outlook. The transition need not be painful for you as a singer, provided that you keep an open mind and are willing to explore new methods. Overall, there is less rigidity to rock interpretation than in classical music, but there is no less discipline required to master it.

In the theatre, the techniques and the freedoms of rock performance practice are regulated by the needs of characterization and storytelling, and by the need for consistent performances over time—every rock concert a performer gives may be a bit different, but in the theatre, every performance, though acted with spontaneity, should be pretty much the same. When singing theatre music of any kind, the thought processes and techniques of acting strongly affect musical values, reshaping and enhancing each individual's realization of a song. In a presentational situation, musical values may have a stronger impact on performance choices, and those choices may be more ad hoc, but still, the bigger conceptual picture of a stage show is paramount. On the other hand, when singing rock songs, whose musical styles and performance practices are so in the forefront, it can seem especially counterintuitive to value things extramusical over those that are musical.

In this chapter, we will examine rock songs from a musical standpoint, accountable though theatre music is to needs more all-encompassing than the music alone. Just as we briefly looked at acting at its most elemental levels, let's do the same with singing, beginning with the musical content you'll be singing, and paying particular attention to rock songs.

Melody

The aspect of music that occupies singers most is *melody*. Melodies are made up of several components, and in rock, preeminent among them is rhythm. There are many manifestations of rock, but what they all have in common is rhythmic propulsion. It functions in all rock melodies, and not just their accompaniments. This distinguishes rock from most earlier forms of popular song.

One can define melody as a series of pitches arranged in rhythm, over time, organized in a musically articulate fashion, and in the case of a song, combined with text. Whenever you sing, you *interpret* a melody, that is, you make choices, usually conscious but sometimes not, of how to sing it. More than any other instrument, the voice is unique to each performer. In the musical theatre, your interpretive choices are motivated by character and situation, and underlaid by your knowledge (understanding), musicianship (ability), and musicality.

Melody is your primary focus because the melody is your "part" in the "score" of a song. As a rule, it is the solo part, the lead voice, what is referred to in polyphonic (multi-voiced) counterpoint as the *cantus firmus*, the literal translation of which is "fixed song." All other parts, instrumental and sometimes vocal, those which make up the "accompaniment," are designed to work alongside the melody, supporting, enhancing, and highlighting it.

Melodic rhythm refers to the sequence of note durations over time in a melody. In rock, the melodic rhythm, and usually the precision of that rhythm, are far more important than in most popular songs of earlier eras. Often the melodic rhythm is the primary rhythmic motor for a song (as in "One, two, three o'clock, four o'clock rock/Five, six, seven o'clock, eight o'clock rock . . ."), and it is always of great importance in the collective rhythmic texture. *Melodic rate* is the amalgam of note durations (half notes, quarters, eighths, sixteenths, etc.) in a phrase or melody: melodies made up of many notes with short durations are said to have a fast melodic rate, while melodies consisting of fewer notes and longer note durations have a slow melodic rate.

The shape of a melody, its ups and downs of pitch, is known as its *contour*. Melodic contour in song is connected to text and text setting, and helps evince the meanings of words, phrases, and entire lyrics. The pitches used in a melody, or the melody's *pitch content*, usually belong to one or more *modes*, or *modalities*. Rock melodies, as opposed to being mostly diatonic with some chromaticism, as were the songs of the Golden Age, favor pentatonic scales, blues scales (also found in Golden Age songs), Mixolydian and Dorian and other modes, and sometimes the modal idiosyncrasies of certain nationalities or ethnicities. (See Example 1.)

EXAMPLE 1

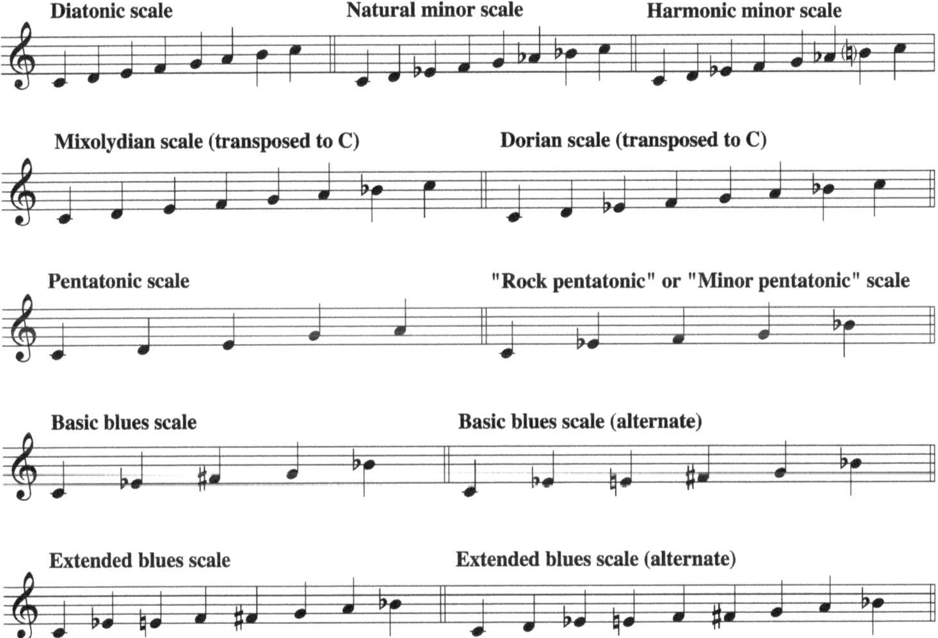

Most of the time, for a theatre singer, the most important aspects of melody are, first, its *relationship to the lyric*, and second, its *phrase structure*. Melodies, like speech, are made up of musical *phrases* (as well as sentences and paragraphs). The way a singer treats a phrase is called *phrasing*. Musical phrasing, like speech, involves vocabulary, syntax, and punctuation. These take the form of rhythmic *motives* (smaller fragments of melodic ideas that recur and develop) and *patterns* (repeated motives or smaller fragments of rhythm or melody), silence (rests), melodic rhythm and rate, and other elements, such as dynamics and articulation.

Most melody is supported by underlying *harmony*, or more specifically, harmonic progression, a series of chords in a musically rational order. Most rock chords are either triads or sevenths, and rock can claim nearly exclusive ownership of the open fifth chord, known also as a "power chord," a triad missing its third. Notes in a melody can be part of the harmony, extensions of the harmony, or in conflict with the harmony. More often than not in theatre songs there will be some connection between harmonic progression and textual choices.[1]

Analyzing a song will quickly reveal its *hook* (or hooks, see chapter 2), defined as the central notion and a concise musical and lyrical expression of a song's essential purpose, or idea. The strong presence of hooks in rock songs raises questions for theatre singer, such as: assuming a hook is repeated often, should your actions and subtext remain the same with each iteration? (Usually not, as this would result in dramatic stasis.) Does the summary nature of a hook require that you associate it with a similarly broad action, or can your action be more specific? (It depends on the situation, but the mere prominence of a hook demands that you treat it somehow differently.) Is the idea behind the hook shared among other characters, and if so, how does this affect each individual? (Sometimes a lead singer will want to blend in more to a larger ensemble vocal texture that shares a hook, and at other times will want somehow to emerge from that texture as a principal, by way of volume, phrasing, or embellishment.)

Examining the *form* of a song will help you gauge such matters as pacing and build, where to hold back and where to let go, where there is a climax (or anticlimax), where there are lulls, and so forth. In theatre music, for several reasons—because songs are like scenes, because song forms can be complex, because other theatrical elements are in play, and because many songs involve more than one singer—negotiating song forms is sometimes a collaborative effort. In *Sister Act*'s "I Could Be That Guy," for example, the lead singer has two instantaneous costume changes that are almost as important as the song's lyrics, and he sings in rhythmic and lyric counterpoint with a group of backup vocalists.

You analyze the *groove* of a song to assess what role the vocal line plays in creating and perpetuating it. As noted, the singer's melodic rhythm is sometimes the driver of the groove, and always plays some part in forming the groove.

Singers are keenly aware of *range* and *tessitura*, of how melodies fit into their individual voices. Range refers to the span between the lowest and highest pitch of a melody, or in vocal terms, of a singer's voice. Tessitura denotes the range that specific melodies or phrases occupy. We may say, for instance, that a song is in an alto range, which means that the pitches in its melody fall approximately between the F below middle C and the C above it. If, during that melody, pitches tend to lie in the upper or lower part of the range, we say that the song has a high or low tessitura, respectively. Range and tessitura vary widely from song to song in both rock and theatre songs, and composers will write

---

1. Excellent texts on music theory for musical theatre singers include John Bell and Steven R. Chicurel's *Music Theory for Musical Theater* (Lanham, MD: Scarecrow Press, 2008) and John Franceschina's *Music Theory Through Musical Theatre: Putting It Together* (New York: Oxford University Press, 2015).

in certain ranges for certain performers. Vocal *registration*, related to range and tessitura, is a matter of singing technique. It refers to particular mechanisms that singers use to produce notes in a certain range, or register. "Chest" voice, or "belting," and falsetto are examples of vocal registration.

Songs with very small ranges can still be highly expressive. Annie Lennox makes the most out of a very few neighboring pitches in the lead vocal of "Sweet Dreams," as does David Bowie in "Rebel, Rebel." Madonna, a very communicative singer but whose vocal range is limited, sings material with similarly limited melodies, but she does so with consummate senses of rhythm and style, in songs such as "Like a Prayer" or "Vogue." Small ranges in rock songs transferred to the theatre are often widened using vocal arranging techniques, as in "Are We the Waiting," from the stage version of *American Idiot*.

By contrast, some commercial rock songs are very "range-y," and some pop performers have made a career out of their extremes of range, from Minnie Riperton's high coloratura soprano down to Barry White's *basso profundo*. A high male tessitura is very commonplace in rock, and there are many iconic "rock tenors" willing to climb ever higher, such as Steve Perry or Adam Lambert. Songs with conspicuously wide ranges have always garnered attention: in early pop-rock, Harry Nilsson wowed his listeners with the octave leaps in "Without You," and more recently, Ariana Grande soars into the stratosphere on a regular basis in songs like "Why Try."

Such vocal virtuosity is not necessarily prerequisite to performing traditional musical theatre material, nor is a wide range. At least two of Rodgers and Hammerstein's favorite leading women, Gertrude Lawrence and Mary Martin, were actors first and singers second; the composers kept their material simple and in a limited range. Rex Harrison and Robert Preston easily overcame their musical shortcomings by devising equally communicative speech-song, and Lin-Manuel Miranda (as a performer) is their theatrical offspring, a better singer, but one who still traverses freely the border between melody and speech.

Some rock musical theatre material, on the other hand, does require more than a minimal vocal range, and sometimes sits in a very high tessitura, or less often in a low one. Transposing is usually an option, but not always, as when the tessitura is an essential feature of the song, or when multiple singers are involved. Regardless, rock theatre vocal ranges may hold challenges. In *Tommy*, the song "Cousin Kevin" harps on a downward chromatic motive ("I'm the school bully . . .") in a relatively high tessitura, and singers can fatigue quickly on such a repetitive pattern, especially at a loud dynamic with such menacing lyrics. "An Unexpected Song," a pop ballad from *Song and Dance*, has a notoriously low hook, which after hitting bottom leaps drastically upward. Digging out the low note is tough enough, but in the second half of the song, which has modulated up a fourth, the problem becomes the note at the top of the leap, which is also the final "glory note" of the song. All in all, the melody spans two octaves plus a whole step, and its most important notes are the two at the extreme ends of the melody, on the hook.[2] (Another famous range-stretcher from Webber's catalog is "Gesthemane," from *Jesus Christ Superstar*.)

Most often, the wide range of a melody or a spectacular vocal effect will be an expression of a character's strong emotional state. Conspicuous vocal or musical prowess is not necessarily a hindrance to believability, but it has to occur under the right dramatic circumstances. Examples would include the spectacular climax of "Defying Gravity," Simba's celebratory vocal obbligato in "He Lives in You" (see Part III), the penultimate section of "On My Own," from *Les Miserables*, and in a lighter vein, "Cheeseburger in Paradise" from *Escape to Margaritaville*.

Many rock melodies (especially blues-based melodies and some pop songs) are subject to *improvisation*, defined here as liberties a performer takes in pitch and rhythm that diverge from a predetermined melody. Yet in rock, it's sometimes hard to find the line between predetermination and improvisation. First off, what "predetermines" a rock melody? It's not usually how a song is notated, if it is notated at all; musical notation is often inadequate to communicate the exact sound of many rock melodies. On the other hand, some songwriters notate their melodies exactly as they want them to be sung—yet if a singer reads the notation with absolute accuracy, the performance might seem mechanical. In the case of a song that's best known from a recording, it might be what's heard on the recording—but what if there is more than one recording?

A theatre singer's interpretation of a rock melody varies according to dramatic and character needs, in addition to musical style. Your task will be a case-by-case, song-by-song determination of how much interpretation, reinterpretation, or improvisation is allowable. How important is precise rhythm to enacting the style? Is a vocal rhythm or groove untouchable throughout a song, or can it be manipulated over time to achieve more a believable performance? To what extent will diverting from written or originally sung rhythms jeopardize the groove? Under what circumstances are musical and vocal embellishment effective performance techniques, and how far can you go before believability is threatened?

There are two more details of melody important for singers to consider. Melody is not just sung pitches and rhythms; what makes melody artistic and communicative is the way a singer (or any musician) attacks, sustains, and releases each note, and the relative power, or volume, of every note and phrase. These qualities, called *articulation* and *dynamics*, function in all musical notes and phrases. Articulation applies mostly on a smaller scale, dynamics on a larger scale. Articulation in vocal melodies is also closely related to vocalism (see chapter 5). Without articulation and dynamics, music would be dry and mechanical, yet much of the time singers are not aware of them as discrete elements.

Instrumental musicians learn, and observe when they read music, a vocabulary of articulations—accent, staccato, tenuto, legato, and others. Most specific musical

---

2. Even the illustrious Bernadette Peters, who originated the role, seemed uncomfortable at both ends, as you can hear on the original cast recording.

articulations in the sung melodies of popular songs are determined by text and textual content, and singers do not consciously apply them except to reinforce conveyance of a word, phrase, character, or emotion (or once in a while as a purely musical requirement, more common in group singing). You'll note that there's not a lot of staccato in rock theatre singing, nor is there much legato. Staccato and legato are musical concepts, and musical theatre is more than just music. Most of the time, a theatre singer is articulating words, sentences, and other particles of speech, and musical articulation is the result.

Dynamics in a theatre rock song, indeed in any theatre song, are also a product of context, such as the overall energy level of the song, specific demands of style, or the intensity of feeling in a given phrase or section. In rehearsal, singers, music directors, and directors generally follow the natural fortes and pianos, crescendos and diminuendos, and everything in between, that a melody and a story prescribe. Singers adjust levels of loudness and softness to convey the beats of story and character, and to give shape, arc, climax, and humor to a song. Notated vocal melodies do not usually display specific articulation or dynamic markings (again, with exceptions).

Rock music is generally associated with loud dynamics. Though loudness can be measured in absolute values, loudness is a relative term. Rock was at first perceived as loud because it *was* loud in comparison to the popular music that preceded it. Within rock music, however, there is a great deal of material that is not loud: acoustic rock, folk, and so on. Furthermore, there is dynamic variety within all but the most "hardcore" of songs, songs purposefully played at high decibel levels for visceral effect. Nonetheless, it is safe to say that rock and rock singing often reach the higher elevations of the dynamic range. Mics and sound systems give singers considerable support, but there must be some power at the source of the sound. Modern sound design and mixing techniques also permit lesser dynamics, all the way down to a sotto voce, to be perceptible to an audience in a rock setting.

Last but not by any means least in a discussion of melody is the lyric attached to it. In rock songs, it seems that melodies and phrases are musicalized utterances of text as often as they are cohesive lyrical statements. Lyrics range from grunts and groans to repetitive hooks and chants to masterpieces of poetic or dramatic expression. Lyrics operate semantically on the large scale, setting mood and tone and telling story, and on the small scale, in turns of phrase and detail. For a singer, the words and the melody are one, most of all in a theatrical context. Keep in mind the maxim that music and lyrics that flow together naturally are the benchmark for effective communication in all song.

Rhythm: Meter, Tempo, and Feel

For study purposes, let's temporarily separate accompanimental and melodic rhythm, interdependent though they are. Upon examining accompanimental rhythm in depth, one can see at least three active forces that propel it.

First is *meter*. Meter is an architectural blueprint, the frame on which rhythms are built. It is a means for listeners and performers to organize and keep track of music over time. Meter intuitively separates groups of beats into measures, and enumerates these groupings in writing with a meter marking. Duple meters, meters grouped in twos and multiples of two, bear the bulk of the load in rock. 4/4 meter, or "common time," is by far the most common. There are also 2/4 (two-beats and marches) and 2/2 (cut time or half-time) meters in some rock songs, and a few songs in triple meters.

Subdividing breaks beats down into smaller parts. In rock, this usually means dividing a quarter note into eighth or sixteenth notes, or into triplet eighth notes. There are both *duple and triple subdivisions* of duple meters. Duple subdivisions are called "straight" or "straight ahead" feels; songs with triple subdivisions are known as having a "swing" or "shuffle" feel. (All these terms are borrowed from jazz.) Depending on the type of subdivision and emphases within the beats and subdivisions, duple meter can take on many different characteristics.

Sometimes, a triple subdivision is actually not completely triple. There is a gradient between strict triple subdivisions and straight eighth notes. There are straight eighth notes played so lazily—specifically, the second of each group of two eighth notes is played so lazily—that they approach a triple feel. (Think of it in mathematical terms. An exact triple subdivision is 66.666 … % the first eighth note, 33.333 … % the second. A loose pair of eighth notes might be divided 60%–40%, or 55%–45%, or anywhere in that range.) Musical notation used to represent triple subdivisions varies, and is sometimes confounding, as is the subdivision itself. (See Example 2.)

EXAMPLE 2

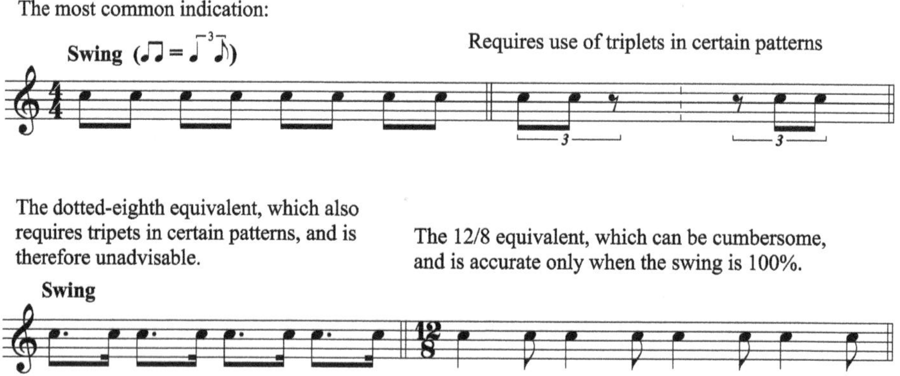

Triple meters, such as 3/4 and 9/8, are atypical of rock. Triple meters have a cyclical engine, rather than one that moves back and forth, like a backbeat or clave. (See Example 3.) It is easy to confuse a triple meter with a triple subdivision of a duple meter (6/8 or 12/8 time, mostly) when in a slow tempo. A true triple meter's accents, if there are any, can fall on either offbeat, as in a folk or gospel three-beat (one-*two*-three or one-two-*three*), or on every downbeat, as in a waltz (*one*-two-three).

Adventurous rockers occasionally experiment with odd meters such as 5/4 or 7/8, or compound meters—3/4 + 3/8, for example. Their inspiration seems to arise from more "sophisticated" jazz and classical genres, but alongside their metrical imbalances, these songs also usually have accessible melodies and strong hooks. Though not necessarily intended as hits, some, such as Pink Floyd's "Money" or the Beatles' "Strawberry Fields Forever," have attained wide renown, and their oddities are part of their appeal.

Tempo is a measurement of the pace of the beats and meter, that is, how fast or slow they move. Tempo is customarily measured in beats per minute, and indicated as a metronome marking. It may be enforced by a click track, especially in modern pop, and increasingly in the musical theatre. Meter and tempo both can change at any time, and in rock theatre songs, quite often they do, much more often than in commercial music. Uptempo rock songs greatly outnumber slow ones, and the majority of theatre songs are uptempo, as well.

Lastly, there is *feel*. Feel, like groove, is an elusive concept, and is wrapped up with meter, tempo, and groove. Unlike meter or tempo, feel cannot be quantified. Feel is a means of describing a rhythmic style in terms of sound, and often by referencing other feels. Feels are shared among songs, though some feels are objectively more distinctive than others. They are often described in dance terms, and certain feels are associated with certain tempos.

Tension and Resolution

Music is a temporal art form, one that progresses, or unfolds, over time. Rock moves through time more tangibly and determinedly than most other forms of music. It is driven by a rhythmic engine that needs to be powered. Its fuel consists of small patterns of tension and resolution, pushing back and forth like pistons in self-sustaining motion. Tension and resolution also occur on a large scale, in melody, harmony, and structure. In music, tension and resolution are also often described as expectation and satisfaction, or conflict and release.

Perhaps the easiest way to comprehend tension and release as a rhythmic motor is to imagine a single tone or click, repeated again and again with precisely the same duration—eighth after eighth, quarter after quarter, whatever. Eventually, tension will build, and you, the listener, will want that note to change in some way. The longer it continues, the greater the tension, and the more you want it and expect it to change. (It's like the maddening leaky faucet that keeps you awake at night—as long as the drip is not perfectly regular, you might be able to go to sleep.)

There are two prominent small-scale rhythmic patterns of tension and release that underlie a large portion of the rock literature. Their origins and pervasiveness are a perfect example of the spread of rock's aesthetic roots.

First is the *backbeat,* a holdover from early American cakewalks, foxtrots, and other forms of swing, jazz, country, and the blues, spanning the racial divide. A backbeat is simply an accent on the second beat of a duple pattern. The most familiar to rock listeners is a 4/4 meter with a backbeat, that is, with accents on the second and fourth beats. That's where the drummer hits the snare drum—on two and four—and that's where you (should) clap when clapping along with rock songs. How much accent there is on the backbeat varies song by song. On one extreme, there is "We Will Rock You," on the other, "I Saw Her Standing There." The backbeat alternates resolution (the downbeat) and tension (the offbeat) on a minuscule scale. (Example 3 shows some common backbeat patterns.)

The other is the *clave,* literally translated from Spanish as "key." In this context it refers to a key that unlocks a forward-moving rhythmic progression. Widespread throughout the Latin musical diaspora, this alternation of syncopation and regularity lies buried under the surface of many rock songs, as well. Example 3 shows a basic clave, a reverse clave, and a rhumba clave (which contains an additional syncopation).

The syncopated half of a clave poses a question, and the unsyncopated half provides the answer, or the other way around. The clave is fully exposed to the ear in songs such as "Bo Diddley," "Faith," and from the musical *Grease,* "Born to Hand Jive." The introductory bars that precede the opening vocal of *In The Heights* are a clave rhythm played solo by the percussionist (on *claves,* a percussion instrument, two rosewood sticks beaten against each other).

EXAMPLE 3

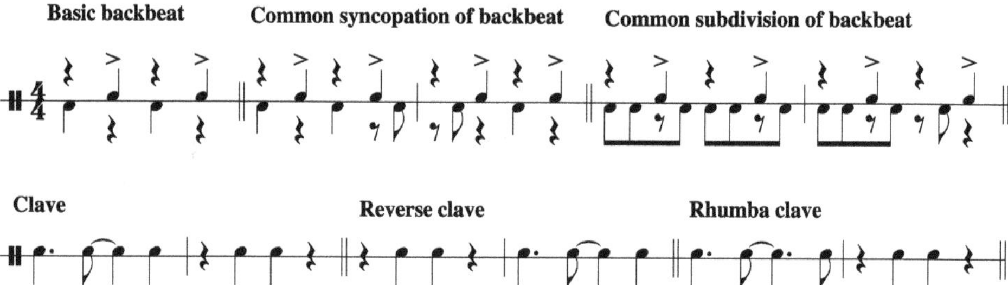

All rock melodies strongly connect to their accompanimental motors, usually riding upon them for the duration of a song. It's a very helpful exercise for you to learn to sing, drum, tap out on your body, or otherwise enact various backbeat and clave patterns. These are also great activities for group warmups. Creating variations on the patterns ("jamming") will become almost instinctive as you absorb them. Most important, focus at all times on keeping a solid tempo, always keeping foremost in your thought process the meter and especially its subdivisions. Mastering the grooves that underlie a melody, that is, the rhythms you do not sing but which support you, will help tremendously in rocking the grooves that you do sing.

Melodic Rhythm and Rhythmic Accuracy

Melody is the predominant voice in a musical counterpoint, and at the same time is part of a larger-scale rhythmic fabric. There are many ways that melody and accompaniment interweave rhythmically to create this fabric, but because rock's machinery depends on constancy of forward motion, the maxim of performance practice is that notes and words be placed precisely *on* beats and their subdivisions, not after them or nearby them. Melodies must be sung with near-absolute *rhythmic accuracy*, unless otherwise indicated. There are in actuality quite a lot of indications otherwise, mostly for expressive purposes, but rhythmic accuracy is the rule of thumb.

Whereas accompaniment in rock (and in all song) tends to be reasonably consistent over the life of a song, melody usually has more variations, which in part explains its more conspicuous presence in the texture. It "leaps out" by virtue of its differences, and, of course, because it is attached to the words. Because of its attachment to the words, and because melody resembles language (sounds, phrases, and sentences voiced as a means of communication), melody takes on many of the qualities of speech. To some extent, melody is organized speech given musical properties, such as motives, pitch, dynamics, and so on. It takes the things we say and feel, and makes them into music.

Another quality melody shares with speech is that it sometimes transcends words and allows music to take the expressive lead. Like a sigh, a grunt, or a howl, this is especially manifest with slower melodic rates, when there is embellishment and melisma, in vocal percussion, and in several other qualities of rock melodies. Even when melody is expressive in these ways, its rhythm and its relationship to the groove are still operative, sometimes more so.

Therefore, in light of the rhythmic mandate, as well as its counterarguments, one of the first issues you face when preparing any rock song for the theatre is discovering the rhythmic nature of its vocal line. Primarily: how precise a rhythmic approach does the song demand, and will your acting choices entail freedom of rhythmic interpretation? In most cases, the answers can be derived from analyzing the text and music.

One axiom is that any rock melody that purposefully outlines a meter deserves accurate rhythmic delivery, a melody such as the beginning of "Rock around the Clock." Here's another elementary example, from Loggins and Messina's "Your Mama Don't Dance" (Example 4), which like "Rock around the Clock" is in a swing feel. For a straight eighth rhythmic melody, listen to "Johnny B. Goode," also discussed in chapter 6.

EXAMPLE 4

The melody outlines the meter and its subdivisions. It also outlines the feel, using on-the-beat rhythms and one brief syncopation, while the accompaniment plays a different, simpler, repetitive pattern. If the vocal line here were to stray from its precise orientation, the counterpoint, the groove, and even the meaning of the lyric, and its conveyance, would crumble.

By contrast, listen to the opening measures of Marvin Gaye's "Let's Get It On" ("I've been really tryin', baby . . ."). In this context, inaccuracy, better described here as vocal freedom, is what makes the melody communicative. Writing down the vocal line would have little purpose, as it could only be a loose transcription of what is actually sung, and the song is best learned by demonstration or by ear. In fact, almost every published version of the melody has a different written rhythm. In this example your rhythmic decisions are based on style, emotion, musicality, and effective communication.

Many songs that demand rhythmic rigor also meld it with some sort of vocal liberty. An excellent example is Aretha Franklin's recording of "Respect." Franklin delivers certain syllables and phrases with precision and a great sense of groove, but others she extends, or lets lag behind, and others she elaborates on freely. In this song, the vocal does not always define the groove, but always enhances it. In the pop literature, and in the theatre pop literature, as in "Respect," we hear a good deal of "backphrasing," or extending the notes and phrases of a melody past their expected metrical orientation.

Beyond just singing correct rhythms, how can you achieve *vocal groove*? What makes your voice an instrument in the rhythm section as well as an expressive vehicle? Where does the rhythm live in a melodic line?

One might think that it has to do with where you place consonants, because of their inherent percussiveness. In truth, it's more about where the vowels land, because only the vowels have any significant note duration. Consonants are short, even instantaneous, and when extended, their extension is very noticeable, as in a drawn-out unvoiced sibilant ("sss") or voiced fricative ("vvv"). When underemphasized, consonants lose their ability to communicate.[3]

In order for you to be in the groove, again as a rule of thumb only, the short life of a consonant should slightly precede the beat, and the vowel should land squarely upon the beat. Try this with this first phrase of "Your Mama Don't Dance." If you consciously place the consonants on the beat, before long, the melody will lag behind. Instead, if you think of the consonants as exploding into the vowel, and land the vowel precisely on the beat, the groove will come to life.

Style and genre will help in determining how accurately a melodic rhythm should be interpreted. Certain pop styles, for example, will lean toward the rhythmically strict ("I Think We're Alone Now," Tommy James and the Shondells, or "Wannabe," the Spice

---

3. Consonant and other percussive sounds actually do have duration, but it is very brief. One advanced aspect of groove is the notion of playing "on top of the beat," or, its opposite, "laying back." These subtleties are the result of where in the brief duration of a brief rhythmic event a musician plays or sings a note.

Girls), but once pop and r&b start to merge, vocal freedom and embellishment find their way in (Prince's "When Doves Cry," or Des'ree's "You Gotta Be," for example). Hard rock, a blues-based genre, usually demands a blues-like rhythmic approach, in which certain lines that define the phrases are sung in time, but others that speak to the emotion of the song depart from the underlying groove (Heart's "Barracuda" or Emf's "Unbelievable"). Electro-pop and a good deal of early rap call for machine-like exactness, but that does not rule out expressive touches, as in Pet Shop Boys' "West End Girls" or Usher's "Yeah!"

There is one absolute certainty: rhythm, in particular the placement of vocal rhythms within a groove, must be an uppermost concern in any rock performance that strives for authenticity. Rhythm is the lifeblood of rock, and groove is its beating heart. Any performance that just goes through the rhythmic motions will immediately be suspect. In jukebox musicals in which one is recreating a performance, rhythmic authenticity is even more crucial, mainly, choosing the appropriate levels of rhythmic accuracy and vocal freedom proscribed by genre and historical context. In preparing a rock song, whether it was written for the pop market or the stage, fully analyze and characterize all aspects of its rhythm(s), melodic and accompanimental, to decide on the right vocal approach for you, for the song, and for the show.

A Note on Classicism in Rock

Despite the depth and breadth of its revolution, rock is still a part of the continuum of Western tonal music that reached an apex of originality and design in the eighteenth and nineteenth centuries. For much of our musical history performers and composers have been operating under the strictures of classical harmony, melody, and form. That's one reason why rock and rap were such marked departures (as was twentieth century concert music).

Yet classicism is ever-present in rock. We see rock classicism in intent, style, and approach, in the music of the Beatles, the Moody Blues, Queen, Rush, Rufus Wainwright, Imogen Heap, and Outkast, among many others. Of course, there is classicism as well in the theatre, which grew directly from classical roots. Not only its melodiousness, but its formality, its techniques, and its forms are among the many classical elements still in operation in the theatre music of today, such as: arias and harmonized love duets, Mozartean multi-voiced production numbers, meticulous writing and arranging for voices and instruments, and the connection of melody and motive over a large-scale form.

Whereas classicism might persist in these ways, in rock, it has not been carried over into vocalism (see next chapter). Indeed a classical approach to singing rock is rock's greatest adversary, and is immediately obvious when an opera singer sings a rock song as he or she would a classical aria. Rhythm, populism, and freedom are the hallmarks of rock, and craft only followed the initial emergence.

Singers do need to analyze and understand a rock melody just as fully as they would a classical piece, but they must sing the song as a rock song.

Melodies by Genre

Let's look at how all of these melodic elements work together in action. The following is a series of descriptive analyses of the melodies of selected commercial and theatre rock songs, grouped by genre, with some performance advice for each.

Rock 'n' roll

"Jailhouse Rock," released in 1957, was one of Elvis Presley's early hits. This iconic song is a hybrid of blues and country, known as "rockabilly." Its lyric manages to celebrate incarceration, by attaching it to rock 'n' roll music. The melody begins by rhythmically outlining the meter and groove, in a clave-like alternation between an on-the-beat phrase ("The warden threw a party at the . . .") and a syncopated phrase (". . . county jail"). The accompaniment punctuates every other bar. In each of the first three phrases of the verse, the melody hangs briefly on a high blue note (the flatted third) before it descends. On the fourth line ("You should've heard those knocked out jailbirds sing . . ."), the melody clings to the high note with increasing emphasis, leading to the chorus. At the chorus, the melodic phrases shorten, giving way to a steadily pulsing boogie-woogie groove and blues-like chord changes. The singer is an instrument in the band, and evokes in his delivery of the melody and lyric a particular setting, a "vibe." When "in tune" with the vibe, the singer is able to inhabit an authentic persona, who is singing about, or better still, singing *with*, the rockin' prison band.

Quite similar in sound and melodic structure to "Jailhouse Rock" is "Heartbreak Hotel," another country blues–inspired Elvis Presley song from a year earlier, but one that sings of sadness. A milder counterpart is "Rock around the Clock." Despite its twelve-bar blues form, the latter song's squarer phrasing, less bluesy modality, and less edgy lyric push it closer to pop. Its relative melodic simplicity within an otherwise typically rowdy rock aesthetic is likely what has made it so immensely popular for so long.

These are exemplars of rock melody, by virtue of their rhythmic content and modalities. Furthermore, a rock-based heightened emotional state motivates their content and style. Performance practices of their style must therefore be observed, in this case, those of country music and the blues. Notes are not attacked or released cleanly; instead, they are slid into or pulled off of. Other pitches are bent while being sustained. The breath, the throat, and the glottis have a greater part in vocal production, and idiosyncratic enunciation of words seems acceptable. (Note that in "Rock around the Clock," a less emotional song, Bill Haley is rather unemotional, and sings with less gritty vocalism and clearer diction than Elvis.)

Songs in an early rock 'n' roll feel have populated the theatrical literature since the nostalgia craze initiated in 1972 by *Grease*, for years Broadway's longest-running show. (The hit television series *Happy Days* started its long run two years later, perpetuating the nostalgia fervor.) Later, original rock 'n' roll songs were rejuvenated as the basis for theatrical revues like *Smokey Joe's Café* and *All Shook Up*. So was their musical style, in book shows such as *Hairspray, Memphis,* and *Zombie Prom*, among others. As recently as 2015, the song "Stick It to the Man," from the musical *School of Rock*, paid tribute to "Jailhouse Rock" and its cousins. Composer Andrew Lloyd Webber's chorus, instead of following a blues pattern, opts for a (very Webber-like) classical melody and harmony. Regardless, in melodic content and tone, the two songs strongly resemble one another.

Look to these original versions of songs and their original singers as a guide to performance practice. You can most effectively interpret all such melodies with full-on commitment to the original rock aesthetic from both musical and emotional standpoints, and with an understanding of how each song fits into that aesthetic, and of course by bringing your own personality to bear. (It's worth noting that there were not as many women as men singing in this style during this early phase of commercial rock.)

Hard rock

"Somebody to Love" is a 1967 hard rock song from San Francisco "acid rock" band Jefferson Airplane. Lead singer Grace Slick's soulful vocal interpretation is remarkable given the confinements of the song's range and its repetition of only a small set of pitches, all essentially drawn from the blues scale. Slick's vocal approach alternates between absolute rhythmic accuracy and drawn-out backphrasing. When delivered in this way, the melody is at once conversational and musical, and also brilliantly conveys the song's darkly shaded, trippy storytelling, as well as its bluesy ancestry.

By contrast, from the same era, the Steppenwolf rock hit "Born to Be Wild" also features a melody packing a hard rock punch, but one with much more regularity and predictability. Phrased first in short, rhythmic chunks, its melody gradually evolves to a more expansive breadth, but never fully "breaks out." There is virtually no vocal improvisation, and the melody stays in Dorian mode throughout. The lyric moves from succinct and direct ("Get your motor running/Head out on the highway . . .") to lyrical and philosophical ("Take the world in a love embrace/Fire all of your guns at once and/Explode into space").

On the other end of the interpretive spectrum, steeped in despair, are hard rock songs such as "Piece of My Heart." Erma Franklin's original 1967 version (more soul than hard rock) was already quite passionate, and the singer rode the powerful rhythms and rising contours of the melody to towering emotional heights. Janis Joplin, with Big Brother and the Holding Company, took the song even further, intensifying and electrifying the sound, vocally and instrumentally. With fierce blues inflection and intonation, Joplin stretches the melody to its limit, peppering it with (apparently drug-induced) snarls, moans, and stutters.

As hard rock progressed, its melodies retained both their rhythmic drive and their raw emotionalism. Tamer, preplanned melodies continued to coexist with improvisational outbursts. Led Zeppelin was particularly progressive, Van Halen and the Cure more pop-oriented, AC/DC and Black Sabbath were particularly nasty, Kiss and R.E.M. a bit tongue-in-cheek, and Gun N' Roses, Nirvana, and Rage against the Machine all very sincere.

Songs in the theatre rarely reach the level of raw force of hard rock melodies and their singers, but there are exceptions. The melodic vocabulary of "The Acid Queen," from *Tommy*, permits the singer to convey the character's ominous seduction by means of hard rock–based vocal interpretation and embellishment. Some theatre songs combine or alternate melodic exactitude and freedom as a way of balancing storytelling with energy, as in "Heaven on Their Minds" from *Jesus Christ Superstar* and "The Heat Is On in Saigon," from *Miss Saigon*, or as a show-wide convention, as in *Rock of Ages*.

Pop and pop-rock

Songs on the lighter side of rock have always been the most marketable; thus their "pop" designation. Much of their success lies in simple, thoughtfully crafted melodies. One of countless examples from the 1960s is the skiffle-inspired Herman's Hermits song, "I'm into Something Good," by Carole King and Gerry Coffin. ("Skiffle" is a UK-based genre with guitar grooves influenced by American rockabilly and country swing.) The melody starts by presenting a simple, rhythmic phrase, the first half on the beat ("Woke up this morning . . .") and the second half syncopated (". . . feeling fine"), another clave. The melodic rhythm repeats exactly in the second phrase, while its contour rises. The third phrase is twice as long, and returns to the lower register (appended with an offhanded "oh yeah"). The fourth line, the title/hook, rises through an arpeggiated triad in four quarter notes, then descends in syncopation to the tonic. It's a melody that uses its major-key diatonic sound and its jumpy rises and falls of contour to support the cheerful nature of the lyric, but still it favors the pentatonic scale, which comprises the majority of the pitch content. This modality, and the bouncy backbeat, and the melodic clave patterns give the song it its vaguely rock-like sound. Other pop artists of the 1960s devised similar songs, but rocked considerably harder: the Dave Clark Five, the Turtles, the Zombies, and of course, the Beatles.

Tony Hatch (writing for Petula Clark), among others, created more elaborate and instrumentally lush structures such as "Downtown." Its melody starts out low and static, but almost immediately reaches an obvious refrain/hook ("When you're alone/And life is making you lonely/You can always go/*Downtown*"). The melody then climbs through two stepwise, almost legato phrases, but it is a false build. The dynamic dips, and then builds again over a rising two-note alternation.

Finally the melody reaches its peak at the primary hook (there are several), where the notes lengthen for three identical iterations of the title, each followed by a lower, eighth note response, the last of which resolves to the end of the form. (Note the subtle inclusion of call-and-response that invited the audience to sing along.) The song is like a microcosmic piece of theatre, a complete story with ups and downs, told with sincerity, and with design elements (the orchestration and vocal delivery in particular) helping to set time, place, and mood.

Once listeners were acclimated to the louder sounds of rock 'n' roll and early rock, pop-rock more easily entered the mainstream. In the 1970s, 1980s, and 1990s, ABBA's "Dancing Queen," Wham!'s "Wake Me Up before You Go-Go," and Cher's "Believe" covered similar pop ground as their predecessors, but added electronic synthesis and new recording techniques. In these three songs, vestiges of rock are still apparent in the grooves and the lyrical content, but the melodies are neatly composed, diatonic, squarely delivered, and audience-friendly. For you as an actor, there's not a lot of interpretive room in songs like these. Instead, just contribute your unique sound and be attentive to the vocal groove, as the original singers did. Find a story of your own to tell as subtext to the lyrics.

You can find more expressive ground to cover in pop that is influenced by hard rock, soul, and r&b, which have less rigid melodic tendencies, and all of which share roots in the blues. "Power pop," for example, was by the 1980s a staple, and is still with us today. One example of an early song of this genre that has crossed over into the theatre is "Holding Out for a Hero," a signature 1980s hybrid of rock, pop, r&b, and disco, first heard in the original film *Footloose*. The recorded version of the song begins in tempo, but as in many theatrical adaptations of uptempo pop songs, the stage version begins in a free tempo, colla voce (literally, "with the voice," meaning that the voice leads the accompaniment). In both versions, the melodic phrases of the opening verse are in a naturally conversational eighth note rhythm, entirely in stepwise motion, and include syncopations and anticipations that give stress to certain syllables ("Where have all the *good* men *gone*/And where are all the *gods* . . .," etc.). This sounds perfectly naturally when sung at tempo, but out of tempo seems stilted. (Make sure that when you sing it, you do so at a realistically conversational pace.) Gradually the melody ascends, leading to the chorus. The melody in the chorus falls more squarely on the beat, and in less conversational, more musical phrases. This is the primary hook, musically and lyrically. Like a paragraph of text, you move from the specific to the general, following the rhythms and contours of melody, the internal logic of the lyric, and the rise of emotion to a logical climax. The unsyncopated "I need a hero . . ." leaves no doubt as to the singer's determination to find the ideal man. These lyrics are a short essay, set to pitch and rhythm in such a way that their meaning is immediately accessible.

The turn of the millennium saw the fusion of pop with r&b, rap, hip-hop, and other genres, which returned vocal stylizing and freedom of vocalism to the forefront. Britney Spears, Mariah Carey, Christina Aguilera, Justin Bieber, Nicki Minaj, and many others (note the new preponderance of female singers) all have very individual timbres and inflections, and are all prone to elaborate improvisation.

Modern pop has found a happy home in the commercial mainstream musical theatre. Theatre and commercial pop songs share a great deal, including many performance practices. Pop's part-time tendency toward exaggerated vocalizing is not usually among them, but it, too, sometimes has found its way in.

Pippin came to the Broadway stage in 1972, and its pop-theatrical score included melodies and grooves such as "Magic to Do" and "Corner of the Sky." "Magic to Do" uses its shifting modalities (mostly minor in the verses and major in the choruses) and a funky-ish melodic rhythm to imbue a historical tale with a rock attitude (there are several rock musicals that are adaptations of Greek myths and dramas and Shakespeare plays). The folk-rock melody and feel of the enduring "Corner of the Sky" help to elucidate the archetypal, rock-era character's "there-must-be-something-more-than-this" need for existential fulfillment. The lyric's scripture-like tropes are arranged in simple, musically tight phrases, rising to an expansively melodic chorus.

Thirty years later, Stephen Schwartz penned another well-crafted pop-theatre standout, "Defying Gravity." It shares the sensibilities of his earlier work, but with a modern posture, extravagant vocalism, and with an ever-shifting background of exultant pop-rock grooves. Most of what you need to effectively execute the song is built into the melodies (and accompaniments), and therefore you can focus on characterization and intention, and on vocal production.

The songs from the 2016 musical *Dear Evan Hansen* are descendants of *Pippin* and *Wicked*, with a post-2010 acoustic-pop flair. Most theatre music disallows vocal improvisation for its own sake, and *Dear Evan Hansen*'s score is no exception. What appears to be extensive improvisation is actually carefully preplanned, and the riffs, melismas, and repetitions are components of the storytelling, even when they are purely musical. Ben Platt's well-known interpretation of the song "Waving through a Window" is authoritative because of his trust in and proficiency with the melody, the immediacy and naturalness of his delivery, and his unique vocal sound. Singers of all pop theatrical numbers can benefit from this model.

More specific, conversational lyrics in semi-satirical theatre pop songs such as "Revenge Party" from *Mean Girls* or "Bad Idea" from *Waitress* seem by necessity to relinquish some of their rock bite, because their first requirements are to define character and move the plot forward. ("Bad Idea" has a hard country-rock feel, but is in a rarely heard 6/4 meter.) Still, their melodies conform to the pop-rock model: patterns of melodic rhythm and contour that help to articulate the lyrics, which progress from specificity and conversation (verses) toward generality and lyricism (hooks and choruses). As they become more general, they invite in vocal and melodic liberty, or the appearance thereof.

Blues and gospel

The term "blues" has evolved to refer to blues-inspired songs of many types, not just traditional twelve-bar blues. There's a little blues in a lot of rock songs, in their subject matter, pitch content, and performance practice. Sometimes it is overt, as in Cream's "Crossroads," or the Rolling Stones' "Love in Vain" (from the original by Robert Johnson). Other times it appears only in the bend of a note, or a cry in the voice. Obviously, the blues informs some genres more than others.

Blues melodies tend to be in regular phrases, often with repeated or parallel texts, sometimes involving call-and-response. Each phrase consists of fragments and motives from the blues scale, somewhat loose in rhythm and pitch, but highly emotionally expressive.

Blues scales are a dissonant departure from diatonic and pentatonic scales, and blues melodies are fraught with feeling. Blues is the music of an emotional state of mind. It originated as an expression of hardship and depression in the Deep South late in the nineteenth century, and evolved from African American work song, field chants, and spirituals, as well as from American folk music. (Big Mama Thornton's original recording of "Ball and Chain" is a perfect example.) Even when a blues singer holds back emotionally, his or her emotion finds expression in the modality, phrasing, and vocalism. When singing the blues, you must genuinely tap into the emotion that motivates it. There is truth to the old saying: "You gotta pay your dues if you wanna sing the blues."

After its initial influence, the blues' strong presence in rock began to fade, particularly in pop. Bona fide blues never lost its audience entirely, however, and maintained its influence in hard rock, and later in sub-genres such as punk-rock, heavy metal, and grunge. The blues had a notable revival in the pop market in the 2000s with artists such as Adele and Amy Winehouse. It also still inhabits the free improvisation that singers add to non-blues-based melodies.

Neither has gospel disappeared entirely from view, having an eternal tie, so to speak, to the religious community, and to a lesser extent to soul, "white soul," and some soul-pop crossover songs, such as those by Elton John and Van Morrison. Though the vocabulary and performance practices of gospel have not changed significantly in the modern era (it has gotten a little funkier), it now reaches extraordinary levels of production and musicianship. Gospel performance practice, and to a slightly lesser extent blues performance practice, encourages demonstrative elaboration on simple phrases and lyrics, spurred on by profound faith, feeling, and vocal chops. Gospel melody is hard to pin down and notate, even though much of it is derived from simple hymn tunes, and is mostly diatonic and pentatonic. Gospel has crossed over into pop songs in the hymn-like melodies of Jackie Wilson's "Higher and Higher," Bill Withers's "Lean on Me," Paul Simon's "Love Me Like a Rock," the Beatles' "Let It Be," and Paul McCartney's "Maybe I'm Amazed."

Gospel music and the blues, perhaps because of their innate evocations and freedoms, occupy only a small share of the rock theatre repertoire, except as specialty numbers. The musical theatre industry is still largely segregated. Therefore, most theatre songs in these styles are either cameos within primarily Caucasian or integrated productions, or are relegated to shows targeted at African American audiences. (Ironically, one of the only full-on gospel musicals ever to reach Broadway, *The Gospel at Colonus*, was composed by a white man.)

One exception is the musical *The Color Purple*, which has over time found a mixed audience. A notable blues-infused song from that show is "Hell No." It begins out of tempo, with a free, non-metrical text set to a free, non-metrical melody, like a blues- and gospel-inflected recitative. As the first verse begins, a funky, somewhat sparse rhythm kicks in, and the band locks into a deep groove. There, the first four melodic phrases have a vague sense of rhythm, but their rhythms are driven by and their contours shaped by the lyrics: "I feel sorry for you/To tell you the truth/You remind me of my mama/Under your husband's thumb." As in many musicals, these opening phrases hover between song and speech, but here, in addition to being effectively communicative, they strongly evoke an authentic blues style. The melody remains firmly within a blues scale throughout, and as the song unfolds, we see that the song form is in fact a traditional twelve-bar blues. The title/hook of the song, such as it is, falls at the end of the form. It is again spoken as much as sung, and its melody shaped more by its defiant intent than by any musical specification. Blues performance practices—freedom of phrasing, limited ornamentation, and vocalisms such as grace notes, bends, and slides, and so on—are entirely right for this stage song.

Blues and gospel melodic style also characterizes the duet "I Got Four Kids," from *Caroline, or Change*. In this song, the harmony holds stubbornly to a single chord, until two crucial and striking moments. Pitches are trapped within the blues scale suggested by that chord. Parallel to the singers' plight, the melody is a prisoner. The persistent, wailing phrases, which feature repeated bits of text and non-verbal improvisation, beautifully express the characters' frustration, by evoking in their melodies the musical roots of blues and gospel.

A less authentic example is the very well-known and well-traveled burst of gospel-like styling in the second half of "Seasons of Love," from *Rent*. The increasing embellishments to the melody in the later verses announce the song's progression from a rhythmic ballad to a spiritual, and the soaring vocal obbligato over the final chorus and coda transforms the spiritual to a testimony. When sung truthfully, without earnestness, by employing authentic gospel riffs and inflections, and not ignoring cultural rightness, the audience is left in tears.

Soul and r&b

Soul and r&b have had a slightly easier time in the musical theatre than blues and gospel, in part because their melodic content is more structured and easily singable. (They've also gotten a boost from the recent jukebox shows glorifying those genres.) Soul and r&b melodies tend to be organized into the kinds of musical and textual shapes one associates with conversation and communication, as opposed to those generated by emotion. They consist mostly of simple, rhythmically based, symmetrical phrases, each neatly matched with a line of text, their delivery tinged with blues vocal inflections. These are more useful melodic structures for storytelling than the free-form building blocks of blues and gospel. Just as important, every singer has a distinct vocal personality that alters the essence of the melodies he or she sings, and together, singer and song determine the threshold of interpretive freedom.

The catchy melody of Sam Cooke's "(What a) Wonderful World" is a simple series of seven related, parallel phrases, all but the last in the same rhythm and contour, all pentatonic. The rhyme scheme is an elementary AABBCCA. The bridge melody is a bit more arioso, but is just as succinct. The song rides a gentle rock backbeat over a vaguely tropical bass line throughout, and the vocal line never strays far from the pocket. Nor does the singer.

Otis Redding's "(Sittin' on) The Dock of the Bay" has a similar melodic structure, in a compact verse-chorus form. Notable in its melody are the alternating rises and falls of contour, recalling rolling waves on the sea, and accentuating the character of a man contemplating his own rise and fall from a place of loneliness. Even here, despite an intensely soulful interpretation, Redding's rhythms stay close to the swaying groove that drives them, and there is very little vocal improvisation, only in the bridge.

Many great soul and r&b songs have an innate sense of the theatrical. Examples include the Temptations' "Papa Was a Rolling Stone," Smokey Robinson and the Miracles' "The Tears of a Clown," and Stevie Wonder's "Living for the City." Others harken strongly back to their African American blues roots, for example, Aretha Franklin's "Chain of Fools" and "Think," while others verge upon pop. Motown, a musical style delineated by a record label and its geographical location, is a hybrid of pop, soul, r&b, and rock. For decades, the "King of Pop," Michael Jackson, and his royal family, including Whitney Houston, Prince, and many others, contributed too many dramatically striking r&b hits to list here. In their more demonstrative pop songs, melodic embellishment adds to the drama, and highlights the musicianship and emotionality of these accomplished vocalists.

The songs from the musical *Dreamgirls* span the full expressive range of soul and r&b melodies. Throughout its score, *Dreamgirls* songwriters Henry Krieger and Tom Eyen find a balance between conversational and motivic melodic structures. "Family" recalls the simplicity of a Motown ballad, yet it is entirely communicative as a theatre piece. Like the songs described above, the melody is in short motives, almost entirely pentatonic, shaped by phrases of text into a typical melodic sentence: "It's more than you/It is more than me/No matter what we are/We are a family." The song gradually builds through a Recitative-ABABC form, but saves its chorus (C) and primary hook for last ("We are a family/Like the highest tree"). In the lyric, conversationalism progresses toward lyricism. In spite of the rhythmic motives in the verse, the fact that this song is also a scene calls for rhythmic freedom in these phrases, and its style permits such freedom, within limits. As we have observed in other songs, these opening lines help to bridge dialogue and song, and are intentional in nature, not just musical. At the climax, the melody locks into the groove, as the feelings of different characters unite. The soul and Motown songs that form the opening sequence of *Dreamgirls* capture perfectly the era, style, and melodic content of the music that inspired them, but have structures and idiosyncrasies that ensure their identity as theatre songs (mixed meter in "Move" and the recitative-like beginning of "Fake Your Way to the Top" are other examples).[4]

In a comedic setting, but with similar tone and techniques, there is "Feed Me (Git It)," from *Little Shop of Horrors*. The song pays homage to Motown, and looks backwards to the blues: "Feed me, Seymour/Feed me all night long," sung rhythmically in a blues modality. The "all night long" portion of the phrase is a melodic/textual blues trope in which "all" is articulated as a slowly opening diphthong ("aah-ooh-wl"), connected by portamento to "night," and a pull-off (a horn-like brief downward slide) at the end of "long." In a lighter comedic vein are "Take Me to Heaven," from *Sister Act*, and "Biggest Blame Fool," from *Seussical*.

"When You're Home," a duet for the young leads in *In The Heights*, is a stylistic mashup with r&b as its source. Styles and their corresponding melodic approaches shift according to dramatic moment and character. The song's melodies blur the line between conversational phrasing and rap, and also feature a pop hook. The modality, too, is a mashup: diatonic, Mixolydian, and blues scales coexist in the musical language of a diverse neighborhood. The character of Nina has earlier in the show been established as a melodic singer, and her budding love interest, Benny, as a melodic rapper; both cross into each other's musical territory as their romance unfolds.

---

4. As a young audition pianist for the original *Dreamgirls* workshop, I observed Michael Bennett take an entirely acting-based approach to his direction of the singers, while composer Henry Krieger was deeply focused on groove. (He also offered me invaluable guidance on how to rock at the piano.)

The song begins with an accompanied, rhythmic recitative; its melodic and textual phrases are unpredictable and irregular. An r&b/funk groove commences to signal the start of the first verse, but these melodic tendencies continue. Dialogue provides the basis for melody; though it is pitched and rhythmic, it is conversation, or rather, discussion. The first chorus is the only fully intact statement of the title/hook, and for those eight bars, lyricism takes over. But as the second verse begins, the melodic irregularities resume. The hook melody then returns in the second chorus with more freedom, motivated emotionally by Benny's increasing interest in and flirtation with Nina. A salsa feel drives the stop-time bridge, in which Nina recalls her Latino upbringing. There the melody is more regularly phrased and rhythmically organized, but is heavily syncopated and in a minor mode, indicating the character's underlying tension, and meshing with the Puerto Rican feel. The song winds down briefly into a ballad-like, dolce section for Benny, where, in keeping with the mood, his melody is gentler, more lightly syncopated, and contoured for sentimental rather than conversational effect. The song ends with what appears as a free-form vocal duet, an ecstatic call-and-response improvisation on the central melodic and textual ideas of the song. (Actually, these melodies are very carefully arranged, as are the vocal lines throughout the song, in phrases and rhythms carefully designed for optimal dramatic and musical effect.)

"Helpless," a modern r&b/pop/hip-hop hybrid from *Hamilton*, reveals the many levels of its lead singer's character and situation by alternating between her nervous two-note melodies and a warm, sighing hook. With the all ironies that make the dramatic context of this song interesting and poignant, a clear, focused telling of the story and observance of the written melody are at the heart of an effective performance. To that, of course, one adds personality, and style. Personality may be a matter of rightness, but style can be derived from the works that inspire Miranda, in this case, certainly, Beyoncé and Destiny's Child, Mary J. Blige, and many others in the modern soul, r&b, and rock genres.

Lin-Manuel Miranda and his creative collaborators are quite aware of the difficulty of achieving musical precision while finding truth in acting, and plan their shows (*In The Heights* and *Hamilton* especially) so that when the acting and singing (and choreography) are enacted as intended, they fully support the actor's believability and conveyance. In these significant exceptions to rock law, singers can entirely trust the meticulously written note.

Rap and pop-rap

Rap, born as a live musical form but raised in the recording industry, has an innate theatricality of its own. Aside from its celebrity culture, its songs are monologues and conversations, and their lyrical and musical content reveal character and intention. Yet the dissimilarities between mainstream rap and theatre song have, until recently, left rap mostly on the fringes of commercial musical theatre. Rap is very self-aware, whereas theatre songs are mostly decidedly not (unless they purposefully are, as when they spoof themselves). Rap songs are verbose, whereas theatre songs are concise. Rap can ramble and sidetrack, but theatre music must stay on its storytelling route. Rap is often monotonous; theatre music is constantly changing. Rap aims to excite and incite its audiences, while theatre tells stories. (Rap songs also sometimes tell stories, some of which, especially when enhanced by video, are like small musical theatre pieces. Eminem's "Stan" is an excellent example).[5]

The progression from older-school African American music styles into rap is evident in early rap melodies such as Funky 4+1's "That's the Joint." In this song, the rhythm and contour of the melody are text-based, and form a repetitive rhythmic motive: "Are you ready for this/Are you ready for this/Well, we just can't miss/With a beat like this." As the song progresses, the regularity of the phrases dissipates, and longer, freer sentences of melody take over.

As rap and hip-hop moved into the mainstream, their melodic constructions separated into freeform "spoken word" over a beat, and melodic or quasi-melodic hooks. As often as not these two approaches appear in the same song, as in "Fu-Gee-La" or "Keep Ya Head Up," or overlaid as in "Walk This Way" or "I'll Be There for You/You're All I Need to Get By."

The bitterness and profanity of gangsta rap made conservative, family audiences wary, but combining rap's rhythmic texts with melody and hooks helped it find its way, eventually, into musicals (as did its entrance into the consumer mainstream). Of course, almost no theatre score remains entirely in one musical style, and rap is no exception. Even *Hamilton* is not all rap. Perhaps the first authentic rap musical was the rap-tap dance show *Bring In 'da Noise, Bring In 'da Funk*, in 1995. There are rap numbers or sections in *Dreamgirls, Starmites, Altar Boyz*, and several other shows from the 1980s onward, but Miranda and his collaborators elevated the theatrical incarnation of rap to an art form, rather than a novelty.

When rapping in the theatre, as when rocking in the theatre, the vocal approaches made available by the style provide you with new options, but do not supersede traditional approaches. A traditional rap delivery is most useful when it helps to define character and tell story. When a character and story does deserve to rap, authentic delivery is crucial. *Bring In 'da Noise . . .* is rap in its natural habitat, whereas the rap in *Hamilton* is a convention; both must be rapped as a rapper raps or they will come off as untruthful. On the other hand, the rap in the middle of "What I Was Born to Do" from *Bring It On*, in which a series of characters identify themselves via rap verses, does not hold to any standard of authenticity,

5. https://www.americantheatre.org/2016/03/18/rap-broadways-new-jazz/.

and needn't. When a character has no intrinsic rap aesthetic, all that remains is the rap skeleton: words spoken in rhythm over a certain style of accompaniment. Characterization by the singer can enliven the performance, but not give it true rap-ness. Rap in this case is but a temporary usage, and is thus more interpretable.

"One Night in Bangkok," a clever rap-pop number from *Chess* (1984, a concept album made into a stage show), raps because its singers are using rap as an expression of cynical character (in the verses) and pop as a sales pitch (in the choruses). Rhythmic pattern and contour are driven by natural emphases of speech (so is mainstream rap, to some extent), but delivered according to what will best convey the intention. The choruses are rhythmically mechanical, whereas the verses allow some freedom. Murray Head's quirky vocal interpretation of this song on the original recording is a perfect illustration of the importance of personality in a theatrical song drawn from a pop context.[6]

Elaborate pop-rap numbers such as "My Shot" from *Hamilton* and "96,000" from *In The Heights* illustrate brilliantly how individuality of character changes the musical rules. Lin-Manuel Miranda found in these and other songs a way to weave the elaborate vocal textures of commercial rap into his stage storytelling, often with the inclusion of other styles, as is typical of musical theatre.

"96,000" begins with its hook, spoken at first, then melodizes and filters the hook through a cast of characters, one by one. Each character has his or her own musical dialect. Rap, r&b, and reggaeton[7] are the main ones, with their respective melodic bents. The rap is a combination of exact and free rhythm, and very conversational. Its contour is a product of syntax, semantics, dramatic context, and the nuances of each character-rapper's individual voice—Benny's rap-off with Usnavi, for instance, and Sonny's stunning display of his rapping skills. The r&b, for Benny, is more expansive and soulful, as it was in "When You're Home." Vanessa, the standoffish object of Usnavi's affection, sings an angular melody in a reggaeton groove, the bright tempo and idiomatic backbeat of which evoke at once the urban and the Caribbean, as well as the character's outward aloofness. In the middle of the song, Vanessa's brief folksong-like arioso ("If I win the lottery/You'll never see me again") is a peek into her vulnerability. The reggaeton groove returns in the final section, where multiple melodies join in a climactic counterpoint. In a coda, these threads meet in dramatic and melodic unison on a continuously repeated two-pitch motive, impelling the song to its close. Character, style, and story, are built into the melodies and feels; and the

---

6.   When rap songs are written down in theatre scores, notes are usually symbolized by x's rather than with pitch-specific noteheads, though x's may be placed higher or lower on the staff to indicate higher or lower pitch ranges.

7.   Reggaeton originated as an underground genre in Puerto Rico in the 1990s, a blend of several upbeat Caribbean grooves that accompanies rapping and simple, catchy melodies.

music is inflected with the regionalism of every character's ancestry (including Manhattan). The rap is grooving but loose, and playfully overconfident. The r&b melody is smooth and sexy. The reggaeton motives are rhythmically tight and funky. The arioso is dolce and legato.

Ballads

There are songs in slow tempos in all genres. A slower pulse usually corresponds with a slower pace to the melody, but not always (hip-hop, for example), and does not necessarily mean that the melodic rate is slower. Calling any song a "ballad" usually just indicates the song's slow, or slowish tempo. The term "rhythm ballad" denotes a song that has a strong groove despite a slower tempo. The vast majority of rock ballads and theatre rock ballads are rhythm ballads.

In general, there are no substantive differences between the melodic makeup of ballad melodies and their faster counterparts within their genres. Slower tempos, however, leave more space for improvisation, and the sentimentality of many ballads justifies improvisation. Sam Cooke's "You Send Me" is a marvelous early example, and the trend continued through the 1960s with songs such as Aretha Franklin's interpretation of "Natural Woman" and Joe Cocker's wailing take on "A Little Help from My Friends." From around 1970 to 1990, pop ballads were more melodically rigid (as were uptempo songs), but still allowed in plenty of emotion. The Young Rascals' "How Can I Be Sure" and the Righteous Brothers' "You've Lost That Lovin' Feeling" are examples from the 1960s, and from the 1970s, the Carpenter's "Superstar" and Billy Joel's "New York State of Mind." The 1980s gave us Foreigner's "I've Been Waiting for a Girl Like You" and Lionel Richie's "Hello," and the 1990s contributed Bryan Adams's "(Everything I Do) I Do It for You" and Savage Garden's "Truly Madly Deeply."

By 2000 the merger between pop and r&b (and to a lesser extent rap) was complete, and ballads readmitted vocal embellishment, at times to such a degree that melody and text were obscured by vocal pyrotechnics. Again, this is not usually an option for a theatre singer, unless such vocalism is germane to the dramatic moment. As in commercial pop ballads, and as in many of the examples cited in the preceding paragraphs, melodic rigor does not disallow emotion, and does not prevent you from somehow altering a melodic approach to fit your unique interpretation.

Early theatre rock ballad examples include the still-standard "I Don't Know How to Love Him," from *Jesus Christ Superstar*. This song's very square, major key, stepwise melody, floating over a gentle folk groove, perfectly conveys the emotional naïveté and unrequited love of the character. In this and similar pop ballads, the best approach is a straightforward one, in which you feel the emotional content deeply, but do not display it too overtly, and sing the music without undue elaboration. Marvin Hamlisch and Carole Bayer Sager's "Just for

Tonight," from the musical *They're Playing Our Song*, typified the slick, slightly soulful pop ballads popular on the AOR charts in the 1970s and 1980s. (The story is about a pop songwriting team.) Karen Carpenter, Michael Bolton, Melissa Manchester, Carly Simon, and others are models of this singing style, closer in approach to traditional theatre singing than most rock vocal approaches. Clear delivery of lyrics and light improvisation are its hallmarks.

Parallel to the commercial music timeline, freer vocal interpretation returned in post-2000 theatre rock ballads, such as *Aida*'s "Elaborate Lives," *The Lion King*'s "Shadowland," and *Wicked*'s "I'm Not That Girl." As in other examples, much of what seems to be improvisational in these theatre songs is actually predetermined, and only slight variations are allowable. By contrast, some of the folk-rock ballads from the musical *Once* are presentational, by virtue of their context in the story. Because of this, and because their lyrics are less specific to the moment than in character- and plot-driven theatre songs, you can sing these songs with considerably more musical liberty.

Chapter 6 contains annotated examples of rock songs, broken down by meter and feel, with additional thoughts on performance approach(es) to each song and style.

5

Singing Rock

Vocal Production and Vocalism

What makes a vocal a rock vocal? Obviously, it depends. In this book I group together the vastly divergent singing tendencies of artists such as Bob Dylan, Ray Charles, Pat Benatar, Chris Cornell, Janet Jackson, Shawn Mendes, Nicki Minaj, and Drake. My argument does not equate these artists, it merely acknowledges each of them as a participant in a massive stylistic movement.

Your voice is the musical instrument that brings rock-based characters to life. To accommodate and communicate the diversity of rock styles now populating the stage, you may have to adjust how you perceive and use your instrument, in several possible ways. Identifying the qualities shared by all rock material and those specific to certain styles will help to understand the many different rock vocalisms, how they operate, and how you can make them work on the musical theatre stage. From examining seminal rock songs, singers, and characters, as well as their histories and circumstances, a rock-based rationale behind the vocal approach to almost every song will become apparent.

All singers, whether they are aware of it or not, work from the precept that the words they sing have properties that suggest how they can or should be sung.

> Insofar as speech is concerned, the formation of a sound image and its reproduction . . . reaches a state of such automatism that the meaning if a word becomes synonymous with its sound. Thus the sound becomes an automatic expression of its meaning. The same automatism, if attained by a singer, will form his most valuable attribute as an artist.[1]

---

1. Sergius Kagen, *On Studying Singing* (London: Rinehart & Co., 1950), 39.

The colorful, explicit language and linguistic styles of rock make this all the more evident, and all the more crucial to believability. Consider, for example, the many ways rock singers articulate the words "love," or "you," or "me." Each singer modifies his or her treatment of these words according to musical and lyrical context and personal tendencies. From the way they are sung, listeners infer quite a lot about what these words mean, the character singing them, and the story being told. They learn about the performer, as well.

Rock speaks in the vernacular, a language of the general populace, and sometimes in a localized dialect or patois—as examples, the sound of the street, the mountains, the bayou, or the islands. This is in stark contrast with the urbanity of Golden Age theatrical language styles (except when writers characterized ethnicity, nationality, or social standing through lyrical styling, as in "Ol' Man River" or "I Cain't Say No"). Ideally, all characters on stage use language in a way that is natural to them, but rock techniques and mannerisms add layers of potential artificiality. If your character should not sing like a rock singer, but does, that is not believable. If you sing a rock song in a legitimate vocal style, that is not believable, either. Again, it is a matter of examining each specific song and character and the way they operate, and finding the appropriate vocal balance to properly represent them.

Singing is a very inclusive act. Audiences accept all sorts of singing voices, and judge singers on the basis of vocal rightness as much as vocal excellence. Both the rock and musical theatre galaxies are full of stars who are not the greatest of singers, nor trained singers, but they are all believable performers. Some rock singers are screamers, some are light crooners, and some just speak expressively in rhythm. Some musical theatre performers are actors or dancers for whom singing is a sideline. Each musical theatre setting is unique, and each dictates a different level of vocal ability and different ways of producing sound. Rock musicals are no different.

In practice, it's not absolutely essential for all singers to understand their means of *vocal production*, the mechanisms that give sound to the human voice. Some singers eschew such knowledge, preferring either to trust their natural abilities, or just to let it rip. This is not as common in the musical theatre as in rock, as the great majority of theatre performers receive some sort of vocal training or coaching. Awareness of how one's voice works does help in controlling and exploiting its possibilities. On the other hand, it also can understandably engender harmful self-consciousness.

The same observations apply to a singer's *vocalism*. Vocalism refers to all aspects of the sound of a voice: its resonance and timbre, its personality, and its involvement in forming musical constructs. Certain people have certain natural vocalisms, such as a country singer, for example, or a singer in a mariachi band. Most rock singers don't consciously change their natural vocalisms from song to song, though there are exceptions—for example, compare Paul McCartney's sound in "And I Love Her," "Lady Madonna," and "Uncle Albert/Admiral Halsey." Musical theatre actors, on the other hand, will adjust their vocalism to suit character, period, and musical style, obviously limited by what their voices and personalities are capable of.

Each voice is unique, and each person's means of producing and manipulating his or her voice is unique. Vocal uniqueness is a huge asset in rock music, because many songs sound similar to one another. It provides distinction, even identity, to a good portion of the literature. In the theatre, too, uniqueness is an advantage, but is tied up with the issue of rightness. Actors can expand the scope of their rightness by adding rock singing to their field of understanding and ability.

Vocal Production and Vocal Health

As is true of acting values, rock only modifies the way you produce sound—your technique won't need an overhaul. All vocal production is the product of a physiology that everyone shares, modified by variables belonging to individuals—singers and characters—and songs. When performing rock in the theatre, you are extending vocal techniques you already use.

In a few sentences, for reference, here is an outline of the basic functioning of the human voice when singing.[2]

A singer takes in breath, or inhales. Inhalation fills the lungs with air and pushes the diaphragm, a muscle just below the lungs, into its lowered position. Reflexively, exhalation follows: the diaphragm returns its original state, and in doing so pushes the air out of the lungs through the trachea, larynx, pharynx, nose, and mouth. (That's also how people breathe.)

Singing is a multi-part process of controlling the exhalation, or *airflow*, by means of various forms of *resistance*. Resistance produces the sustained tones that make up sung melody. The outgoing air vibrates the vocal cords (*phonation*), resonates in the upper torso, nasal cavities, and mouth (*resonance* or *resonation*), and is enunciated with the jaw, lips, soft and hard palates, teeth, and tongue (*articulation*), all in service of creating an outgoing sound (*projection*). Resistance in the chest and abdomen is known as vocal "*support*," and allows longer phrases to be sung without breathing midway. By repositioning the larynx, singers alter pitch and register, as well as *timbre*, defined later in this chapter. Volume is controlled primarily by the strength and speed of exhalation, but also using the vocal folds, resonators, and articulators. (Speaking operates much like singing, but with less resistance to exhalation. Speakers are also usually much less conscious of the process of producing sound than are singers.)

---

2. For a complete understanding of vocal technique, I refer you to the wealth of information available from books, online videos and courses, your friendly local voice teacher or vocal coach, and the excellent university faculties who dedicate the entirety of their energies to this discipline.

Sound travels to the listener by means of *amplitude,* a term that denotes the amount of air being displaced from the sound source, in this case, the voice. A soft vocal sound, a low *volume,* can still "carry" well when sufficient air is released and there is sufficient resonance to effect a higher amplitude. Not to be confused with amplitude, volume is a measurement of how loudly a listener perceives sound, usually measured in decibels (db). The sound of a singer's voice is also greatly subject to the effects of the space in which he or she is singing—room, hall, church, etc.—and, in rock and modern theatre vocal performance, to the microphone and sound system.

In training the singing voice, the different operations of vocal production are treated both separately and as one complete mechanism. The long-term goal for a singer, as in all technical training in art, is to obscure the technique and effort of producing sound, so that the listener hears only music. Again, this speaks to naturalness and believability. The healthy paragon of this mechanism puts no undue strain on any part of the singer's physiology. A well-developed vocal mechanism is achieved through exercise and practice of proper breathing, resonation, and diction. As with all muscular skill and development, those abilities must be maintained over time.

It is no misconception that some commercial rock does involve singing loudly, and can encourage potentially dangerous physical habits. Some rock stars seem impervious to such hazards, and some have been famous for exacerbating their vocal self-abuse with other vices. Unfortunately, many a singer has succumbed to vocal fatigue of some kind, and even polished, careful singers have experienced vocal tragedy. On the other hand, just as many rock singers continue to sing with their usual rock panache, including their bad vocal habits, for decades. They may, however, transpose their songs down as they age. One of the "secrets" of maintaining healthy rock vocal production over a long career is actually quite simple: rock singers keep their material within a comfortable tessitura. If it seems that there a lot of male rock singers singing a lot of very high notes, it only means that there are more tenors in rock than baritones or basses.

Healthy vocal production is essential for you as a musical theatre singer, in the long term and on a daily basis. Musical theatre as a practice and profession is demanding on the voice, and stamina is a major concern for singers of all ages, especially for younger voices. You will sing constantly in rehearsal, auditions, lessons, while practicing, and in front of audiences. Your voice will tire sometimes, and cannot be used indefinitely even when singing correctly. The emotionalism of acting also sometimes endangers healthy vocal production, because unbridled vocal production can truthfully convey certain extreme emotional states. How you manage these challenges is crucial to both effective performance and an enduring career.[3]

3. Kristin Linklater's timeless text *Freeing the Natural Voice* is still a great resource for theatre singing, and greatly helpful for rock singing.

Maintaining your vocal health is an ongoing responsibility. It goes beyond caution to healthy living in general—exercise, nutrition, rest, all the things everyone is supposed to do, but for singers are compulsory. Your vocal health begins with maintenance of your instrument and ends with using your voice in a way that gets the job done, and allows you to do it again the next day. Prudent and forward-thinking singers consciously look for ways to navigate potentially dangerous vocal requirements as safely as possible. For stage singers singing rock, this is a mission statement.

In truth, however, you really needn't worry that singing rock the way it should be sung will shred your cords or make your eyeballs pop out, and certainly you should not try to sing that way to emulate rock stars. Too much concern over your voice can put undue stress on your vocal mechanism. First and foremost, when you're singing rock, sing naturally. Chilina Kennedy, an experienced actress in rock musicals who has played over a thousand performances as Carole King in *Beautiful* on Broadway and Toronto, agrees: "Fear of hurting my voice can make me tight, and this can lead to bad habits. The freer and easier I can be with my sound, the better for my vocal health overall. It's pretty simple, really, I take care of voice by resting it, not drinking too much alcohol and sleeping well. I also drink plenty of water and warm up before every show."

Once you learn to adjust your natural vocalism correctly, if you need to at all, singing rock is not necessarily any more perilous than legitimate singing. Make no mistake, though, singing rock on the theatre stage (indeed all stage performance) does require physical fitness, and endurance. You'll not only sing more often than commercial rock singers, but you'll also sing while dancing, in costume, under the lights, observing onstage traffic patterns and avoiding set pieces, and you'll stay on stage for two-plus hours at a time, as many as eight times a week. You may not dance as hard while singing on stage as Britney Spears or Madonna, but those two get to lip sync when necessary.

How does vocal production change when singing rock music, and how can you practice its techniques? Let's break it down, and try out some techniques in miniature, using warmup exercises.

First is breath. Making a more powerful sound generally means using more air and exerting greater air pressure. The high ranges of rock, as well as some of its typical resonances, require extra breath support. In rock, breathing is also a musical element, the same as a note, and is often done in rhythm. You can start by working on taking bigger breaths, inhaling them faster, and exhaling them from with more force from the chest and diaphragm. Breathing exercises will help expand your lung space, and develop the intercostal muscles that aid inhalation and the abdominal muscles that control exhalation.

The following is a series of preparatory breathing exercises. Whenever doing breathing exercises, especially those favoring unvoiced consonants (consonants that do not engage the vocal cords: "t" versus "d," or "k" versus "g," for example), make sure the larynx remains lubricated, by swallowing and drinking small amounts of non-viscous fluids frequently. Take frequent breaks, so you won't hyperventilate.

Exercises 1a–b: Both these exercises involve unvoiced sound only. Exercise 1a is a breathing calisthenic, done in rhythm. In Exercise 1b, on the inhalations, 1) form the mouth and lips to an "ooh" shape, as if (pardon me, it is a book about rock music) smoking a joint, or 2) spread the lips into a horizontal smile, or an exaggerated "eeh" shape, and inhale through the teeth. On the exhalations, form the mouth to a relaxed "ah" shape. Keep the rhythmic pulse steadily in your head, or clap it out gently, with the hands in front of the sternum and the elbows lifted slightly outward.

EXERCISES 1a-b

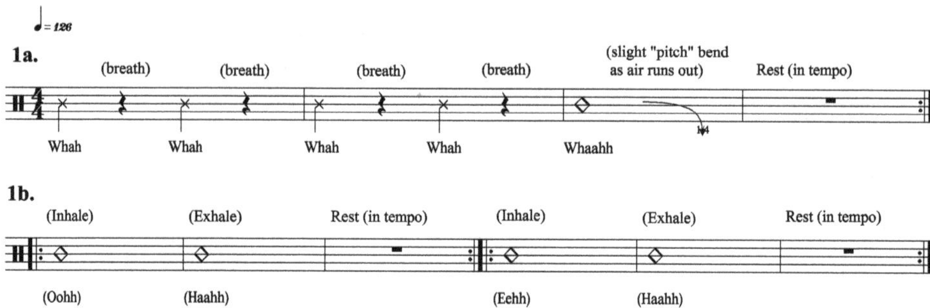

Exercise 2: The rhythmic inhalations and exhalations here are staccato. Keep time strictly. If you get bored with repeated quarter notes, make up some simple alternate rhythms. After doing these exercises with breath alone, begin to gently voice the sounds (vibrate your vocal cords). On the exhalations (short and long both), use pure, open vowel sounds (ah, ooh, eeh). Always be sure to keep the throat relaxed during both inhalation and exhalation. If you feel it tightening, slow down for more control, or stop entirely and diagnose the problem. You are training the breath to do the work of creating vocal power, while acclimating the throat to staying out of the way. This sort of conditioning is beneficial to all sorts of singing, not just rock.

EXERCISE 2

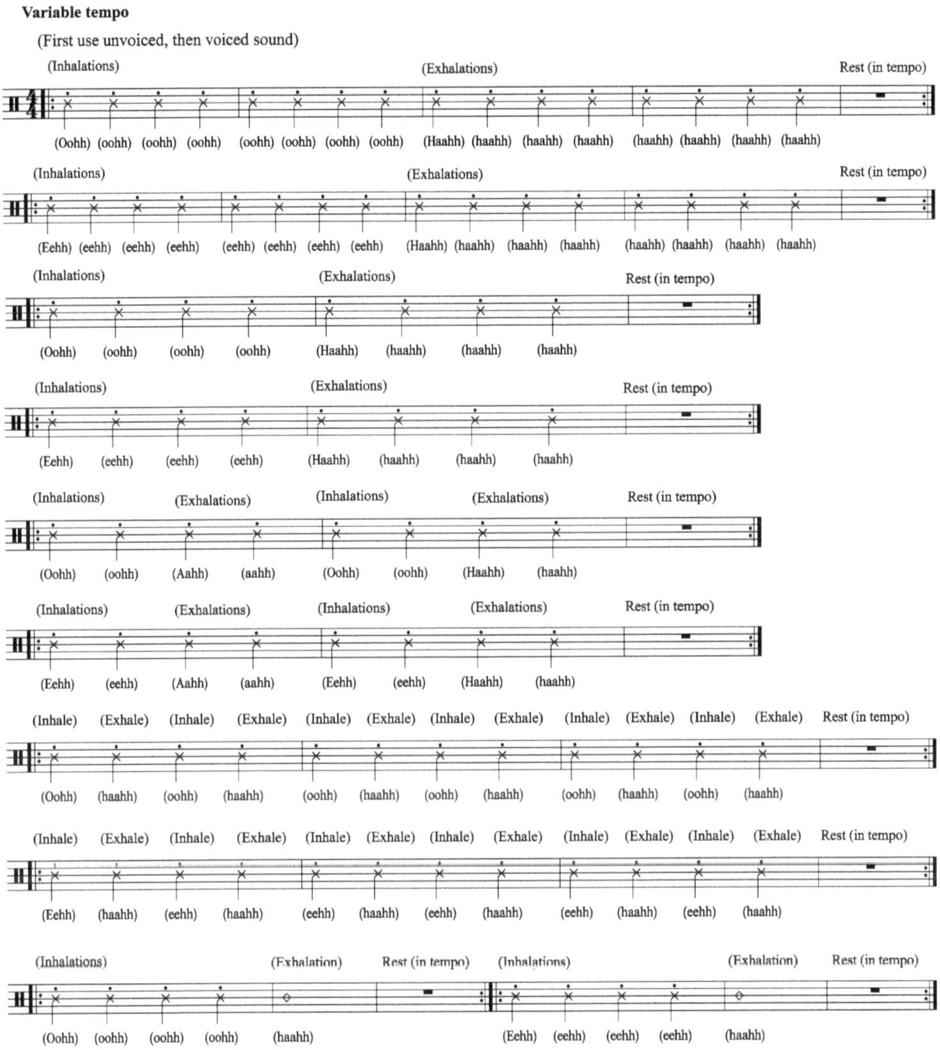

Exercise 3: To further engage the vocal cords and more readily connect your breath to a voiced tone, try this "doo-wop bass line" exercise. Accent the "sh" portion of the phoneme. Alternate the "shooh" sound with a "shah" sound, and try putting a non-explosive "p" at the end of the staccato notes (close your lips to a "p," but do not "pop" the "p"). Make sure to observe the rest at the end of the second bar exactly in time. Do the exercise in multiple keys, and try it in a very low register, like a bass guitar.

EXERCISE 3

The following exercises explore resonation. There is a huge variety of vocal resonances in the rock vocal repertoire. Some will come naturally to you, and some not. Resonance in the chest area, from above the pelvis up through the shoulders, is the first phase of projection. It is a natural mechanism whenever speaking or singing at any dynamic level above a whisper. Exercise 4 helps you explore a strong chest resonance.

Exercise 4: With your jaw open but relaxed, inhale fully and energetically through your mouth, then use the entire breath as you send the sound outward. Begin on a moderately high pitch in your speaking range, and allow the pitch to fall as you exhale. Start with medium to long note durations, and then increase their length. Focus on the musculature of your abdomen and diaphragm, feeling the sustenance that originates there. Note the resistance that might naturally occur in the larynx; consciously relax your throat as you release the sound. If you start to tighten up, relax by doing the exercise unvoiced, softer, or on a lower-pitched sigh.

EXERCISE 4

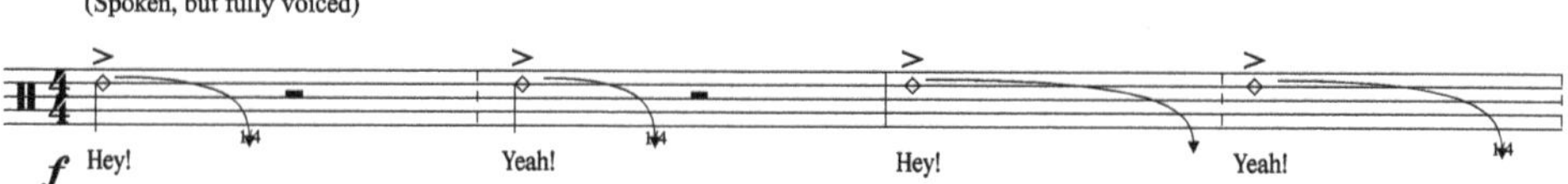

Traditional voice training dictates an open, fully relaxed larynx, through which singers sustain long, expressive tones ("bel canto" singing). By contrast, in some rock singing, especially harder rock material, the throat is actively involved in vocal production. Some singers simply have what one would call a throaty sound; singers such as Rod Stewart and Melissa Etheridge are identified by their rasps. Others, such as Joe Cocker and Britney Spears, seem to squeeze their sound through their vocal cords, using them to sculpt words and melodies, and their phrasing. Some vocalists seem to actively manipulate their sounds by positioning the larynx to create a certain resonance; Michael Jackson and Macy Gray are obvious examples. The most common approach to post-2000 pop vocal production and vocalism is a mix of smooth, airy sounds and throaty articulations, evident in the work of artists such as Carly Rae Jepsen, Rhianna, Drake, and many others.

This aspect of rock vocal production also relates directly to text and meaning. In the rock language, using the throat as an articulator in shaping specific words and phrases is common, for entirely aesthetic reasons. Obvious examples are the many harsh interpretations of "yeah (yeah, yeah)," "all right," and "baby." Throatiness in some form seems to suggest either sexuality or extreme angst. Despite the fact that these implications have become vocal clichés, they have proven to be effective means of conveyance. An audience hearing a yowling pronunciation of "oh yeah" will understand that the singer is speaking rock. They might also recognize if he or she is speaking rock fluently.

What I have so far referred to generally as the "throat" is actually a series of anatomical parts. Starting above the trachea, the tube that connects the lungs to the throat, is the larynx, a structure of cartilage and muscle that houses the vocal cords. The vocal cords are symmetrical folds of soft tissue that the muscles of the larynx control. The glottis is the doorway to the vocal cords, and the epiglottis a small flap of cartilage that protects the glottis. Above that is the pharynx, a series of resonant passageways leading to the resonating cavities of the sinuses and mouth.

It's a natural tendency at times to tighten the larynx or reposition it higher or lower when speaking, and in forming speech-like interjections ("errrrrr," "auugghh," etc.). It's quite easy to make sound with one's larynx without using much breath support. Try it, by letting out most of your breath, and you'll see how many different sounds you can articulate using just the vocal mechanism from the throat upward. (Explosive consonants, which require air pressure, are the exception.) But if you do this for too long, you'll find that your throat tires from being tensed, and, of course, at some point you'll need to breathe. In small quantities and low volume levels, this action causes no harm.

When air is taken in and projected outward more forcefully, however, as in some rock singing, a tense throat is an obstacle, and a prime source of vocal trouble, unless used thoughtfully. Rather than being a product of the throat itself, healthily powerful vocal production in rock results from how the air moves through the throat, and how sound resonates in the various cavities. Your vocal cords are not necessarily tighter, but greater volumes of air are passing through them more quickly and powerfully, and the air pressure in all areas of resonance is greater.

To understand the involvement of the throat in producing sound, let's use an exercise that voice students may be familiar with, often called the "creaky door." This exercise simply uses a tight and slightly spread "ee" vowel to imitate the sound of a creaky door opening slowly. It's not necessary to use an extremely high pitch or head voice, just pitch it wherever is comfortable, and do it softly. First, make the sound as you did when experimenting with unsupported sounds; in other words, don't breathe before the exercise, and don't support the sound with outgoing air. Next, inhale before the exercise, and use the outgoing air for support. The creaky door sound is harder to make because your throat naturally relaxes. The more you tighten your larynx, the greater the creak, because the air is being stopped off, like staving off the opening of an inflated balloon. You'll also find that it is more difficult to reach higher pitches and greater volumes, and to do so will require more air. On the other hand, once the higher pitch or greater volume is attained, it will have greater amplitude. This is what you might hear with a rock tenor singing loudly in a high tessitura, or in a rock female singing in a resonant mix.

Next, try speaking a few open vowels ("ah," "ooh," "eeh"), alternating between a breathy attack (a slight "h" before the vowel) and a gentle glottal attack. See if you can mix the two articulations, or control the transition from one to another. Here, you are using slight tension in the throat to project sound, but not interfering with healthy airflow.

The following exercises use phonemes similar to those found in rock lyrics, and bits of sound bordering on words, focusing on the throat as a harmless source of articulation.

Exercises 5a–b: Sing these exercises mezzo-forte, not forte, but be aware of projecting your sound outward. Let your mouth and jaw widen without actively spreading them wider. Inhale at every rest. In Exercise 5a, inhale through your nose with an open jaw, then immediately relax your glottis into a closed "ng" shape. On the exhalation, keep the "ah" vowel wide open. Think of the word "guy," but don't close off the diphthong. In Exercise 5b, inhale through your mouth only. "Ah-seh" is equivalent to the words "I say," in rock parlance. Try giving each "ah" sound a slight glottal attack, but continue to move the air through the larynx. (You can change up the words to "I know," "I see," or a nasal "Unh-hunh.") These exercises are written in minor modes typical of a rock bass line, but feel free to alter the pitches as you like.

EXERCISES 5a-b

Chambers in the pharynx offer various possibilities for resonance, which increase exponentially with the addition of the sinuses, nose, and mouth. You can brighten or darken your resonance by changing the balance among these different resonating cavities. This is usually known as *placement* of the tone. Different placements result in different *formants*, which are harmonics brought out by resonance. A variety of terminology is used to describe the sounds (timbres) that result from different placements and difference combinations of formants, words such as "brassy" or "forward," and "warm" or "covered." Whereas these are subjective descriptions, they all refer to the acoustic structure of the sound: "bright" sound emphasizes the higher harmonics of a tone, while "dark" sounds emphasize the lower. In the same way as differently shaped brass instruments produce different timbres, you create formants in your voice by shaping your resonating cavities in different ways and combinations and passing air through them with different levels of force. You can explore the possibilities of resonance with the following exercise.

Exercise 6: As you sing through this arpeggiation of a dominant seventh chord, experiment with different placements of the sound. Both the "ey" and "ow" diphthongs are very flexible, and very commonplace in rock lyrics. Do the exercise in multiple keys, and at both soft and loud dynamics, but do not extend the range past where it is comfortable for you.

EXERCISE 6

Another way to find the possible resonances in your voice is to imitate different sounds and types of singers. For example, if you cast yourself as a guard at the Wicked Witch's castle in *The Wizard of Oz*, and sing their famous "Oh-wee-oh" chant in character, you are likely to use a darker resonance that closes off the nasal passages and the front of the mouth (except perhaps on the "wee"). If you quack like a duck or make the sound of a baby crying ("Waaahhh"), you are pushing the epiglottis over the vocal cords to create additional resonance in the pharynx. If you make a mechanical, robot-like sound in a monotone, you will be using the resonance of the nasal passages. To add nasality and forward resonance in the oral cavity and on the hard palate, form a trumpet bell with your lips and imitate a singer with a strong southern accent (Reba McEntire, for instance, or Merle Haggard). Try making the sound of a didgeridoo, a jaw harp, or an electric guitar playing country music. These forward-based resonances are often aptly called "twang."

All resonances are applicable in rock, in different proportions, depending on the style and content of each song and each phrase you sing. Certainly, forward resonance is quite common in rock singing, and "twang" allows many singers to achieve higher notes and greater amplitude, provided that the twang is properly supported by breath. The several forms of resonance that Exercise 7 targets will be useful in different rock contexts.

Exercise 7: Repeat this entire exercise three times as follows: 1) use a breathy, dark sound at a soft dynamic; 2) use a natural, relaxed, speech-like resonance—whatever is a natural placement for you—at a moderate dynamic (*mf*), and 3) sing forte, consciously bringing the sound forward and upward, engaging oral and nasal resonances, and using the front of the mouth to propel the sound outward. Do the exercise in multiple keys, beginning low in your range. As you move into a higher tessitura, note the strength of airflow and positioning of the larynx required in each register. Make sure each repetition is equally supported by the breath; begin each time through by inhaling deeply, take a full half note–long breath at each half note rest, and conserve air throughout the long exercise.

EXERCISE 7

The technical process of vocal articulation culminates in *diction*, defined here as the production of meaningful sound through *enunciation* and *semantics*. Rhythm and text are the infrastructure of rock melody (as opposed to line and beauty, as in bel canto). The vital force behind the melody of any rock song is a singer singing the words (intelligible or not) in rhythm, and in the groove to the extent the song dictates.

In singing rock, clarity of diction and manipulation of diction, as well as being communicative, have the advantage of giving the upper part of your vocal mechanism, the primary articulators, a greater role in projection. Enunciation connects the upper vocal mechanism to the lower, because consonants, especially unvoiced consonants, must be impelled from the diaphragm, and articulated by the lips, teeth, tongue, and forward-resonating cavities. The more intensive your enunciation is, the greater your amplitude will be. It is possible to create consonants with no significant release of air propelling them, but their sound cannot carry (as shown in earlier demonstrations). When connected to the remainder of the vocal mechanism, however, diction can operate both independently and as part of the whole.

The warmups in Exercise 8 promote a focus on good enunciation, while strengthening your breathing apparatus.

Exercise 8: Using unvoiced consonants in pulsing rhythms (indicated by "t"), open first into longer exhalations, then into resonating vowel sounds (both indicated by "tahh"). Then, voice the initial consonant sound: "t" becomes "d," etc. Vary the initial consonant to your liking, using all of the articulators: the soft palate (velum) for "k" and "g," the hard palate (alveolum) for "t" and "d," the tongue for the sibilant "s" and "z," and the teeth for the fricative "f" and "v." Do this exercise first with a fully relaxed jaw and larynx, then again with your mouth shaped in a smile (still relaxed), which will lift the cheekbones and raise the larynx for a brighter sound. Find other rhythms for this exercise to your liking; one alternative is shown.

EXERCISE 8

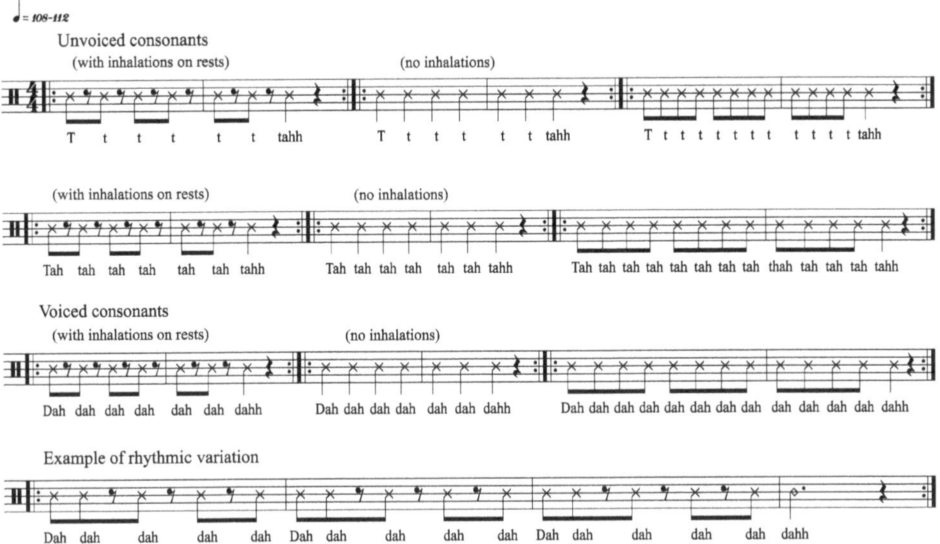

In both rock and theatre music, diction is often exaggerated or stylized. You can formulate exercises out of certain words, varying their articulation and resonance, examining how each affects the meaning and intent of the word, as well as your vocal mechanism.

Exercises 9a–b: In Exercise 9a, clearly enunciate the opening consonant of each word ("Do you love me"), and clearly shape each vowel, as shown. Slightly emphasize the explosion on the release of each word, making sure the second eighth note of each two-note grouping is slightly staccato, but don't breathe until the rest at the end of every other bar. Exercise 9b is more legato, but your enunciation should be just as distinct. Do both exercises in multiple keys, at a moderately strong volume. Feel the change in resonance as you climb through the arpeggio, and keep the air moving through the whole of your vocal mechanism at all times. You will find that extra support and energy may be needed for the top notes, so conserve breath as needed. Try replacing the text with "Nev-ah wan-nah be-wi(t) dout-cha" ("Never want to be without you"), or other lyrics of your choosing that suggest the same rhythms.

EXERCISES 9a-b

Exercise 10: This exercise brings together breathing, airflow, resonation, and diction with text, rhythm, and rock modality. Inhale strongly in rhythm at every eighth note rest. Clearly enunciate both consonants and vowels, and feel free to shape them idiosyncratically as you proceed through the exercise—a dentalized "t" in "tell," perhaps, or an especially bright "yah." Note the staccato marking on "Not," which indicates that the "t" is stopped, rather than explosive, which shortens the note. "Gonna" is a popular rock word to experiment with; among other things, the "g" sound directs your articulation to the soft palate, where you can create a gentle growl without reaching lower into your throat for tension. Keep the melisma in the second half clean and open; it is there to show how the diction-energized vocalism can be applied to legato, as well. Re-articulate the initial "wh" only where indicated. It's fine to scoop into the notes at the peak of each phrase, and to slide a bit between pitches. In place of "Not gonna tell yah," try other lyrics: "I'm on a side road," "Gimme a hug, yo," and "I love my main man."

EXERCISE 10

Power in rock vocal production is the result of strong airflow, proper breathing and resonation, and informed, careful articulation. These are also qualities of effective theatre singing, so you might already have a head start in learning to believably rock. The dynamism associated with rock is available to all vocalists through practice and refinement of techniques such as the ones addressed in the preceding exercises, and many others that you will discover through your exploration of the repertoire, your training, and your career.

Vocalism

For some singers, the musical and stylistic challenges presented by rock music are greater than any technical difficulties posed by rock vocal production. Rock has performance practices that most people don't learn in voice lessons, or in the study of general music. To some people, they come naturally, or have been absorbed through a lifetime of experience. Others learn them by immersion in the material and its aesthetics: listening to and absorbing a song list of enormous and ever-expanding size, studying with teachers and coaches well-versed in those styles, and, of course, practicing and performing.

In theatre singing, you will always characterize your voice to some extent, that is, you'll modify your vocalism to suit the role you are playing. On the other hand, you cannot subdue your voice's natural qualities. For singing rock in the theatre, therefore, having rock qualities to one's natural sound is of tremendous advantage. This translates to a methodology for those who are not natural rock singers: first work on being a rock singer, so that singing rock while playing a character is not artificial.

Vocal technique and musicianship come together in *vocalism*, and come to life in melody. Style, character, and storytelling are all at least partially defined by vocalism. We can break vocalism down into interrelated components.

Timbre is a term that refers to the tonal qualities, or tonal color, of a sound. It is a result of different combinations of harmonics associated with a fundamental tone, known as formants. Loudness and range factor into timbre, but they are also independent characteristics of vocalism. Timbre is affected by individual inflection (including localized accents), articulation, diction, and improvisation.

Like many musical qualities, timbre is somewhat subjective. It is usually described metaphorically; I did just that when I referred to timbre as "tonal color." Timbre in its musical context also occurs over time, and can change. Every sound has what is known as an *envelope*, that is, a beginning, middle, and end, or what happens during the life of a sound. (In electronic synthesis this is called "ADSR," an acronym for "Attack-Decay-Sustain-Release.") Timbre can be manipulated for musical intent, usually on a large scale, as when a singer chooses a certain tone color for a particular song or character, but also at times within melodies and phrases.

Earlier I mentioned that a bright, forward sound is common in rock singing. It is, but it is only one of many timbres in the lexicon of rock vocalisms. Most of all, vocal timbre depends on each person's vocal physiology, and the natural resonances of his or her tone. Obviously, a bass has a different timbre from a soprano, but there are also obviously timbral differences within those vocal ranges. Likewise, a booming, stentorian voice differs in color from a meek, airy one. Some of these qualities are within your control, and some are not. A singer's natural timbre is usually evident in his or her speaking voice, but not always (for those of you who remember, need I mention Jim Nabors?).

By altering your resonance, you change your timbre. To explore your natural resonance, try singing "long notes" (notes of very long duration, a term borrowed from instrumental warmups) on a single vowel while actively changing your placement. (Don't change the vowel, just the placement.) Sing in a comfortable range, not at the extremes. Inhale deeply to start, initiate the sound with the air, and keep the airflow moving through the sound, with no part of your mechanism overly tensed by the changes in shape.

One significant quality of traditional musical theatre vocalism is prohibited in many rock styles: *vibrato*. Vibrato is a slight modulation of pitch during a sustained tone, which (at least in Western music) is thought to give life and beauty to the tone over time. Unlike a note sung in *straight tone*, that is, without vibrato, vibrato keeps a tone in a constant state of change; therefore it is considered more expressive. Of course, straight tones can change over time, as well, and often do in rock vocalism, by bending pitches, altering vowel sounds, or changing placement, among other techniques.

Vibrato is endemic to bel canto singing, and throughout the classical and jazz literature, any instrument that is capable of producing vibrato, including the voice, uses it extensively. In traditional musical theatre, the use of vibrato is stylistically correct, perhaps a vestige of classicism. The legendary vibratos of Ethel Merman and Patti LuPone helped their voices rise over the orchestra and fill the house; what's more, their vibrato was part of their stage personae. Vibrato as a power source is largely obsolete in the modern musical theatre, as all voices are amplified, and even a relatively small straight tone can be mixed so that it is clearly audible. (Regardless, the more signal the sound system has to work with, that is to say, the more output there is from the singer, the more powerful a sound will be.)

Many stage singers, especially when singing correctly and robustly, possess a natural vibrato, and some have trouble suppressing it. So do some rock singers, and some exaggerate it for effect, mostly as an expressive tool, providing long notes with energy, just as in legit singing. Vibrato in rock vocalisms, however, is derived more from its instrumental counterparts, such as bending the strings or using a whammy bar on an electric guitar, or overblowing a saxophone.

From the early days of rock, it has been mostly singers crossing over from pop or gospel who regularly sing with vibrato. Those who sing emotionally charged pop songs, especially gospel- and soul-influenced songs, singers such as Gloria Gaynor, Celine Dion, and John Legend, freely use their vibrato, both as a constant tone quality and for additional expression. Some singers, such as Björk or Tori Amos, employ it only when musically or stylistically appropriate. It is also common in presentational pop vocal performance, where the voice (rather than the song or character) is the focus. Despite these many manifestations, in rock, vibrato is more an attribute specific to songs and singers than an essential element of vocalism.

Singing rock on the theatre stage will accommodate vibrato in music that is under the influence of soul and gospel styles and singers, and others related to them. It is also permissible when it effectively conveys emotion. Some singers (Billy Joel is one example) embrace or induce classical-style vibrato to bring additional expression to soulful melodies. (Joel may have pushed too hard in this effort, as his voice tired considerably over time.)

On the other hand, vibrato would be out of place for most of the music in *American Idiot* and *Rock of Ages,* in a 1970s pop throwback show, or when playing Bob Dylan in a Dylan revue. Furthermore, when singing in an ensemble, especially in harmony, straight tone makes for a better blend, and in most styles, a more convincing group vocal. Listen to the group vocals in *Hair* or *Jersey Boys* as examples. Many singers possess a natural vibrato, and use it without upsetting the style of their material, such as ABBA's female half, Agnetha Fältskog and Anni-Frid Lyngstad, who also reduce their vibrato when singing together. *Mamma Mia!,* the musical, is relatively vibrato-free.

Although theatre singers use vibrato for the same reasons as rock singers (and legit singers), you must learn to defeat it as part of your rock vocal education, and learn to sing comfortably in a straight tone. Even if some rock styles permit it, many do not, and its absence is inborn.

There are two sources of vibrato: vibrations in the diaphragm and the muscles that surround it, and vibrations of the muscles surrounding the vocal cords. The diaphragmatic vibrations are slower; the laryngeal vibrations are quicker. Different proportions of vibration in these two areas result in a faster or slower rate of vibrato. Vibrato also has depth (or width, or breadth; any of those terms will do), that is to say, the extent of the pitch modulation varies. Vibrato is often confused with tremolo, which is a modulation of volume, not pitch. Tremolo is the result of the vocal folds quickly opening and closing; at its most pronounced it has a machine gun–like effect. It sometimes mixes with vibrato in a singer's voice; Elvis Presley and Freddie Mercury are good examples.

One of the fastest routes to reducing vibrato is to restrict your singing to a small tessitura in the middle of your range. When singing in a range where vocal production is most like projected speech, your natural vibrato is at its minimum. Another easy way, but one that disallows long phrases, is to use your entire breath to create a very short burst of sound.

Other than these rather drastic solutions, you can reduce vibrato in two main ways, either opening up or closing off the vocal folds to minimize their vibration. With either technique, it is important to maintain a constant airflow, and therefore that you will probably run out of breath faster. The best illustration of using air in this way is the male falsetto, which has no natural vibrato because the vocal cords are in a completely relaxed position, and air is flowing through them very quickly.

The first method closes off the vocal cords somewhat, as in a twang. To find this technique, do a five-note up-and-down scale on a very forward hum, focused mainly in the teeth and lips. Think "hmm" rather than "hum," or make a face like a pug dog. After doing the exercise a few times, open the jaw slightly—not the lips or cheeks, just the jaw, and leave the tongue flat, the tip touched to the back of your bottom teeth—and sing the scale on the syllable "maah" with very forward "aah" vowel (note the twang). The back of your jaw will lift, gently tightening your vocal folds from beneath, and disallowing those muscles from vibrating. Increased airflow will simultaneously prevent your diaphragmatic muscles from vibrating.

In the second method, the vocal cords are opened somewhat. To access this sound, which might feel to you like a falsetto or head tone, as described above, bring a great deal of air gently through relaxed vocal cords. Sing in a moderately high part of your range, and imitate a choirboy or a Renaissance liturgical chant on a fully open (but not stretched) "oh" or "ah" sound. Or hoot like an owl, but a very gifted owl who can make different vowel sounds. Feel the sound float atop the airflow. Your vocal cords are still engaged, but are naturally relaxed, as in speech, and thereby resonance is lessened, and both diaphragmatic and laryngeal pulsing decrease. While sustaining a long note, increase the airflow further to keep the cords from unduly engaging and vibrating, and to keep the diaphragmatic muscles preoccupied.

Rock singers do sometimes subdue vibrato by consciously exerting pressure on the throat, thus counteracting vibration in the larynx. This risky procedure may be in the nature of a character you sing on a theatrical stage. My advice: if you try it, don't overdo it. Find a way to do it convincingly enough to capture the effect, without shortening your theatrical shelf life. You certainly needn't do it as ferociously as rock singers fronting a band might. And by all means, let the microphone help you.

One last aspect of vocalism worthy of discussion is the connection between notes within a phrase. When notes are connected smoothly to one another, this is known as *legato*. Legato is present in the majority of vocalisms. The reason is that we speak legato, or more accurately, we do not speak in what is the opposite of legato, which is staccato. Our words are mostly connected to one another, in one breath, until there is a punctuation— or simply a need to breathe, but somehow our internal wiring seems to know how long we can speak sensibly before needing a breath; we don't usually run out of breath in the middle of a thought. Therefore, we don't sing that way. Of course, within our spoken legato there are many other articulations, dynamics, and emphases at work. Legato falls under the umbrella of articulation, but is not always discussed as such because it is not always conscious.

In classical vocalisms, "line" is of huge concern, and line is a close cousin of legato. In rock singing, on the contrary, the melody, the words, and the feeling behind them take precedence over line or legato. Unless a singer is trying to make a specific musical point, he or she sings in the same way as he or she speaks, or an enhanced version of it. Even a very melodic singer singing a smooth line in rock is not thinking about line or legato; instead, his or her thought process focuses on making the words and notes sound at once clear and musically phrased.

The more common technique of connecting words and notes in rock, though often no more consciously executed than legato, is *portamento*. Portamento refers to sliding from note to note, and in rock (largely because of the blues) we may extend the meaning to include sliding into, out of, and around pitches. (Only instruments without keys or frets or other such pitch divisions can use portamento; the voice is perhaps its finest purveyor.) Rock singers connect many of their notes with portamento; in a way, it supplants legato. Words and phonemes with unvoiced consonants at their beginnings or ends cannot be connected with portamento, because portamento requires uninterrupted vibration of the vocal cords. Nevertheless, in some rock vocal performances, it seems as if portamento is in use at all times.

There is a strong relationship between portamento and *melisma*. Melisma simply means multiple notes sung to a single syllable. It can be two notes, or twenty. In contemporary song, melisma takes on tremendous importance as an element of expression and improvisation. It is often composed as part of a melody, utilized by writers for expression, and in keeping with certain styles. Most vocal embellishment and improvisation takes place on a very few syllables or sounds. It is where much of the portamento that we perceive in rock vocalism actually happens.

Melisma is everywhere in post-1990 pop songs. From the marriage of r&b, a style derived from the typically melismatic genres of gospel and blues, to pop, a highly rhythmic melodic style driven by vocal personality, a new vocalism was born. We will name it "melismatic rhythmicism," an approach in which the notes of the rhythmic portions of the melody are connected via portamento, and in which both melody and melisma are sung rhythmically, or at least with groove in mind.

Exercise 11: A good way to practice portamento is by using diphthongs to assist in sliding between notes. This technique also simplifies and makes perceptible to you the function of your larynx in changing pitch. In this exercise, when singing "my," "wow," or "hey-yey," slowly close off the diphthong as you slide up the octave, and use the two halves of the diphthong to assist you in sliding as you move through the faster notes. As in earlier exercises, make sure you inhale deeply and maintain strong breath support to sustain the long phrases, and to keep vibrato at bay.

EXERCISE 11

Using the rock song repertoire, you can devise additional vocal exercises that replace traditional scale and arpeggio patterns with content typical of rock. From this sort of research and practice, you can integrate rock vocalisms with rock's musical attributes.

Begin with the many rock songs listed in this book. What melodies and phrases seem most to define their styles and their vocalisms? Sing them for yourself, and learn how your individual instrument handles them. Are there improvised or quasi-improvised musical utterances (sounds we've met before, such as "oh yeah," "whoa, whoa," "awright," or "yooowww!") or familiar fragments of melisma that would make for good vocalizing? Make yourself an exercise routine based on your favorites. This is also an opportunity to determine which styles and vocalisms best suit you as a performer.

In addition, "cop" (that's music lingo for "copy") some bass lines and guitar riffs and other instrumental elements, and use them as exercises, too. The lead guitar in rock is very much akin to the voice, and the bass is the foundation of many song rhythms and feels. I also recommend physicalizing your warmups whenever possible. Again, watch some of your favorite artists in performance, and how they move. If you can, add elements of movement to your warmup; after all, you'll be moving when you perform. Here are some ideas to get you started.

- Replace your diatonic warmup exercises with ones based on scales as in chapter 4, Example 1.
- Replace triadic arpeggios with dominant 7th and 9th chords, minor 7th and 9th chords, and major 7th and 9th chords.
- Practice bending into and out of notes (imitate an electric guitarist bending strings), and learning how to control the bend. Selectively add vibrato to notes that sustain.
- Because blues inflection is so essential, simple riffs such those in Exercises 12a and 12b should be a staple of your vocalism collection. Think of this exercise as emulating a guitar, or a trombone with a plunger mute.

EXERCISES 12a-b

- Exercises 13a and 13b are examples of bass lines that make good vocal exercises. (You might recognize them.)

EXERCISES 13a-b

- Seek out melodies that contain typical rock motives in a limited tessitura, and sing those motives as warmups, staying in a range comfortable enough for you that you can "rock them out." Here are few that would qualify: "Rescue Me" (Fontella Bass), "Lean on Me" (Bill Withers), "Sweet Home Alabama" (Lynyrd Skynyrd), "Hey Jude" (the Beatles), "Party in the U.S.A." (Miley Cyrus), and "Eye of the Tiger" (Survivor).

Microphones and Other Electronics

Earlier I referred to the use of amplified instruments and higher microphone levels on singers as a benchmark of rock. Here, a little more relevant detail. (There are some excellent writings on the subject of electronic vocal amplification in the theatre, from professionals with far more technical know-how than I could ever claim to contribute.[4]) An overly detailed discussion of the topic here would be superfluous, except as it applies to you as a rock musical theatre singer. The question for you is a simple one, and one not exclusive to rock: how will microphones and amplification affect your voice when singing on stage?

First, there is your rock-based accompaniment. The standard pop-rock instrumental grouping has not changed much over time. It is made up of one or two guitars (electric or acoustic or both), bass (upright or electric, mostly electric), a drum kit, usually along with additional hand percussion, often a keyboard or two (pianos, electric pianos, electric organs, and later synthesizers), and sometimes orchestral instruments: trumpets, trombones, and saxophones ("horns," in rock terminology), strings, and the occasional woodwind. Bands grew in size and variety as rock composers' imaginations expanded. Theatre music, at the time when rock music was taking hold, was anchored firmly to its pit-sized house orchestras on Broadway: between twenty and thirty players, configured

---

4.   The definitive text is probably Deena Kaye and James LeBrecht's *Sound and Music for the Theatre: The Art & Technique of Design* (New York: Focal Press, 2016), but there are several others.

like a mini-symphony orchestra plus rhythm section, or like a big band with strings. (In-house radio, television, and recording studio orchestras were much the same.)

This traditional, union-enforced orchestral template was inconsistent with the new sound of rock. What's more, the piano, which had always been the preferred accompanimental instrument of theatre rehearsals (and still is), and had through the years served so well in generalizing the sound of a pit orchestra, was not always up to the task of representing a rock groove made up of drums, bass, and guitars. At first, the existing house orchestras, with modifications, accompanied the new rock shows, and some larger pit bands still do (when musically appropriate, as in studio r&b style of *The Color Purple* or the "Philadelphia Sound" of *Sister Act*, for instance). Bit by bit, though, theatre orchestras mutated, and shrank, into what eventually became today's typical outfit: a large rhythm section, with additional small orchestral sections proscribed by the musical style or by the dictates of the producers (union minimum orchestra size requirements are usually irrelevant in today's theatrical environment). Synthesizers are now doing far more than their own work as electronic keyboard instruments. They are also replacing orchestral musicians (string players, most commonly) by triggering high-quality samples of actual instruments. Sound synthesis, sampling, and sequencing (loops, prerecorded tracks, and other computerized musical and sonic output) have been raised to an art form in shows like *Hamilton* and *Natasha and Pierre*, orchestrations that deploy them with stylistic rather than budgetary incentive.

Next is the amplification of your voice. Theatre sound design evolved alongside its music, and followed the change in musical style. Prior to the mid-1970s on Broadway, area microphones on stage would slightly enlarge singers' voices, but stage singers had bigger voices then, and were trained to project them to the back of the house. Conductors conducted and musicians played with extreme sensitivity to the singers (they still do, ideally, even with amplification), and the very architecture of orchestra pits did a good job containing the orchestra's volume. Since then, there have been many technical advances in amplification. Perhaps the most meaningful one for the theatre was the remote wireless body microphone, which permitted lighter-voiced singers to fill a stage with sound—one no longer needs Merman-esque pipes when a mic is an inch from one's lips, and when the sound operator is riding the faders at the mixing board. Sound design is by now a nearly equal participant in the delivery of music to an audience in the theatre, and every singer and instrumentalist is subject to its effect.

Both musical theatre vocals and rock vocals go through microphones, but different kinds of microphones. Rock vocal mics are usually high-end and full-sized, either hand-held, or placed on a stand when the singer is playing an instrument. In the 1980s, when certain pop singers began to get very physical on stage, they began to wear what have become known as "Madonna mics," wireless microphones securely affixed to a headpiece or neckpiece, allowing them to move about freely while singing.

In the current musical theatre, almost every singer has a small, high-quality radio frequency microphone either taped somewhere near his or her mouth or concealed inside a wig or costume piece. (Principal singers often have two, in case one fails.) Part of your pre-show routine is getting "mic-ed up," and when the mic is somehow built into a costume or wig, that can be an elaborate process. In certain musicals, more rock-like mics have been used—*Rent* was the first Broadway show that had Madonna mics, and *On Your Feet* and other bio-musicals have used handhelds. In the original *Spring Awakening*, handheld mics were a design feature, helping to embed the large-scale symbolism of rock as youthful rebellion. (They were also cleverly used as phallic symbols, which might be considered germane to the rock aesthetic.)

Rock never had the requirement that voices needed to be heard over an orchestra, as its vocals were amplified from the get-go, and the level of the accompaniment was always close to the level of the lead vocal. Still, rock singers tend to sing dynamically into their microphones, and so do most musical theatre singers, as if there were no microphone. This is the correct approach regardless of style. Although singers of softer and jazzier rock sing at lesser dynamics, their voices may still be formidable—James Taylor and Fiona Apple, for instance.

Microphones and sound systems can be a huge boost to singers without a lot of natural power, or whose voices can benefit from some sort of transformation at the mixing board, most notably, equalization. Equalization, or "EQ," can de-emphasize undesirable frequency bandwidths and formants in singers' voices. Your microphone, however, is not a part of your vocalism. It's the sound designer's and operator's priority to make you sound good. Your job is to sing with clarity and project your sound into the mic and sound system. All musical theatre vocals, amplified or not, sound best when the singer sings with his or her full dynamic range, enunciates clearly and often exaggeratedly, and "sings out" to the audience, that is, projects his or her voice as if it were not amplified. Theatre is still a living, breathing art form, and therefore any vocal performance that relies too heavily on technology as a means of vocalism or conveyance automatically injects a layer of artificially, and defeats theatre's essential purpose.

In other words, musical theatre rock singers, don't change what you usually do because your voice is amplified. Unless you're holding a handheld mic, your amplification is out of your control. Sing as you always have, and as strongly (or not) as you always do.

There is one complication, one that many performers might have already experienced. Musical theatre sound design does not use onstage vocal monitoring, to prevent feedback. As a rule, you will only be able to hear yourself sing within your immediate space, and as your sound returns to you acoustically from the room or hall in which you are singing (sometimes there is a lag). Some singers find this befuddling. If you cannot hear yourself clearly, you are prone to the rock taboo of singing behind the beat: the few microseconds that you spend trying to hear yourself delays your rhythm just enough to push you out of the groove. Keep this in mind as you apply the rhythmic approaches to melody described earlier.[5] One recent solution is the use of in-ear monitors, which allow

---

5. Interestingly, many singers attest to feeling the beat in the stage floor slightly before hearing it, and rely on the tactile beat more than the auditory beat as a guide.

singers to hear themselves perfectly, but can be cumbersome and do not reflect the actual way in which one hears one's voice when singing live.

Your technical rehearsals and production sound check (assuming you have them) are very helpful in dealing with the lack of monitoring. During sound check, wander the stage, and use your voice in all the ways that you will be using it in performance. See how you sound to yourself in the performing space. Make sure your mic is comfortable to wear and does not alter your vocalism by being in any way physically intrusive. Above all, make sure that you still feel as if you are singing naturally, as if you were not amplified, while singing with your mic on. If not, turn to your sound designer and operator (and perhaps your hair and wardrobe teams) for help in finding a solution.

Chilina Kennedy, whom we met earlier in this chapter, puts it all into focus: "It's less about the mics and more about the sound that's coming back to me from the house and the monitors. This is especially true when I'm singing a pop or rock show with heavily amplified sound. The more I can hear myself and the *band*, the more I can trust that the sound I'm making is enough and that it sounds the way I want it to." Like a great rock singer, Chilina has an impeccable sense of groove, in large part because she makes sure she can hear the band, and makes sure she's singing with them.

Song Examples

To close this chapter, let's look at some examples of different vocalisms in some well-known rock voices. The following is a list of rock singers (and songs) with distinctive sounds, annotated with: 1) a few words describing vocal timbre, 2) more specific comments on overall vocalism, and 3) suggestions for singers wanting to learn from or emulate those vocalisms, or who want to sing these and related songs.

Little Richard ("Tutti Frutti," "Long Tall Sally")
Timbre: shouty and guttural, brawny.
Vocal approach: Little Richard's approach is offhanded, barely finishing phrases, sometimes pulling off or punctuating the ends of notes with a guttural or falsetto explosive; works almost entirely in blues scales (note the preponderance of flatted thirds in these songs); sings with intensity even when singing nonsense.
Singers: be careful!—if you adopt this approach, try to do it within the comfort zone of your range, and pull back from Little Richard's relentless fortissimo to no more than a forte.
See also James Brown.

Frankie Valli ("Walk Like a Man," "Dawn (Go Away)")
Timbre: pinched and brilliant, like a piccolo trumpet.
Vocal approach: Valli uses falsetto but places the sound in the upper jaw and hard palate, adding a potent nasal resonance that helps connect the lower and higher

registers (even though the break is considerable); the doo-wop influence in the music means that the vocals are always rhythmic, and rhythm is used as vocal punctuation (note the backup "Walk/walk" and the "ooh" descant in the break of "Walk Like a Man").

Singers: you'll find that the list of actors playing Frankie Valli in *Jersey Boys* is very short. It takes an unusual vocal mechanism to perform this technique convincingly.

See also Geddy Lee (Rush).

Johnny Cash ("Ring of Fire," "I've Been Everywhere")
Timbre: earnest, steely, dark.

Vocal approach: Cash's potent speech-like vocalism lies somewhere between preaching and chanting; his tone is resounding but not highly resonant, giving it a mix of loudness and intimacy; timbre is consistent in both the conversational midrange and the extreme low range, where most of his songs lie; booming, sometimes pained enunciation of each word often leaves him behind the beat, adding a sense of detachment from his often sober topics, or transcendence above them.

Singers: fill your entire mechanism with sound, tell the story as if giving a speech on melody, and avoid vibrato entirely.

See also Tennessee Ernie Ford.

Diana Ross ("You Keep Me Hangin' On," "Theme from Mahogany")
Timbre: mild, shimmering, sensual.

Vocal approach: one of the sweeter and more graceful voices in soul and Motown, Ross's soprano-like sound was one of the most beloved and instantly recognized in the genre, in part because in bypassing most blues vocalisms, she found wider appeal (i.e., was able to cross over into a white market); her voice is mostly in a forward nasal mix with some lighter head tones and a slight natural vibrato; while quite soulful, it rarely breaks out, and seems never to rise above mezzo-forte.

Singers: like Ross, it is possible to bring a great deal of feeling into a vocalism that is very unadorned. She is not a storyteller, rather, she shows that it is possible to embrace the beauty of a tone and the contour of a line, and communicates largely through personality and manner. Her rhythms are accurate and grooving but never forceful, or forced.

See also Jewel.

Jim Morrison ("Break on Through," "Riders on the Storm")
Timbre: gruff; warm, but wooden.

Vocal approach: almost as if reading poetry to melody, Morrison's blunt vocalism only occasionally ventures into brighter resonances and harder-edged blues vocalism; when it does it borders on frightening vehemence.

Singers: Morrison's thought process epitomizes the "artistry" of rock; perhaps not a paragon of healthy vocal production, but you can take a lesson from his dedication to a life engrossed in multiple art forms and intellectual pursuits beyond music—poetry, philosophy, mysticism, and so forth—and how those things can motivate a persona or character and a vocalism; but please, do it without the self-destruction.

See also Kurt Cobain (Nirvana).

Art Garfunkel ("My Little Town," "Disney Girls")
Timbre: angelic, silky, airy.

Vocal approach: a natural baritone employing a countertenor-like falsetto; the folk-pop version of bel canto, but with more Renaissance purity than classical vibrancy; most often heard in perfectly blended duet with equally smooth-voiced Paul Simon.

Singers: Garfunkel's natural straight tone and feathery vocalism can only take you so far stylistically, but it is admirable for its clarity and lack of ostentation. It is, however, a difficult vocalism to maintain, because it largely disallows chest resonance while requiring an increased airflow, like a true falsetto.

See also Dan Fogelberg.

John Lennon ("Whatever Gets You through the Night," "I Feel Fine")
Timbre: glottal and nasal, with a very fine grain.

Vocal approach: Lennon varies his tone and vocal character song by song, but the Liverpudlian nasality is always present; a deep attachment to the blues shades all of his vocalisms, as does his affinity for simple melody; Lennon sings as he speaks, with frankness, humor, and passion; the emotionalism is muted but still very palpable.

Singers: the quality that made all of the Beatles' vocals (except perhaps Ringo's) so remarkably artistic and musically important was their fully allowing their personalities into their sound, while adapting their vocalisms to the truth of each song—whether warmly melodic, agreeable and catchy, or hard-edged and biting.

See also Elvis Costello.

Joni Mitchell ("A Case of You," "The Circle Game")
Timbre: muted, ethereal, flutey.

Vocal approach: classical, folk, and jazz approaches meet in Mitchell's voice in both tone and phrasing; generous improvisation and ad hoc interpretation of rhythm; extensive exploration of high head tones in unabashedly free melisma; along with the sense of independence is an earthiness that keeps her voice accessible, and friendly.

Singers: It's quite difficult to reproduce Mitchell's original performances, either in vocalism or musical content. You might want to simplify them somewhat, imagining them without her interpretations, and convey the melodies and lyrics with due respect to the original, but in your own sound. (Note how many singers have covered Joni Mitchell songs in very different ways.)

See also Linda Ronstadt.

James Taylor ("Shower the People," "Don't Let Me Be Lonely Tonight")
Timbre: buttery, mellifluous, gentle.

Vocal approach: like a troubadour, or a great campfire singer, Taylor's vocalism is plain and unfettered, evenly distributed in resonance, and crystal clear; his tones have virtually no envelope, rather, they float on by, riding the tight but understated rhythms and euphonious lyrics, in harmony, as it were, with his accompanying guitar.

Singers: there is a sadness, a brooding quality, even in Taylor's upbeat songs; this sense of melancholy under a serenely romantic exterior is the hallmark of his charm as a performer and songwriter. Attempts to bring undue emotionalism or musical embellishment, indeed any sentimentality at all, to his material and style usually fall flat; even Taylor himself has trouble when he tries. Keep it simple and let the gentle grooves guide you.

See also Don McLean.

Tina Turner ("River Deep—Mountain High," "I Can't Stand the Rain")
Timbre: husky, vibrant, tangy.

Vocal approach: a natural singer with mostly on-the-job musical training, Turner's unbridled dynamics and vibrato dominate her sound; gaining greater control as her voice matures, she retains a bright but covered resonance that she manipulates like the mute on a brass instrument; her brash shaping of words and phrases is constantly surprising, yet for her always truthful; her physicality resembles and supports her vocal performances.

Singers: Note that Turner often does her studio recordings in one take; she points out that in concert, she only has one take, so she thinks of concerts and recordings as alike. Going into the session, or the performance, she has already absorbed the song so deeply that she can make it happen at any given time. This is the paradigm both for rock self-assurance, and for putting one's all into every performance— and being ready to do so.

See also Chaka Khan.

Elton John ("Goodbye Yellow Brick Road," "Tiny Dancer")
Timbre: honky, springy, saxophone-like.

Vocal approach: pervaded by a forward "meow" resonance, the timbre is constantly moving back to front; at the same time it is dynamically active and very melismatic; phrasing is free and embellished but very grooving; text is slurred, often to the point of unintelligibility, in a homemade country rock–British blues dialect, what Sir Elton himself called "honky-tonk."

Singers: As with many of the entries on this list, there is an inextricable connection between song and singer in the catalogue of Elton John and lyricist Bernie Taupin. The subject matter is often so obscure, and the vocal styling so distinctive and connected to the text, that many songs only sound right in John's voice. Choose a song from his catalogue that tells a reasonably clear story, or give an unclear lyric a well-considered story. You can incorporate those attributes of Elton John's vocalism that belong to the song, but don't try too hard to sound like him.

See also Jake Shears (Scissor Sisters).

Luther Vandross ("Never Too Much," "Here and Now")
Timbre: mellow and rich, buoyant.

Vocal approach: a pure tone and pure style born in church and gospel music, rhythmic but somewhat free, with melismatic touches, and a light vibrato; baritone with an unforced high mix and a light falsetto; it is a legit voice that has perfectly crossed over, bringing a strong sense of rhythm to the melodic forefront, replacing legato with portamento, and improvising with taste and truth.

Singers: Vandross's background in ensemble singing probably contributed greatly to the musicality and effortless vocal production he brings to his solo material. He allows his naturally lovely tone to work for itself; he merely sings, and sings groovingly. Quite often, the "secret" to successful rock performance is the right voice singing the right melody with a good sense of rhythm and sincere underlying emotion. In this case, his is also an objectively attractive voice.

See also Gladys Knight.

Cher ("If I Could Turn Back Time," "Strong Enough")
Timbre: sultry, covered, fluttery.

Vocalism: a full-throated but airy tone with a dark nasality, a reverse twang, as it were; mostly contralto-like, but with occasional bursts of brilliance; a slight tremolo or laryngeal shake when sustaining; a very straightforward pop musical and vocal approach, with solid rhythm and occasional light embellishment.

Singers: there is no reason not to re-think Cher's sound in your performance of much of her material; hers is a distinctive voice applied to pop songs, rather than a voice that necessarily belongs to the songs she sings.[6] What is important

---

6.   There are exceptions, especially in her earlier repertoire, and now that her life is a Broadway show, her songs' place in the rock theatre literature is considerably more complicated.

to learn from Cher—a major taste-setter since hippiedom's move into the mainstream, and "the only act to have notched a No. 1 single on a Billboard chart in each of the last six decades"[7]—is her independent spirit, her pride in her uniqueness, and her commitment to a rock aesthetic despite an unusual and unspectacular voice. Cher may not be the most accomplished singer, but she's a genuine rocker.

See also Paula Abdul.

Peter Cetera ("Hard for Me to Say I'm Sorry," "You're the Inspiration")
Timbre: bright and reedy, oboe-like.

Vocal approach: extreme forward resonation (twang) takes Cetera's already high tenor to new heights, with clarity, power, and apparent effortlessness in all registers; primarily straight tone; a rhythmic pop melodic approach with minimal improvisation.

Singers: Cetera's voice and a vocalism by themselves seem to carry all the necessary feeling of his romantic material. Together, highly melodic and grooving melodies, an attractive, distinctive tone, a sincere, uncomplicated delivery, and the singer's winning vocal personality perfectly embody the power-pop style. If you, too, have a voice that conveys emotion just with its sound, use it in a similar way. Sing rhythmically, with minimal adornment, and genuinely feel the feelings of the character.

See also Bryan Adams.

Willie Nelson ("Always on My Mind," "My Heroes Have Always Been Cowboys")
Timbre: forward but round, warm, buzzy, like a cello.

Vocal approach: almost mumbling at times, a slight strain pervades Nelson's slightly throaty twang; a constant wide, loose vibrato highlighted in many long, sustained notes; gentle country phrasings that rarely land exactly on the beat.

Singers: the maturity in Willie Nelson's sound and the tender, understated freedom of his rhythmic approach exemplify the country balladeer. Though he always seems to sing softly, his sound has a distinct resonance that is able to convey a sense of intimacy even to a large crowd, and the sincerity and depth of his feeling is never in question, even if his mind seems to be elsewhere as he sings.

See also Rod Stewart.

Steven Tyler (Aerosmith) ("Dream On," "Walk This Way")
Timbre: like a wail, narrow and fierce.

Vocal approach: supported mostly by the upper chest, Tyler's sound is pushed from his body like a megaphone; he accesses an unusually high male register by adding more forward resonance, and pushing harder, sometimes just shrieking;

7. https://www.billboard.com/articles/news/473595/cher-shines-with-no-1-in-sixth-consecutive-decade.

musically in the groove, but sheer energy sometimes propels him into some uninhibited improvising.

Singers: almost unavoidably, this sort of vocalism will lead to trouble, and in Tyler's case, did. Nonetheless, he and similar artists may be the first thing people think of as definitive of rock vocalism. The trick is to capture his spirit while saving yourself to sing another day. Again, transpose songs to comfortable keys, and don't try to replace airflow and support with mere volume.

See also Robert Plant.

Whitney Houston ("Saving All My Love for You," "I'm Your Baby Tonight")
Timbre: velvety, creamy, shades of blue and purple.

Vocal approach: a legit vocalism, but tinged with gospel and blues tendencies, including ample embellishment; an ever-present but warm vibrato; impressive range and an uncanny ability to hit the same pitches in different vocal registers, including a powerful high chest resonance and a light soprano; very specific diction and a great sense of groove.

Singers: Most of Houston's recorded output displays transcendent vocalism, natural musicality, and personal and vocal charisma of the highest order. She is more often envied than imitated, but her repertoire is great for theatre singers to work on, with its stylistic mix of pop, r&b, and soul, all very popular styles in musical theatre. You can do her material your own way. It's hard to know if her long-term vocal troubles were due to her renowned self-abuse, but certainly the loss of control over her life extended to her singing career.

See also Gloria Gaynor.

Amy Lee: (Evanescence) ("Bring Me to Life," "Call Me When You're Sober")
Timbre: luminous, smoothly polished, zesty.

Vocal approach: natural, free, and spacious, unaffected and relaxed, with a huge range but little variance in timbre; vibrato is usually pushed aside by a steady airflow; musically very rhythmic and in the groove, but her melodies often have slow melodic rates, which feeds into her expansive vocalism and occasional exoticism.

Singers: beyond Lee's superb musicality, her control over her airborne vocalism is impressive. Her physical, musical, and emotional investment in every song is immediately apparent in the way her sung melodies rise above the ardently rocking instrumental accompaniments. Also striking is her use of elaborate melisma without its ever seeming gratuitous; it seems always to be sincerely inspired by intensity of emotion.

See also Alanis Morissette.

Billie Joe Armstrong (Green Day) ("Good Riddance (Time of Your Life)," "Still Breathing")

Timbre: blunt, raw, well-worn but unsoiled.

Vocal approach: quintessentially punk-pop in its blend of plainness and power, like melodized speech; a balanced resonance with a strong forward element and no vibrato, in a baritone or low tenor range; no-frills, rhythmic pop-rock musicality; note the singularity of diction, a "California accent," if you will, in this and many similar vocalisms and nearby genres, which includes a sneering, toothy resonance on certain vowels and dentalized or sibilant "t" sounds.

Singers: the plain honesty of Armstrong's voice, and his rebellious musical spirit—highly committed yet never over the top—is a great model for many rock songs, certainly those of this now commonplace form of melodic hard rock. Keep it simple, put the song in a key where you can rock it, and find the appropriate attitude; you can convey a strong point of view without being overly demonstrative.

See also Michael Hutchence (INXS).

Katy Perry ("Teenage Dream," "Chained to the Rhythm")

Timbre: glossy, feisty, crackling.

Vocal approach: confident full-on alto-like belting with occasional light head tones; many notes seem to originate in or be propelled by the throat, like a vocal cough or cry, despite a wide, athletic resonance, great clarity of diction, and ample airflow; an excellent example of the melismatic rhythmic approach of modern pop.

Singers: try to capture Perry's energy while adopting a more benign means of vocal production. Her spirited rhythm and phrasing and shiny tone are accessible without the laryngeal pinch in much of her vocal production, and the songs themselves are largely unchallenging. (In modern pop performance it is important not to forget the significant role the microphone plays in a singer's sound; that is one reason that more current pop artists did not make this list.)

See also Britney Spears.

6

Rock Songs

A Selective, Annotated Survey

The rock music literature is vast. It features countless genres and variations thereof, and a remarkable diversity in subject matter, lyric styles, melodic styles, rhythms, and ethnicities. Rarely does one demarcation suffice in describing one certain song; rather, most songs are hybrids, and many are mongrels.

Because there are so many possible permutations, the following chronological list of songs from the rock literature only scratches the surface. It offers a recounting, in context, of some of the essential elements of rock that you as a musical theatre singer are likely to come across. You may or may not want to include these songs in your repertoire, and by nature certain songs will be excluded from certain performers' reaches or rightness. Included with each song are highly condensed bits of performance advice. Note how frequently an original performance informs your potential approach to a song and to related acting values, musicianship, and vocalism. From this list you can extrapolate performance practices applicable to other songs, including theatre songs written in or inspired by these styles.

Songs in Duple Meters with Duple Subdivisions

"Johnny B. Goode" (Chuck Berry, 1958)
High-energy, early blues-rock-rockabilly. 4/4 time; twelve-bar blues form. Guitar-driven eighth-note pulse. Simple, mostly metrical melody centered around a very few pitches. *Performance tips*: This is a narrative song, so tell the story plainly, and with truth; it's a seminal version of the rock star legend. In keeping with roots rock style and the hard, deep groove, keep your vocal rhythm steady and venture

from the beat only minimally. The many repeated notes in the melody are an excellent opportunity to employ a diction-based approach to your vocalism; use them to "dig in."

"Tossin' and Turnin'" (Bobby Lewis, 1961)
Upbeat r&b-rock. 4/4 time; extended verse-chorus form. Straight-ahead crossover backbeat with a loose eighth-note pulse. R&b melodic and vocal style, combining rhythmic singing and free improvisation, with rhythmic backing vocals. *Performance tips*: The lyric is a story told in blues-related form and the music rocks a blues vocabulary, but there is a pop lightheartedness in the tone. Tell the story in your own voice, and have fun in a party-like vocalism, as if you were leading a singalong. You might enunciate the words more clearly than in the original recording, but a little blurring and slurring is more than acceptable in this ebullient tune, the lyrics of which are unambitious, and intended as amusement.

"Up on the Roof" (The Drifters, 1962)
Calypso-tinged pop-soul rhythm ballad. 4/4 time; AABA form. Constant eighth-note feel with backbeat. Gently rhythmic melody; soulful lead with doo-wop backing vocals. *Performance tips*: Never should your vocal approach be overstated. The mere warmth and ease of the melody convey the sincere, gentle sentimentality and urban escapism of the character; don't try to do too much with it except to tell your own version of the charming and identifiable story, and keep it in the toe-tapping groove. The song is equally effective in James Taylor's slow ballad interpretation, and can work in a brighter tempo as well.

"I Get Around" (The Beach Boys, 1964)
Uptempo surf-pop-rock. 4/4 time; ABAB form. Guitar-driven eighth-note pulse, with some stop time in the B section. Elaborate vocal arrangement around a melody replete with hooks. *Performance tips*: Though composed as a group song, you can cover a lot of the melody with a solo voice. Treat this as a character song—the singer is a rock archetype, the freewheeling California dude; he has a strong independent spirit but is cool, confident, and smooth. Note the breathiness and slightly lazy groove in the original vocal, still with a rock sensibility in its text-based delivery and its strong connection with the instrumental accompaniment.

"For Once in My Life" (Stevie Wonder, 1968)
Bright Motown-pop-rock. 4/4 time; ABAB form. Bass-driven eighth-note pulse. Expressive melody; note the very slight slackness (a bit of swing) in the eighth notes (pre-funk). Motown melodic style, highly rhythmic but enhanced by the singer's distinctive phrasing. Large backup vocal group. *Performance tips*: Stevie Wonder's vocal performance and arrangement are definitive (the song misfired in attempts by various other artists prior to his timeless interpretation). Emulate

the style of the young master, his innocent, understated emotion, his airy, free vocalism, and his unrelenting attention to groove. Observe the limits of vocal freedom he establishes.

"Fortunate Son" (Creedence Clearwater Revival, 1969)
Straight-ahead country rock. 4/4 time; verse-chorus form. Insistent four-beat with a light backbeat, and a multi-guitar eighth-note pulse. Earnest country-rock vocalism. *Performance tips*: This is a protest song written in a southern musical and lyrical vernacular, and should be delivered with down-home frankness. Though it is possible to bring your individual perspective to its performance, the grooving vocal rhythm and countrified blues inflections as heard on the original recording can't be ignored. Rock attitude, in this song a strong and committed political point of view, translates perfectly to rock singing.

"Evil Ways" (Santana, 1969)
Mid-tempo Latin-rock fusion. 4/4 time; AAA form. Backbeat plus reverse clave, both propelled by a constant four-beat (on the cowbell). Lead vocal with group singalong-style backing vocals. *Performance tips*: The subtle edge of the original vocal comes from the singer's slight emotional detachment, probably the best approach to this highly rhythmic, blues scale–based melody. In keeping with the lyric, the singer seems to be scolding, rather than emoting. Deliver the song honestly, cleanly, and with constant attention to the insistent Latin-rock groove. Because the melody is so simple and limited in range, you might improvise on it slightly, as long as your vocabulary is in keeping with the style. This is a good song for an actor or dancer with limited singing experience or vocal range.

"Love the One You're With" (Stephen Stills, 1970)
Upbeat acoustic rock-jazz fusion. 4/4 time; verse-chorus form. A unique feel and multilayered groove with driving, syncopated eighth-note guitar and bass parts on top and implied clave, backbeat, and other patterns underneath. Rhythmic rock-style lead vocal with harmonizing backup singers. *Performance tips*: The syncopated melody is in rhythmic counterpoint with the quick-paced accompaniment, but moves at a slower rate, so it must be sung with rhythmic accuracy. The lyric is a poetic rock anthem to free love, and therefore can bear some emotionality and light improvisation, as long as your intent remains clear and the groove is not lost. Listen to the Isley Brothers version, as well.

"Midnight Train to Georgia" (Gladys Knight & the Pips, 1973)
Soul/gospel rhythm ballad. 4/4 time; verse-chorus form. Strong backbeat, more a slow two-beat gospel feel than a four-beat rock feel, despite the time signature. A solo and group vocal arrangement quintessential of its genre. *Performance tips*: Assuming the song is right for you, deeply inhabit the character, imagine

the specific time and place, and tell your story. Trust your interpretation of the text and your imagination of the scenario to shape the phrases naturally, and to conjure up its vivid imagery. Observe a moderately free, gospel style approach to the vocalism and phrasing. Note the character's ambivalence; this is an interesting subtext to enact.

"I Shot the Sheriff" (Jimmy Cliff, 1973)

Uptempo reggae-funk. 2/2 time; ABAB form. The slightly swung, double backbeat (two eighths instead of a single quarter), the sparse groove and the distinctive instrumentation and percussion mix make this a song definitive of reggae, while its bluesy melody and minor mode place it at the edge of funk. *Performance tips*: The singer is an outlaw antihero whose story is as timely in the present day as it was when composed. Rock the song with a balance of pugnacity and defensiveness, as did Eric Clapton in his hit re-recording, but do not adopt a Jamaican accent unless you are of Caribbean origin. You can just as easily reset the song in the location of your choosing. Pay particular attention to the rhythmic contrast in the first two lines of the chorus, the first line syncopated, and the second very metrical. Keep both melodic rhythms deeply in the pocket; the words will be very helpful in doing so.

"Sing a Song" (Earth, Wind, and Fire, 1975)

Funk-disco-pop-rock fusion. 4/4 time; verse-chorus form. Truly an amalgam of all these feels: four on the floor plus a backbeat, with plenty of funky syncopation. A light pop melodic and harmonic sensibility, complete with the simplest of hooks. *Performance tips*: Performing the song as a solo requires singing both the calls and the responses in the verses, and making a choice of vocal lines in the chorus/hook. For the most part, the verses, especially the calls, accommodate a good deal of joyous embellishment, whereas the hook should remain relatively intact. Philip Bailey and Maurice White's duet lead vocal is a lesson in how to create vocal groove while maintaining a relaxed vocalism; it would be hard to match their musicality and imagination, but you can groove just as deeply.

"Uptown Girl" (Billy Joel, 1983)

Retro-pop-rock. 4/4 time; extended AABA form. Straight ahead, bright two-beat that bridges early 1960s and 1980s pop styles. Modulations between verses and chorus are typical of Joel's episodic forms even within compact structures. *Performance tips*: There are many levels of character in this song, a love song to someone the singer believes is out of reach, but who perhaps isn't. The singer (Joel himself, singing of his romance with Christie Brinkley) seems to be posturing himself as a rocker to impress his love interest; thus the melodic is unflaggingly metrical (note the doo-wop influence) and the vocalism wide open and exuberant. His approach is undeniably effective, and an excellent model for theatre rockers.

"Say Say Say" (Paul McCartney and Michael Jackson, 1983)
Mid-tempo pop-rock-r&b. 4/4 time; ABABCAB form. Half an unadventurous pop-rock backbeat, and half funk-pop. Vocal stylings and approaches are characteristic of each megastar singer. *Performance tips*: McCartney takes the softer rock side of this split-personality song, and his lyric is persuasive and direct; Jackson has the r&b feel, which is appropriately more emotional and demonstrative. The two singers' vocalisms are precisely in line with the two stylistic faces of the song: McCartney is softly rhythmic and slightly bluesy, Jackson funkily rhythmic, bluesy, and very slightly improvisatory. Both freely use portamento in their phrasing. One person portraying both characters might make for an entertaining reinterpretation.

"Summer of '69" (Bryan Adams, 1984)
Hard pop-rock uptempo anthem. 4/4 time; ABAB form. An "Americana" feel, with a plain, unsyncopated groove, prominent guitars, and a powerful, unflagging backbeat. *Performance tips*: As a fond, poeticized, rock-era reminiscence with a "common man" outlook, the song calls for sincere embodiment of a slightly melancholy character whose native language is rock 'n' roll. The singer is empowered but a bit downtrodden, and his story is very identifiable. Your interpretation should likewise be plainly told yet deeply felt; a little grit and age in your characterization will help. Stick with Adams's text-based, rocking rhythmic approach to the melody.

"State of the World" (Janet Jackson, 1989)
R&b-pop-rock. 4/4 time; extended verse-chorus form. A danceable hybrid of techno-pop-rock and r&b, with a funky bass line and an unremitting electronic drum backbeat. Some light vocal improvisation, but a mostly rhythmic, blues-based vocalism. *Performance tips*: An excellent example of the effective use of a melismatic rhythmic vocal approach. Note the exactness of Jackson's vocal rhythms, and how they fit so comfortably into the groove, while gliding from pitch to pitch, replacing legato with portamento. Adopting such an approach will help you to emotionally convey the cautionary intent of the lyric, more so when set against the hard-edged, mechanized feel of the accompaniment.

"Another Day in Paradise" (Phil Collins, 1991)
Soft-rock rhythm ballad. 4/4 time; verse-chorus form. Pop-rock, new age sound with a vaguely world-beat groove. Shimmering, expansive melodies that ride atop open harmonies and pedal tones (pedal tones are notes, usually bass notes, that

sustain under multiple chords). *Performance tips*: Narrative songs with an earnest tone are common in the early 1990s, and play on listeners' emotions through simple melodic storytelling and evocative harmonies. All you'll need to do is accurately deliver the melodic rhythm and describe the scenario as presented in the lyric, keeping emotion dormant under the modest vocal and musical facade. The original vocal performance is a bit dry, and might accommodate some modest embellishment, particularly on the repeated chorus lyrics, but going too far would disturb the minimalist compositional approach and purposeful detachment.

"Always" (Bon Jovi, 1994)

Power ballad. 4/4 time; verse-chorus form. Strong half-time feel, very straight ahead, electrified but with striking dynamic contrasts; the first chorus cleverly eliminates the powerful backbeat. Free, r&b-based vocalism typical in hard rock ballads. *Performance tips*: If ever you were given permission to let loose with an extravagant vocalism, this simple, powerful lyric and melody over a hard rock groove at a slow tempo might be the time to do so. The song's plain emotionalism needs an injection of rock vocal styling such as the one in Jon Bon Jovi's performance to keep it healthy. Avoid being presentational by telling a genuine and specific story of your own under the rather generalized text.

"I Wish" (Skee-Lo, 1995)

Uptempo rap-rock. 4/4 time; verse-chorus form. A hip-hop sound palette overlaid with imaginative rap vocal rhythms transform this simple rock backbeat into a hybrid of feels. *Performance tips*: Like a primer on how to perform rap, this early retro-rap song perfectly exemplifies both quasi-freestyle rap in the verses and rhythmic rap in the choruses. It also has the rare quality in rap of being a self-deprecating lyric, which makes it more accessible to you as an actor, and more likely to appeal to general audiences. Studying and emulating the original delivery is the best route to an effective performance, and will inform your performance of other songs in the genre.

"Whenever, Wherever" (Shakira, 2001)

Latin-world-rock-pop fusion. 4/4 time; extended verse-chorus form. A true hybrid of feels, including Peruvian-Andean flutes and drums, chorused electric guitar from the 1960s, and a deeply funky, ever-changing groove, all under a distinctive vocal styling. *Performance tips*: Songs whose successful recordings rely heavily on production are not always good choices for singers, but well-written ones such as this, especially those with melodic and vocal interest, can be. It is impossible to reproduce Shakira's unusual sound and idiosyncratic interpretation, but you can emulate the dynamism of her phrasing, her stellar sense of rhythm, and the way she uses consonants and diction to define and lock in her vocal rhythms, almost as vocal percussion.

"Standing Still" (Jewel, 2001)
Upbeat pop-folk-rock. 4/4 time; extended verse-chorus form. Percussive and guitar-driven, fluctuating between the acoustic and the electronic. A relatively slow melodic rate and plaintive lyric make the song feel like a ballad despite its bright tempo. *Performance tips*: It's not necessary to adopt Jewel's throaty shaping of the expressive melody because the melody is quite expressive on its own, but do pay attention to the innate cries and sighs in the contour and how the melody connects to the singer's endless questioning of her situation. It's a good song to act, but also a good song in which to practice emotional self-control, letting the music, particularly the rhythmic content and the vocalism, convey your intention.

"Rehab" (Amy Winehouse, 2006)
Neo-blues-Motown-rock. 4/4 time; ABC form (the A is a sixteen-bar blues, the B a Motown-style verse, the C a short break). A modern exploration of the blues-soul styles of Etta James and Ray Charles (the latter mentioned in the lyric). *Performance tips*: Note Winehouse's unusual approach to rhythmic placement in this song—singing in perfect time but consistently a bit behind the beat. This is a habit borrowed from earlier soul artists, and in this context speaks brilliantly to the reluctant and perhaps inebriated character of the singer. Technically speaking, to form the trombone-like timbres associated with this style of singing, open the back of your mouth and freely employ your lips, without tensing either, in service of shaping the words. This process also explains the lag in Winehouse's beat—it takes time to shape the sounds. Note the similarity of her vocalism to a wah-wah pedal on an electric guitar, which creates a similar sound, and likewise forces a slight rhythmic delay.

"Poker Face" (Lady Gaga, 2008)
Pop-EDM. 4/4 time; extended verse-chorus form. A four-on-the-floor electrified disco feel, with a bit of rap. Straightforward, simple, rhythm-based pop melody. *Performance tips*: Make a strong dynamic and timbral contrast between the verses and choruses, as the melody is quite simple but has a satisfying breakout at the hook. As does Lady Gaga, embrace and enjoy both the seductive teasing of the verses and the proud defiance of the chorus and rap. Stay strictly in the dance-beat rhythmic pocket, with minimal improvisation. Another excellent song for a less skilled singer, perhaps for a dancer who sings.

"Halo" (Beyoncé, 2009)

Mid-tempo modern pop hybrid. 4/4 time; extended verse-chorus form. A melodic hip-hop ballad with elements of hard rock and power pop, in a driving halftime feel with arioso breaks. Mostly rhythmic melody in a very wide range with some melisma, and heavy vocal processing in the recording. *Performance tips*: This is an original performance hard to improve upon. You can emulate (or just admire) Beyoncé's relaxed but unshakable groove, her use of consonants to enhance rhythm, and the expansive, open, vocalism in her legato. Also note that the airiness in her timbre is available in all registers (except the very lowest) and at all dynamics; she uses airflow to its full effect in creating and supporting a variety of resonances. You cannot duplicate the virtuosity (nor the recorded enhancements) of the original performance, but your version can be effective on your own terms, if, like Beyoncé, you sing deeply in the pocket, use diction and rhythmic content to propel your vocalism, feel the emotion of the lyric sincerely while keeping it at a slight distance, and trust the well-written material.

"We Are Never Ever Getting Back Together" (Taylor Swift, 2012)

Upbeat pop. 4/4 time; verse-chorus form. A little bit of everything: acoustic rock, a four-beat modern pop kick drum, a countrified vocalism, some rapping, and more, all adding up to slick post-2000 bubblegum, mass-market pop. *Performance tips*: Bring your own personality to the highly conversational lyric, which leaves some room for embellishment, but doesn't require much. This is a good example of a song originally intended as presentational, but potentially useful for theatre singers, both to give deeper meaning to, and to embrace the frivolity of modern pop. Enjoy the chance to use a higher vocal register, partly as exercise and also just for fun, but also in the independent spirit of the lyric. Though identified as a female song because of Swift's huge popularity, there's no reason a man couldn't sing it just as entertainingly.

"Battle Scars" (Guy Sebastian/Lupe Fiasco, 2012)

Rap-hip-hop-r&b. 4/4 time; extended verse-chorus form. A very melodic rap song, representing a collaboration between a pop artist and a rapper, evident in the hip-hop beat overlaid with rap, rhythmic pop phrases, and a soaring minor-key hook and bridge. *Performance tips*: Find a way to enact all faces of the style without breaking character, and unite the threads of the lyric into a story. The rap is heartfelt but rambling, and can readily be personalized, its rhythms loosened as needed. Keep the simple melodic motives of the pre-chorus precisely in rhythm. Sing the sustained chorus with a soulful rock approach, but don't overdo it, so as not to upset the balance with the rap, or overstate the already emotionally charged lyric.

"Stay with Me" (Sam Smith, 2014)

Neo-soul-rock rhythm ballad. 4/4 time; verse-chorus form. Shades of gospel, roots rock, Motown, and a little hip-hop, in a moderately slow tempo, updated with a four-beat kick drum. *Performance tips*: In keeping with the soulful styles it recalls, this song requires a singer's interpretation to bring its plaintive emotion to life. The almost childlike melody and tone of the verses and the simple hook in the chorus demand individualistic stylization, perhaps even some applied mannerism, as in the original performance. Without your strongly personalized vocal and musical investment, the song is likely to seem awkward and dry. Yet the lyric is clear, so find your own specific story to tell, and musicalize it, using intention and style as your guides. The fragmented phrases will bear well the weight of some free, emotionally connected vocal embellishment, but the melody is still strongly connected to the groove, and for the most part should be sung very rhythmically. The song can be sung by any gender.

Songs in Duple Meters with Triple Subdivisions

"Young Blood" (The Coasters, 1957)

Mid-tempo r&b-soul. 4/4 time; extended verse-chorus form. Blues-rock shuffle feel, with a strong backbeat. Conversational, free-form vocal styling. *Performance tips*: The melody is built on blues scale and phrasing, dictating a free, blues-based vocal approach, but with very clear storytelling. The lyric, too, supports this; it is a slightly tongue-in-cheek version of an archetypal boy-meets-girl-but-the-parents-don't-approve story, a favorite subject of rock throughout its history, here told in a bluesy, sexually charged vernacular. Enjoy it, and tell the story with your own personal panache.

"Act Naturally" (Buck Owens, 1963)

Uptempo country-rock. 2/2 time; ABA form. "Dixie swing" feel (related to boogie-woogie; swung eighth notes in a fast tempo) with lightly bouncing backbeat. Simple country melody. *Performance tips*: The comedic surface of the lyric disguises a self-effacing, somewhat sarcastic character. These qualities should not announce themselves—if they do they will fall on unsympathetic ears—so observe the maxim of feeling your emotion rather than displaying it. An honest, straightforward, rhythmically conversational approach to the simplistic melody is most effective. A countrified vocalism is totally acceptable, provided it is true to your personality, and is not in any way pejorative. This is another good song for a less confident or skilled singer—after all, Ringo Starr made it work.

"You Don't Own Me" (Lesley Gore, 1963)

Pop-rock rhythm ballad. 6/8 time; ABAB form. Strong triplet half-time backbeat feel, orchestral but still rocking. Plainly detailed rhythmic accompaniment that underscores an iconic vocal performance (really two performances; Dusty Springfield's version is also quite well known). *Performance tips*: This song's early feminist statement of philosophy cannot be ignored in the modern ethos. It calls for a confident, pointed, rhythmically driven delivery that is emotionally driven and expressively powerful, but not over the top. Only mild embellishment is warranted, and it must be in service of the singer's defiant declaration. Think of the song as a reaction rather than a statement of purpose; by being reactive, the character is yet more sympathetic, and the slight quaintness in the lyric can take on a deeper intention and meaning.

"Norwegian Wood" (The Beatles, 1965)

Pop-classical rhythm ballad. 6/8 time; verse-chorus form. Guitar-driven folk-pop, with a prominent sitar part (the first on a commercial rock single); moderately slow two-beat with a triple subdivision. Lamenting, slightly countrified vocal and melodic style. *Performance tips*: Most Beatles original performances are definitive of their songs; that is why Beatles covers are not widespread among rock artists. It is hard to separate the melody from John Lennon's vocalism, and to some extent, simply replicating the original phrasing and detached storytelling style will be an effective approach. If you like, the quasi-classical style allows you to sing the melody slightly more legato, provided you maintain the folk-like rhythmic lilt. The shadowy yet evocative lyric (you might research its interesting history) will support well whatever specific circumstances you bring to the story.

"Build Me Up Buttercup" (The Foundations, 1968)

Uptempo soul-pop-rock. 4/4 time; verse-chorus form. The bouncing yet burly shuffle feel and vocal style are equally bubblegum pop and Motown, with a strong rock backbeat throughout. (Notably, the British band the Foundations was one of the only racially integrated pop bands of the time.) *Performance tips*: Adhering to the practices of both pop and Motown, deliver the melody plainly and rhythmically—and enthusiastically, as in the original—with possible slight embellishment at the ends of certain phrases (". . . waiting for you/ Ooh . . .," etc.). Don't be surprised if your audience sings the responses in the chorus ("Build me up," "Let me down," etc.); you might even encourage them to do so, in the exuberant spirit of the melody and groove. This is a fine example of a song that treats heartbreak as a cause for celebratory singing; behind the jocularity is depth of feeling.

"Lido Shuffle" (Boz Scaggs, 1976)

Uptempo pop-rock. 12/8 time; extended verse-chorus form. The insistent triplet figure in the bass and strong backbeat drive this slick, brassy rock shuffle. "Retro" for its time, it is a throwback to earlier shuffles, but with a more rock-based vocalism. *Performance tips*: The syncopations of the melody can be tricky to negotiate, but it's important that they land accurately with the metrically pulsing accompaniment. To assist in your effort, actively shape the descriptive, singable words in your mouth and lips, while supporting the long melodic phrases with constant airflow. This vocal approach, clearly evident in the original performance, makes the melody far more comfortable for you to sing, and by enlivening every note, helps keep your rhythms precise. It also helps to detail your narrative of the rock-based title character. Note that the writer has built an opportunity for improvisation into the hook: "Lido" opens seamlessly into the melismatic "Whoa oh oh oh . . .," and represents an opportunity for you to take some slight liberty.

"Everybody Wants to Rule the World" (Tears for Fears, 1985)

Moderate pop-rock. 12/8 time; extended verse-chorus form. A typically 1980s pop combination of synthesizers and guitars outline a bubbling triple pulse with a rock backbeat. Unembellished pop-rock vocal styling. *Performance tips*: In a melodically limited song such as this that relies heavily on its hook-filled, grooving accompaniment, the voice is an expressive instrument in the rhythm section, and in this case outlines the metrical pulse more than any other instrument. The lyric seems to (vaguely) warn of the dangers of wanting power, a typical stance for a rock-based character. Find a character and story for yourself with which you can address this timeless moral dilemma. To ensure the groove, and to convey the cynicism of the lyric, place the steady dotted quarter notes of the melody with absolute rhythmic accuracy and bite, avoid portamento and legato, and articulate the text with a rock edge.

"Nothing Else Matters" (Metallica, 1992)

Slow folk-hard rock ballad. 6/8 time; extended AABA form. Powerful half-time feel over a constant eighth-note pulse. A mostly subdued hard rock vocal style, more country than blues, but for the minor key. *Performance tips*: The dark but rather unspecific lyric leaves itself wide open to your personalization. The melody starts plainly, but expands and gains power over time; it is a good exercise in using a long form to gauge the arc of your performance. It is entirely permissible in this style, and with this simple but mostly unrhythmic melody, to take musical and vocal liberties, depending on the character you adopt and how you interpret the text. Use dynamics to convey your intensifying emotional state; you don't have to sing from your throat to do so, as in the original recording.

"My 1st Song" (Jay-Z, 2003)

Hip-hop-rap. 12/8 time; extended verse-chorus form. A syncopated, urban contemporary feel and vocal style, hard-edged, in a moderate tempo with triple subdivision and a consistent backbeat. *Performance tips*: When poetry meets rap rhythms (just as when poetry met rock rhythms), rhythm and poetry become symbiotic, and feed one another. In this and many other rap songs, the emotion is subdued but not suppressed, as if the singer does not want to admit the depth of his or her feeling. Instead, it is revealed through rhythmic spoken word. This inspirational rap song should only be performed by someone who shares the experience described by the writers. It could conceivably be cut to suit a different singer, but the story must be told from actual identification with the subject matter. The melody requires an authentic rap vocal approach, at first singing strictly in rhythm in the opening verses and choruses, and shifting to a "freestyle" delivery in the long postlude.

"Breakaway" (Kelly Clarkson, 2004)

Pop rhythm ballad. 6/8 time; extended verse-chorus form. Triple eighth-note groupings on the acoustic guitar and a tenacious backbeat form the motor of this half-time power-pop feel. A catchy groove and a signature vocal performance have made the song a pop standard. *Performance tips*: There is little room, if any, for improvisation in this succinct, controlled melody, which skillfully combines rhythmic conversation with soaring expressiveness. Find a "breakaway" story for yourself, and support it with a clean vocalism throughout. Ride the rises and falls of the melody. Mark the contrast between phrases with faster and slower melodic rates with precision on the quick rhythms and expansiveness on the long notes. Enunciate clearly and gently to mark the rhythms in the verses and tell the backstory. Freely use portamento to phrase the more lyrical choruses.

"Dani California" (Red Hot Chili Peppers, 2006)

Upbeat rock. 4/4 time; extended verse-chorus form. The subtle triple subdivision is in the sixteenth notes of this song, which is a hybrid of several sub-genres of hard rock, including punk, glam, grunge, and others, all adding up to a throwback, backbeat feel. Idiosyncratic vocal styling. *Performance tips*: In this prosaic lyric about a renegade character, a traditional rock approach is most appropriate: rhythmic accuracy and soulful inflection, with a biting and slightly blues-mannered approach to diction. Find a rationale for the surreal and poetically told story, and find a place for yourself in it as a narrator or participant. Then, relate the story of a rock legend as you would the story of any iconic character (from this chapter alone, Johnny B. Goode and Lido are two examples, but there are dozens in the literature, from the Black Magic Woman to Rocky Raccoon), descriptively and with due reverence.

"So What" (Pink, 2008)

Bright pop-rock. 12/8 time; verse-chorus form. A hard-edged, hard rock four-beat with a strong triple pulse. Modern pop melodic and vocal style. *Performance tips*: Like a chant, the childlike verse melody plainly outlines a rock pentatonic scale, and is very metrically oriented. Go with the playfulness, and fully invest in pitch and rhythm despite the repetitions and the offhandedness of the tone. The chorus provides some opportunity for you to break out vocally, but still the melody lands mostly on the beats, disallowing all but the simplest of embellishments. Though the outward tone of the lyric may be disorderly and defiant, you can still perform the song with independence as your intention, which will be more sympathetic. Use insolence and disorderly conduct as actions, rather than as goals, and find the humor in these potentially unattractive behaviors, as Pink successfully does.

"Stressed Out" (Twenty One Pilots, 2015)

Mid-tempo hip-hop pop-rock. 4/4 time; extended verse-chorus form. A strong sixteenth-note triplet pulse with a hip-hop backbeat, plus breaks. Unforced, clean pop-rap vocalism. *Performance tips*: Like many a good pop song, the melody is very effective as originally performed, combining rap with a locked-in pop hook. Use the recording as your guide, but apply your own sound; the original vocal performance is not definitive of the song. The melodic rhythm never strays outside of the pocket. Note vocalist Tyler Joseph's slightly throaty vocalism in the rap, compared with the lighter pop mix and falsetto in the chorus; in the pre-chorus he melds the two vocal approaches. Learning to modulate between these respective qualities of speech and song is a worthwhile effort in learning to capture this style and sing in this commonplace modern fusion of genres.

Songs in Triple Meters

"The Times They Are A-Changin'" (Bob Dylan, 1964)

Moderate folk ballad. 3/4 time; AAA form. Simple three-beat feel, with emphasis on the downbeats. A typical Dylan vocal performance, part poetry reading, part song. *Performance tips*: A populist tone of voice, a poetic, politically charged lyric (it seems never to get old), and wide, persistent renown together define a classic song that can be interpreted any number of ways. Deliver the text with sincere, understated emotion, and give it a clear intention. Shape the simple phrases of the melody in a way that effectively conveys the song's important message, without preaching. You can certainly rethink Dylan's whining deliver of the melody, but even in this loose folk style, rhythm and text should still guide your interpretation.

"Manic Depression" (Jimi Hendrix, 1967)
Mid-tempo hard jazz-rock. 3/4 time; ABAB form. The meter is further subdivided in triplets, resulting in a 9/8 feel, like a heavily electrified jazz waltz. Hard rock-blues vocalism. *Performance tips*: Both the jazz element and the hardness of the hard rock in this song warrant a gritty vocal approach. The small range of the melody will mitigate some of the strain this might put on your voice. Blues inflection as in the original vocal performance is entirely appropriate, even necessary, yet some vocalists have tried to replace Hendrix's unique sound on this song with their own unique mannerisms (Styx, Hollywood Vampires, et al.); this can work, if you do it believably, and without ignoring the fundamental angst of the lyric. The hard rock feel, on the other hand, is immutable, so embrace it fully in your tone and your rhythmic determination.

"Only Love Can Break Your Heart" (Neil Young, 1970)
Country-folk rhythm ballad. 3/4 (9/8) time; verse-chorus form. The three-beat is subdivided in triplets, adding a touch of gospel to the simple mid-tempo country waltz feel. Whining, countrified vocal. *Performance tips*: The innocent lyric states the obvious, without self-consciousness or pretension. Your vocal approach should reflect that; the original interpretation certainly does. Being "folksy" is correct. Give the melody and lyric a down-home interpretation without undue artificial twang or other country mannerisms (unless those are natural qualities of your voice, as they are for Neil Young). As an actor, this means conveying the unaffected words convincingly. "Sing the song to your best friend" may be hackneyed song acting advice, yet is very suitable here.

"Piano Man" (Billy Joel, 1973)
Folk-rock rhythm ballad. 3/4 time; AAA form, with variations and breaks. A folk waltz in a bright tempo, with a barroom/café vibe in the sound, and in the vocal approach. *Performance tips*: The style and story of the lyric, as well as the prominence of the piano and accordion in the sparse instrumentation (not to mention the piano in the title), anchor this song in its friendly neighborhood barroom setting. Relocating the story would likely defeat the song's purpose, and there's no compelling reason discernible in the lyric to do so. The song is clearly sung in the first person of the title character. Play that character, adding your personality, and give him a reason to sing. Honor the melancholy tone and the purposeful theatrical craft of the original. Make this narrative song into a reactive performance, by knowing the people whom you are singing about, and how they relate to your own alienation.

"You Light Up My Life" (Debbie Boone, 1977)
Pop ballad. 3/4 time; verse-chorus form. A slow waltz, with a triple subdivision that adds a little country soul, and a touch of classicism in the beautifully

harmonized verse melody. *Performance tips*: The conservatism of the melody and the downtempo feel are so pronounced that they seem rife for elaboration and personalization. Even Debby Boone's rather by-the-book interpretation in the highly successful original recording lets loose in the last chorus. Subsequent versions by singers such as Whitney Houston and LeAnn Rimes are more representative of the great lengths of expressiveness this melody can bear. Make the song yours, and perhaps add a subtext of loss or disappointment that can add depth and dramatic progression to the rather static lyric.

"Kiss from a Rose" (Seal, 1994)

Classical-pop-folk-rock. 3/4 time; extended verse-chorus form. A moderately slow waltz. The oddly phrased feel of the verses settles into a backbeat in the choruses, but a three-beat feel is the primary motor throughout. Soulful, full-bodied vocalism. *Performance tips*: The engaging melody freely traverses the boundaries of pop, folk, and r&b. The elusive and double-edged lyric, set to melody in lilting rhythmic phrases, likewise leaves itself open to different approaches according to the moment—straight ahead, wistfully soulful, or pointedly rocked out. This is a wonderful song in which to explore this mixture of rock vocal approaches, for all of which Seal is an excellent model.

Songs in Complex Meters

"Whipping Post" (The Allman Brothers, 1969)

Hard blues-rock. 3+3+3+2/8 in the vamp, 3/8 in the verses, 12/8 in the choruses; verse-chorus form. Three feels are at work: a jazzy intro with a dropped beat, a less jazzy 3/8 rock one-beat in the verses, and a traditional rock-blues 12/8 ballad backbeat in the choruses, adding up to a legendary jam song. *Performance tips*: Despite all the rhythmic variety, what is most important for the singer is to authentically embody the Southern blues tendencies of the vocalism. Study the original recorded performances. Deliver the conversational utterances of the verses with relative freedom, and in the appropriate musical and textual vernacular. Use the first "Sometimes I feel" in the pre-chorus to lock into the groove, and the second to empower a more melismatic blues improvisation. In the chorus, once you've set the rhythm in the first "Like I've been tied," you are free to let loose, returning to exact rhythm for the a cappella "Good lord, I feel like I'm dyin."

"Kashmir" (Led Zeppelin, 1975)

Progressive hard rock. Polyrhythmic time: 3/4 (or 3/8) superimposed over 6/4 (or 4/4/ + 2/4). A hard rock ballad in a long, episodic form, a repeated refrain with breaks and two long bridges; a powerful backbeat glues together the multiple feels. There is as much exotica in the modality as in the rhythm. *Performance tips*: The experimental yet essentially rock qualities of this song emanate from Robert Plant's unusual shaping and phrasing, as well as from its metrical and melodic oddities. Plant sings in a pinched and piercing vocalism with exaggerated pentatonic and blues scale-based portamento, and backphrases freely. These elements establish the trippy vibe, and communicate the mystical lyric, which is apparently a monologue uttered by some sort of rock deity or luminary. Embody the otherworldliness to the extent that suits your vocal personality, but make sure to sort out the meter first, and rehearse thoroughly, so that you won't lose your place in the rhythmic maelstrom.

"Outshined" (Soundgarden, 1991)

Mid-tempo grunge-metal. Mostly 7/4 time, with a 4/4 section in the chorus; extended verse-chorus form. In the verses, the lost quarter note every other bar upsets the simple hard rock backbeat. The elaborate chorus has a bit of everything: backbeats, syncopations, and funky unison riffing. An angst-ridden hard rock vocalism. *Performance tips*: As in the other examples of complex meters, this is essentially a rock melody sung over an unusual metrical pattern, and your vocal approach will thereby be the same as in other hard rock songs: a rhythmic, slightly edgy, blues-based vocalism, perhaps with more rasp in this especially electrified context. The story tells of insecurity and inadequacy, again typical of songs with these stylistic tendencies, and again representing a despondent rock-based character.

"Seven Days" (Sting, 1993)

Mid-tempo jazz-pop-rock. 5/4 time, verse-chorus form. A truncated jazz waltz that turns into a lopsided halftime rock feel (accents on beat 4 only) for the choruses. Sting's unique vocal sound has elements of pop, rock, new age, and reggae. *Performance tips*: The apparently purposefully regular poetic meter of the verse lyrics is offset by the odd time signature and by surprising harmonies, which lead the melody on an interesting journey. The story is well-told musically, so you needn't add emotionalism (or vibrato); merely sing the song with clarity and groove. The verse lyrics are classically poetic in syntax and choices of words, personalized but descriptive and almost tongue-in-cheek in their self-effacement, and the chorus lyric is a conspicuously unemotional list. Though the tone is detached, even wry, throughout the song, the chorus melody is soulful enough by contrast to the jazzy verse to reveal your underlying emotionalism. It's as if you were embarrassedly reading a poem that tells of your capitulation to a romantic rival.

"Hey Ya" (Outkast/Andre 3000, 2003)

Bright power pop-funk-hip-hop-rock fusion. Mostly 4/4 but with several 2/4 bars; extended verse-chorus form. A feel that, despite the many genres it refers to, boils down to just a jumpy pop two-beat with some odd phrase lengths. Undemanding melody with a singalong hook, and some elements of rap and spoken word. *Performance tips*: Simply tell the story and embody the character, a person having doubts about a long-term relationship, and espouse the arch but facetious attitude as a way of remaining cool under pressure, and of mitigating the gravitas of the conflict. Use the vocal rhythms, even the odd ones, to "dance" the melody along with the beat-box groove. Make sure the song is appropriate for you before adding it to your repertoire.

"15 Step" (Radiohead, 2007)

Upbeat alternative jazz-rock. 5/4 time; episodic form (AABCBA). The feel is a hybrid of funk, modern jazz, and a foot-stomping, hand-clapping street-corner jam. An "emo" vocal approach—vulnerable, cry-like, straight-toned, and not necessarily grooving. *Performance tips*: If you choose to tackle this rather free-form melody and modern beat poem of a lyric, remember that it's still mostly just a melody in a rock pentatonic mode, albeit in a deliberately esoteric setting, but not nearly as complex as it might at first seem. You can make up your own story to go with the impenetrable yet very singable lyrics, which lend themselves well to a diction- and rhythm-based vocalism.

PART III

Process—Coaching Sessions

As we move into the practice of performing rock songs in the theatre, it's worth reviewing the fundamental principles collected so far.

Commitment to Characterization through Authenticity

Full commitment to rock-based characters entails understanding their aesthetic foundations. Once you know the historical and cultural origin and context of a character, you can determine how stylistically authentic your musical performance should be. Needless to say, for example, there is a significant difference between vocally portraying the characters of Evan Hansen and Frankie Valli, even though both roles exercise their high ranges in a pop-rock style.

Commitment to Performance Practices

Determining your approach to each song based on character and style requires familiarity with *all* rock-related styles and their incumbent performance practices. Because there is so much crossover among and derivation within rock's sub-genres, and because each rock-based character you play is unique, your knowledge must be comprehensive. Furthermore, it will help you avoid techniques that are contrary to rock performance practice, such as legato and vibrato. For the most part, you will employ a text-based rhythmic vocalism for effective communication and conveyance. When melodic freedom is called for, it must occur in an authentic vocabulary of style, with appropriate rhythmicism, pitch, and phrasing. You will always sing with attention to the accompanimental groove, and you must understand the role of the melody, the melodic rhythm, and your vocalism in creating and perpetuating the groove as well as effectively delivering the text and conveying its meaning.

Characterization through Song

Before choosing to perform any song, consider ability, rightness, and correctness of cultural appropriation. Are you as a performer capable of performing this song? Are you the right performer for the song? Would your performing the song be somehow inappropriate? Next, gain an understanding of the writers' and a song's purpose. How does your character fit into a story? What is your character's reason for singing a song at a particular moment? From compositional and dramatic standpoints, what are the determinants of that song's style, form, and content? As in any characterization, define your objective, and as in any song performance, work through your intention and plan your actions. Consider the particulars of language and linguistic style that contribute to your characterization. Above all, find a balance between truth in acting and musicality that maximizes the believable conveyance of your objective and emotion.

The following songs from the rock musical theatre repertoire cover a wide range of styles and contexts. You'll note that I've favored material that has an undeniable rock aesthetic, not any song that might be questioned by virtue of being stylistically watered down or entirely theatrical in nature. In the coaching sessions, I will likewise concentrate on issues that are based in the aesthetics and performance practices of rock music. Still, all of these songs, being good theatre songs, serve a strong dramatic purpose, and function very effectively in their theatrical contexts, and connect strongly with the music, as these sessions will demonstrate.

Although most of these accounts are based on actual coaching and music direction sessions, I have reorganized events to focus on the issues most germane to this book. Naturally, the information and advice I provide is selective; it would be impossible to discuss every detail and nuance of every song in this format.

At the beginning of each session, I include a reference to a printed or published version of the songs being studied. I use mostly lyrics and structural elements (rather than measure numbers) as points of reference.[1] Unless otherwise indicated, the "original" performances that I allude to are those heard on the earliest available recording of a major commercial production of each show.

---

1. In addition to commercially published versions of songs, many actors and musicians in today's industry are party to shared versions of what once were securely protected printed materials. In referring to scores that are only available when licensed, I in no way am condoning piracy. (Fortunately for the art form and the industry, the fact that songwriters today write music that they should be paid for but are not has apparently not deterred them from their calling.)

Coaching #1: "Suddenly Seymour"

(*Little Shop of Horrors*, original handwritten score from the Off-Broadway production.)[2]

The genre of low-budget, pre-digital age horror and sci-fi cinema, which includes the original film on which the Off-Broadway musical was based, may be unfamiliar to you, and the early rock and pop musical styles of the late 1950s and early 1960s (including the girl groups that inspired *Little Shop*'s Greek chorus) may not be atop your playlist. If so, watch some of those films, and listen to that wealth of great tunes in order to absorb the source material that inspired Ashman's stage adaptation and Menken's musical pastiche. An excellently written song such as this illustrates perfectly how you can derive a believable performance by relying on and trusting the choices made by the writers, while bringing your own emotional life into a poignant (and entertaining) event on stage.

The Song

On the surface, this is a love song, a rock duet that unites two unlikely lovers. For the character of Seymour, however, it represents a metamorphosis. The compact form of this rhythm ballad is a simple verse-chorus, three times around, with slight variances in each iteration, and a coda appended to the last chorus. There is a gradual build in dynamics, intensity, orchestration, and to a lesser extent, tempo, from beginning to end. The tempo stops briefly at the climax of the song on the decisive lyric, "Seymour's your man." There is no interstitial music other than the brief piano introduction; the end of each chorus overlaps with the beginning of each subsequent verse, so no time is wasted, and the urgency of the dramatic moment is sustained. The first verse and chorus are Seymour's, the second is Audrey's, and the last is a duet, with the Greek choral trio of female backup singers joining in. In this study, we will focus on Seymour.

The Style

The compositional style is typical of Menken in its contained tonality, its effortless, natural melody, and its satisfying formalism. In tone, it straddles the line between theatrical caution and rock audacity, and gradually transforms from one to the other. All these qualities support the character-driven but stylistically apt lyric as the focus. The music, while highly effective, goes largely unnoticed, in that it just seems "right." Though slightly showy, the music does not in any way steal the show; rather, Seymour and Audrey do, as they should. (Remarkably, the music team for the original production found a key that worked equally well for both the male and female voices. Transposition of the song is rare.) The accompaniment is simple but beautifully detailed; it begins with piano alone

---

2. This version of the score for *Little Shop of Horrors* is not the one currently distributed by Music Theatre International (MTI); the expanded score of the Broadway revival of the show is the one available for rental. Original hand-copied versions of "Suddenly, Seymour," however, are still widely shared, and the revival and original versions of this song are nearly identical, except for the orchestration. Avoid, however, the version printed in the show's Off-Broadway vocal selections book, which puts the song in 2/2 meter, a very confusing change from the original 4/4.

and gradually works in the full force of the small rock group (the original 1982 cast recording adds a guitar to the four-piece Off-Broadway band). The backup singers magnify the penultimate moment with three-part, forte, gospel-tinged echoes of the melody.

The Coaching

Context

Seymour is a "downtown" character with the same "downtown" birthright as the Off-Broadway stage musical and film. A hallmark of the show is the correspondence of the humbly offbeat nature of rock to the black-and-white, sci-fi horror B-movie feel of the original 1960 Roger Corman film. The design and location of the original production—intimate, rundown, and literally downtown (the Orpheum Theater in New York's East Village)—perfectly captured the seedy, creepy essence of the film (it was also the main reason that the wise producers did not move that production to Broadway). So did the style of dialogue and the local linguistic inflections. Most characters speak and sing in urban, New York–like accents, which provide quick entry for the audience into the aesthetic territory. Songs that were heard on the radio and in an urban environment of the early 1960s were the colors on Ashman's and Menken's palette for painting the scene in music.

Characterization

Seymour begins as a drudge (Jerry Lewis) and transforms to a smooth operator (Montgomery Clift). Seymour has experienced little more than the oppressive, underprivileged world where he has spent his life. The plant represents the irresistible Devil to his Faust, offering him a way up and out. Seymour's path toward iniquity ironically parallels his personal growth and eventual self-actualization; therein lies the primary conflict of the story. The farcical nature of the material requires that it be acted with extreme realism and truth. The plot may be absurd, but the emotions are genuine. Depth of character, not caricature, brings *Little Shop of Horrors* to life. If you comment on or exaggerate your performance in any way, the believability, and the humor, are lost (as Howard Ashman, in his role as librettist and director, vociferously dictated in rehearsals).

General Notes

Increases in dynamic, intensity, and tempo indicate the strengthening of character as the song progresses. The change from freer phrasing in the earlier part of the song to singing in the groove in the last verse and chorus convey the character's gaining confidence and attractiveness.

Find your inner nebbish, rather than creating a caricature. You need not exaggerate the character of Seymour, just place him in context. His truth comes from within, and from the situation he is in. It will also be evident in your accent, so make sure there is authenticity there, as well, and not approximation.

Specifics

The opening lines, contrary to how they are written on the page (Example 5), should be enlivened and arhythmic. The opening line in particular does not require explicit enunciation or evenly sung eighth notes, as the score indicates; rather, it's a naturalistic reaction that is also physically manifest on stage. Sing the lines as if they were spoken sentences, in a slightly nasal, forward resonance corresponding to Seymour's speaking voice. By this point in the show, the audience has no problem accepting that the characters sing, yet your delivery of the very beginning of the melody should be speech-like in order to make a smooth transition from scene to song, and to give the song ample room to build later on. While observing the written contours of pitch and the motives of the rhythm, let conversation prevail over lyricism, and spontaneous communication over display.

EXAMPLE 5

Note that Seymour chooses the word "Kleenex" over "tissue"; perhaps he takes tacit pride in having in his pocket and offering to Audrey that iconic full-priced brand (television advertising and branding were new and trendy cultural threads). By giving this word extra value (not emphasis, just understanding), the entire phrase takes on time period–based humor and realism.

The song is largely a scene of mutual (if awkward) seduction, and was originally staged that way, with Audrey and Seymour drawing physically closer and closer through the song, and finally dry-humping their way through the coda, to the hysterical delight of the audience. With the lyric "Show me your face," there is a significant change in Seymour—he is clearly being aroused by the situation, and by the object of his affection. By adding a hint of hormonally based self-assurance to the mix (Marlon Brando), "Show me your face/Clean as the morning" will grow in importance and musicality, rather than sounding clichéd or forced. The rhythm of "Show me your face" should land more securely in the groove, as a further indication of the onset of Seymour's transmutation. By shedding his neediness and gently flirting, Seymour becomes more sympathetic, and Audrey's attraction to him more understandable. Rhythmicism is an indication of an emergent rock persona. The makeover occurs in the real time of the song, as Seymour experiences the new thought process.

There is an implied comma between the words of the title: "Suddenly" and "Seymour." The whole sentence is "Suddenly(,) Seymour is attending beside you." The character's name is not "Suddenly Seymour" (the comma-less version, although the omission of the comma might be because the new, improved Seymour comes on rather suddenly). Adding this comma outwardly, however, will delay the downbeat of the chorus, which should land firmly land in the new, quarter-note driven pulse (the right hand of the piano beats out the time). Therefore, keep the comma internalized, while making sense of the title's syntax. At the chorus, over a now steadier tempo, lock the melody into its written rhythm. This musical transformation further establishes Seymour's increasing determination and evolution into a heartthrob, and a rocker.

There are, in keeping with Seymour's rock-based insurgence, rock-based choices of words in the first chorus: "Don't need *no* makeup," and "*sweet* understanding." The double negative is not really Seymour's; rather it belongs to blues style. Seymour, in this phrase, consciously or not, is adopting a rock patois. It can easily be absorbed into his urban dialect. "Sweet understanding" is a rock trope (as is "sweet" anything). The adjective is most meaningful in light of the emotional truth of the story: sweetness is precisely what Seymour is offering Audrey, an escape from the harshness of her past love interests. Let your understanding of the rock semantics of these lines inform your interpretation, that is, to convey character, imbue these phrases with moderate rock inflection.

The gesture in the accompaniment that follows the second statement of the words "Suddenly Seymour" in the first chorus is Menken's and orchestrator Robbie Merkin's nod to "Superman"—this fanfare-like dotted eighth-sixteenth note rhythmic figure has found its way into several Superman movie and television themes. In Ashman's original staging, Seymour would whip off his glasses and stand up straight in time to the music, leaving Clark Kent behind. You might add this physicalization to your presentation, as well, or internalize it.

Seymour starts the third verse over a persistently grooving accompaniment. Ensure that the first four notes of each vocal phrase are in precise time, so as to establish the groove. That evenness, along with the slight increase in tempo, are entirely in keeping with the character's pounding heart (and loins), and with his growing optimism and sex appeal. Feel free to move in time with the beat. With the subsequent notes in each phrase, the heightened emotional state can take some control over the phrasing, and rhythms can be freer. Many rock singers employ this approach (among them Elvis, Dion, John and Paul, James Brown, Steve Tyler, and Usher): first establish the groove of a phrase by beginning it tightly in rhythm, then let the vocalism take over, with meaning and feeling as your guides. In a fully musicalized moment such as this, a musically based approach helps to convincingly convey character.

In the last chorus, Seymour, after singing mostly as part of the backup vocal arrangement, significantly joins with Audrey on the lyric "Learn how to be more/The girl that's inside you (me)." Here is the culmination of Seymour's self-actualization; for the first time he has transcended his demoralized state. By empowering Audrey, he empowers himself.

Observe the subtle rhythmic change from previous choruses on ". . . be more," now two formidable half notes rather than the earlier syncopated figures. Dig into those note values.

Seymour (and the chorus) continues the last chorus in a call-and-response with Audrey. The two characters confirm their emotional connection, in stylistic terms. Raise your voice above the three backup singers to ensure your preeminence in the storytelling, rather than blending with them. Note the blues alterations in the repeated statements of "sweet understanding" in the coda, and the new meaning of the phrase once your goal is within your reach. Convey the feelings behind them with freer phrasing, increased portamento, and meaning-based diction. This is an example of melody and vocalism reflecting rock-based ecstasy and exhilaration.

Coaching #2: "Take Me or Leave Me"

(*Rent*, original score from the Broadway production, as licensed by MTI.)

This second act sing-off between quarreling lovers puts modernistic everyday language into a rock context. The song integrates a grooving and catchy melody and accompaniment into an effective, character-driven musical scene. Because of its lyrical and melodic style, the song requires active participation by singers with some mastery of vocal improvisation to make it work effectively. There are several parallels to opera in this duet; of course, the story is resourced from Puccini's *La Bohème*, and likewise set in a socioeconomically inequitable environment, with some character parallels. Important in both the story and the commercial phenomenon of *Rent*, the musical, is the notion of stardom. Not just Maureen (like Musetta in Puccini's opera, something of a local celebrity, in part for her promiscuity), but many of the characters in *Rent* either are rock stars, or rock star wannabes, or they act like rock stars, all in the context of an artistic but decadent, ego-driven niche society. Even the writer himself may be considered a rock star in his own right.[3]

The Song

The song is in a bright, stop-and-start shuffle feel. Its form is an extended verse-chorus. The first two-thirds of the song belong to Maureen, the more demonstrative character, followed by a verse and chorus by Joanne, usually more conservative and diffident—but not here—and lastly, a duet bridge and chorus. As in other songs from *Rent*, the writer unapologetically sought out a quasi-authentic pop-rock sound to match the quasi-realistic setting of the play, while still communicating the story through clear characterization and content. A conspicuous hemiola (three beats in the time previously occupied by two beats, in this case three quarter notes replacing two dotted quarter notes; the first quarter note is a rest) in the second half of each measure of the accompaniment (see Example 6a) propels the groove for much of the song, and is plainly evident in the opening measures. The melody in the verses begins in a call-and-response with the accompaniment, as in a

---

3. The history of the show's inception and creation reveals its multiple sources and participants, and the long and somewhat tortuous process of its realization. Writer Jonathan Larson's untimely death contributed to the show's iconic rock theatre status.

blues song. The melodic rhythm locks into the groove at each cadence, and then again in the climb and chorus.

The Style

The feel of the song and its gospel- and soul-tinged harmonies are somewhat reminiscent of Marvin Gaye's "How Sweet It Is (to Be Loved by You)," while its aggressive sexuality and 12/8 funk recall Whitney Houston's "I'm Your Baby Tonight." (That these songs were hits three decades apart is evidence of the timelessness of traditional shuffle feels, and of the long-term influence that r&b and gospel have had on the language of rock.) The lyrical style is conversational and specific to character, but many lines are also emblematic rock phrases: "I walk down the street," "I'm your baby," "So be kind/And don't lose your mind," and even the hook, "Take me, baby/Or leave me." The verse melodies grow freer and more complex as the song goes on—Joanne's verse borders on rap—and the improvisatory element likewise increases throughout.

The Coaching

Context

These characters (I'll address both in this session) live in a generalized version of New York's Lower East Side in the 1980s and 1990s. Research this subculture, and the sociology of Manhattan, before and during its gentrification. Understand the overwhelming societal effect of the AIDS crisis, particularly in the arts. Again, it is essential to view these characters as products of their historical context. Maureen's character was groundbreaking; her sexuality was empowered by two decades of boundary-breaking that led up to this song moment. Being "out" was not as common, or as acceptable, at that time; it was still somewhat fresh, and still less common among women. Likewise, Joanne's yuppiedom was still a somewhat bold life choice and an atypical achievement for a female, especially an African American female.

Characterization

"Take Me or Leave Me" depicts a couple breaking up. As they part, each partner redefines and reclaims her individuality; this is their shared objective. Their intention in the song is to stay together, but the effort fails. That they are a lesbian couple is irrelevant, except perhaps for Maureen's open flaunting of her sexuality as one of her actions, and because of one clever turn of phrase in the lyric at the end of the second bridge (see "Specifics"). Maureen's vocal flair and musical virtuosity are right for her effusive character, but when Joanne turns those qualities loose in this song, it represents her personal empowerment. While Maureen's progression through the song shows her going a bit off the rails, Joanne keeps her feet always firmly on the ground, and states her case impressively, with uncharacteristic musical vigor and zeal. The r&b/gospel style is not really native to either character, but is native to the musical. Assuming that Joanne is African American, in adopting powerful r&b- and gospel-based vocalisms she is reappropriating those musical styles to their rightful origins.

General Notes

The basic melodic pattern consists of a series of somewhat loose offbeat phrases, made up of eighth notes (and rests) grouped in threes, followed by a square, cadential pair of half notes. In the r&b-gospel fashion of this song, the melody does not really carry the groove, and for the most part does not require a strict interpretation. Indeed, if you were to sing the music precisely as written in the score, the result would sound mechanical. Nonetheless, regardless of how freely you phrase it, the melody makes a strong contribution to the groove, and to the rhythmic foundation of the song, in its internal rhythms and its starts and stops.

This song covers relatively little dramatic ground, exploring instead its basic purpose and emotional state in great depth. As in opera, it calls for a "slow-motion" acting approach, in which large-scale feelings or actions are elongated, and accommodate musical expression. Fortunately for you as an actor portraying a specific character, there is sufficient textual content to fill the space.

To learn the rather intricate music, first practice the words alone and the essential rhythmic aspects they suggest, and gradually add in the pitch content, both from the printed page and by listening to original performances (the Broadway original cast is still definitive). Figure out, line by line, or in this protracted acting context, section by section, the character's specific emotions and actions. Let the lyrics and your actions determine how strictly or freely you deliver each phrase.

Specifics

Begin at a very moderate dynamic and energy level. The song comes out of a scene, and needs a good deal of headroom to build into and sustain a convincing altercation over its multiple sections and four-plus minutes.

The 12/8 time signature highlights and confirms the importance of the alternation of straight shuffle time and hemiola; this motor is easily visible in the notation. So that the alteration is perceived by and the groove imprinted on the listener, it falls upon the singer, in the opening verse at least, to carefully observe the rests that precede each vocal phrase (see Example 6a).

The fourth line of the verse, ("Baby's so sweet") lands on the beats, giving bite to the line and connecting melody to meter. The long duration of the first two notes of this phrase, and the fact that the first note resolves so inevitably to the second in a classical half cadence, provides ample motivation for an ornament connecting the two, as you will hear on the original recordings.

Note that the distance between the downbeat and the sung line decreases in the two subsequent phrases, the rests getting shorter: "Ever since puberty/Everybody stares at me . . ." By the time you reach "Boys, girls . . .," the melody starts on the downbeat. The groove is being established so that your melodic interpretation can become less restrictive as you move forward. This is quite useful in your acting plot: your need becomes more urgent as the song progresses, and therefore you are more inclined to jump in sooner in response to the accompaniment.

On the line "(Just remember) that I'm your baby," the vocal rhythm joins in the hemiola with the accompaniment. The vocal and accompanimental rhythms are in conspicuous unison; this supports well the moralistic tone of the lyric as well as providing a clear cadence.

The melody in the choruses plays on the delayed entrances of the opening phrases. The phrases "Take me for what I am" and "Who I was meant to be" begin on the third eighth note of the first triple eighth-note grouping in the 12/8 meter. These vocal entrances coincide with rearticulations of the chords in the accompaniment, which had been rests in the verses. (The original hemiola persists in the second half of each bar in the chorus.) Singing the entrance as indicated not only further solidifies the groove, but also conveys the character's resolve. (See Example 6b.)

EXAMPLE 6a

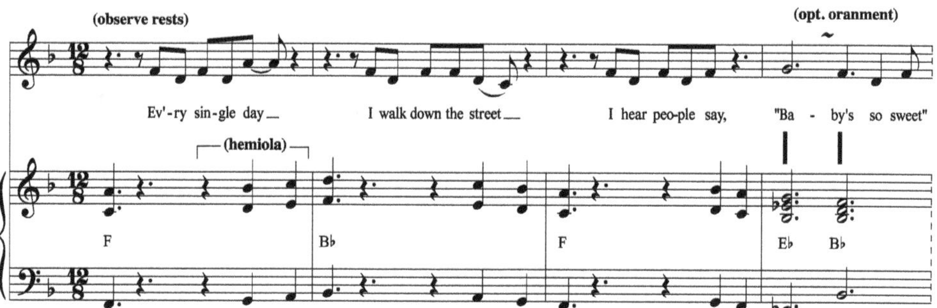

EXAMPLE 6b

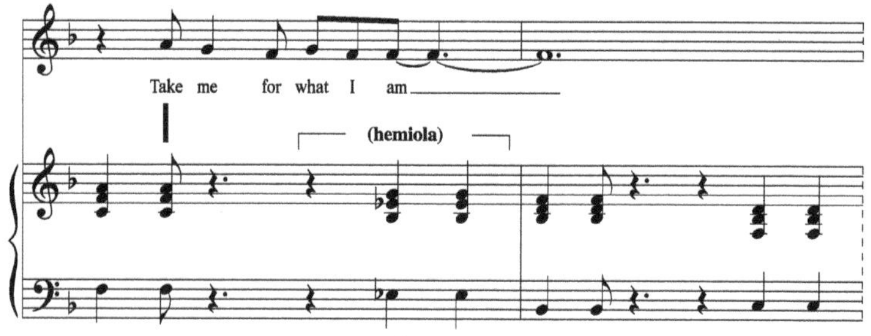

The third phrase of the first chorus, "And if you give a damn," a rather confrontational clause, begins with a quarter note rest followed by three dotted quarter notes. Here the melody outlines the meter, deepening the groove, and giving Maureen's stubbornness even more authority. The three vowel sounds of the first three words are ideal for delivering the rhythm meticulously, as a bassist or drummer would, and for conveying the sarcasm. The squareness is broken up by a return to the offbeat rhythm of "Take me baby . . ." This affords you a chance to lash out in syncopation, then return to the metrical rhythm for the more matter-of-fact ". . . or <u>leave</u> <u>me</u>."

The heightened intensity, musicality, and vocal freedom continue into the second verse and climb, and reach a temporary climax in the second chorus and bridge. In the score you'll see some spoken lyrics ("Folks would kill to fill your shoes," "Cryin' honeybear"), some notated blue notes ("You love <u>the</u> limelight, <u>too</u>"), and more melisma (several iterations of "Baby," and others). These are not exact notational representations. Rather, they are signals that you now have permission to emote more vividly, and thereby interpret and embellish more freely.

Note that in the second chorus, the three notes on "And if you (give a damn)" are now in line with the hemiola, rather than the meter. This slight rhythmic variation is a means for you to rethink your action on a repeated lyric, with a revised text emphasis.

The steady four-beat groove of the bridge underpins a traditional rock melodic structure of alternating short and long phrases, a sort of solo call-and-response. The call is the tension, the response the resolution. The back-and-forth is a way for you to conduct an impassioned question-and-answer interior monologue, while keeping the rhythmic motor chugging. Combine these musical and textual concepts to rock out the bridge.

The vehemence of the bridge cools a little into the short interlude that leads into the last verse. As one might hear in an r&b song, use of a head tone is right for Maureen's mock tenderness on the second statement of the line "Who's in your bed." This dip in dynamic provides an opportunity for the song to build again to another climax, which it shortly does, as Joanne begins the last third of the song.

Another play on the hemiola occurs on Joanne's lyric "Baby, what's my sin." Here at this mid-verse cadence, the vocal line takes the three quarter notes of the hemiola while the accompaniment hangs on its usual half note. This vocal gesture is characteristic of Joanne's rigidity and controlling nature. Deliver it in precise, slightly accented rhythm to ramp up your energy as you proceed in rattling off your list of gripes.

In the second bridge, the steadier rock shuffle groove returns, and the burgeoning free-spiritedness of Joanne can become fully overt and appreciable. Joanne adopts Maureen's linguistic and vocal styles and takes them one step further, re-establishing herself as a worthy opponent. She begins to out-sing Maureen, heightening the conflict and motivating Maureen to re-enter the fray.

The alternation of short and long phrases is now also an alternation between duet and solo. That the two characters are able to sing in harmony and rhythmic unison at all reveals the tenacious but tenuous bond between them. The rhythmic unison of the call must be impeccable, to stand in stark contrast with the animation of the solo responses.

This stanza culminates in the aphoristic conclusion that "Women . . ./Can't live with 'em or without 'em." There is ironic humor in the agreement between these two characters, and, of course, in that they are both women. You can best convey the irony with casual, boisterous conversation, as if two stereotypical men were chatting in a bar or locker room.

The brief accord between characters persists into the first line of the final chorus, but now there is an underlying tension, and the harmonized melisma can help bring that out—it is as if the discussion should be moving forward, but is stuck in the melody. Furthermore, the two voices in the melody seem to want to break free from one another, and they do, as the second phrase turns into counterpoint. This is yet another form of call-and-response, now sculpted into a musical argument. Here the fact that the chorus lyrics are repetitious is almost irrelevant. The basic conflict is now fully melodized, the characters are more adversarial than ever, and their disagreement is coming to a head.

Tension in harmony reappears in the long, rising note on the final "ba-<u>by</u>." It is immediately followed by an anticlimax: each character has made her decision (albeit one still in doubt), and in quiet unison, they release the tension with the final mezzo-piano ". . . or leave me."

Coaching #3: "When I Climb to the Top of Mount Rock"

(*School of Rock*, as reprinted in the Broadway vocal selections book.)[4]

This "I want" song for the story's protagonist establishes his unrealistic objective: Dewey Finn wants to be a rock star, despite limited talent and outright indolence. Still, his wholehearted immersion in and utter devotion to rock music and rock culture infuse him with a good deal of rock authenticity. This song, sung to the world at large, is a chance for his star to shine, at least in his own universe. The material suggests a hard rock vocal approach, yet one that makes the words clear, and displays personality within the melodic and textual constraints. One challenge will be in sustaining a generalized feeling over the long song form. (It might be advisable when performing this song out of its show context to cut it down at your discretion.) Studying and learning to appreciate the rock repertoire and the mythic rock lifestyle that Dewey so profoundly reveres are essential to fully understanding and communicating the song.

The Song

The stage version of *School of Rock* is a mostly faithful transfer from the film on which it was based, and clearly shows the respective musical and lyrical skills and tendencies of composer Andrew Lloyd Webber and lyricist Glenn Slater. In "When I Climb to the Top of Mount Rock" they have fashioned an authentic rock song, with a powerful groove, a simple form, and a strong hook, but with a theatrical bent. Sir Andrew cannot help but espouse original, unexpected sounds, and in this song his inventiveness appears in the odd (yet logical) chromatic harmonic excursions. Slater's lyric is descriptive, and rife with detailed references to rock stardom. The melodic shape is rather square and poetically metrical, over a very meticulously arranged accompaniment. The feel is a bright 4/4

---

4. Milwaukee: Hal Leonard, 2015.

backbeat, with several small rhythmic gestures and shifts in feel along the way. The song embraces, in a subtextual, incipient way, the central notion of the show: that rock music has the power to heal and to bring people closer to each other. At this early stage of the story, Dewey's depiction of the rock world is still very naïve and self-centered. It's an aria for Dewey more than a song that moves the plot forward, and it falls to the performer to create an inner life beyond the lyric.

The Style

The groove and feel of the song recall hard rock and metal artists such as Black Sabbath, Poison, and Blue Oyster Cult. The unusual harmonies add the progressive rock quality of bands such as Led Zeppelin, Yes, and Rush. The storytelling in the first stanzas of the song is slightly reminiscent of Foreigner's "Jukebox Hero." Otherwise, the lyrics, besides the hook, are largely a list of aspects of rock life, with a few familiar rock industry "in" jokes (no brown M&M's; jumping off the stage into the crowd). They also explore in depth the metaphor of Mount Rock, as a symbol of power, as an Olympian height, as a perch for the rich to look down on the poor, as a forum for rock ideology, and as an objective for Dewey.

The Coaching

Context

In films adapted to musicals, such as *School of Rock*, the "textbook" rules of making musicals are often in operation. One of the most important of these is identifying heightened dramatic and emotional moments, essences of character, thematic concepts, and motivic fragments of language or idea that can be transformed into song. The books for most of these shows adhere closely to the original screenplays, presumably because the originals were quite well written, and because changing them might deny audiences' expectations. This song is a perfect example; as an ode to the culture of rock, it serves the textbook function of highlighting the objective of the protagonist and, ideally, making him sympathetic and likable to the audience. The metallic 1970s-1980s-1990s feel of "When I Climb to the Top of Mount Rock" will not succumb to theatricality and specificity if you sing the song as a rock singer would, which is also as the character would, and as the audience will want and appreciate.

Characterization

Dewey is an antihero. His behavior early in the story tags him as somewhat amoral, or at least irresponsible, but he is conflicted. He is not a sociopath; his feelings are hurt by others' low opinion of him, and he wants to do better. Like many rock characters, Dewey is disenfranchised, and poor, largely due to his own neglect. Yet he craves recognition and acknowledgment. He is seeking fulfillment of some kind, though he is not yet aware of it (therein hangs the tale). Beneath his pomp and proneness to failure, he is trying to overcome his insecurity and self-hatred, and this makes him more sympathetic. One of your primary tasks as an actor is to find the character's heart. Audiences will know later on in the story that he has one, by virtue of his personal growth, but in this early number in the show you will be seeking sympathy for an apparently unsympathetic person. Dewey's insensitivity can actually be an asset at this early point in the story, as long as it is not off-putting; his transformation from slacker to proud pedagogue and functional human being is the broad character arc that the audience follows and roots for.

General Notes

Simply slipping into the rock star mantle, that is, singing the song in the mirror with a hairbrush microphone, as it were, cannot on its own convey the necessary depth of character. Instead, you must live out the story of the song in great detail as you sing, or imagine telling the story about yourself in the past tense, as a narrative. (Again, it's important to know your rock history.) Play Ozzy Osbourne instead of Dewey. That's what Dewey is doing. Certainly some of the normally attendant physicality of such a performance is in order, as well.

Dewey's objective as a character shouldn't be confused with the intention of this song. You will have to provide intention, as the song does little more than serve its dramatic function of identifying one crucial aspect of the character. You can make the intention active and immediate, something such as making money or finding a job, or even just getting out of the house, rather than just vainly seeking stardom, as the words suggest.

The song is long and musically a bit involuted, and requires careful vocal planning. It's wise to transpose it so that your high note (A in the original key of D minor) is one you can sing repeatedly, accentuate, and sustain without undue effort. Make sure you understand the chromatic chord changes to G-sharp and C-sharp and how they function (both as independent chord destinations and as chromatic neighbors to i and v in the tonality). Once you hear those pitches in the accompaniment, you'll be able to tune them better in the melody.

Throughout the lyric, especially when outlining specifics, keep your scansion very close to speech rhythms, even when the score contraindicates it. Like many rock scores, even with lyrics as detailed as these, this is expected; there is no compelling reason to resist what sounds natural and makes sense to you as a singer, as long as it also makes sense to the audience. (The changes in the melody for the different lyrics of each verse demonstrate that it is flexible.) When singing rhythmically, as you will be doing much of the time as servant to the poetic patterns, stay solidly in the groove. Don't lag or rush; be part of the rhythm section and keep good vocal time.

You cannot impose a rock-like grit or bite to the entirety of the song; that would quickly get tiresome, losing significance over time, and be hard on your voice. Pick your spots to growl out a lyric or heavily stylize a phrase. There are some words that seem to invoke a more radical vocalism. In the second verse are the likely candidates "...blowing out amps," "...beg for more," and "the party will rage." Your vocalism will point up your objective in lyrics such as "Just wait and see," "...sold out galactic tour," or "...the all-time best."

Above all, have fun with the song. One of Dewey's likable qualities from the outset is his joviality (note the similarity to another archetypal rock-era character, John Belushi's Bluto in *Animal House*). The comedy in the song is easy to find; enjoy it and play it up. For you as a performer, delivering this simple text and quasi-hard rock melody—assuming that you enjoy singing rock—can be playtime.

Specifics

If your intention is to make money, there are dollar signs in your eyes when you are discovered—jump on the bandwagon. Sign that record deal; ride that limo; trifle with your hangers-on. Each of these actions represents fantasy cash in the bank. Play the bravado, play the hustle, play your greed; all are means to your end. If instead you are seeking affirmation, play your gratitude, play your wonderment, play the showering in adoration. Mount Rock (the chorus) may appear to you as a mountain of cash, or a mountain of approval and self-worth. Either way, bring specific actions to the metaphoric description. (These schematics are examples; there are many possible intentions and actions.)

At the half-cadences at the ends of the verses ("Just wait and see," etc.) and the penultimate bars of the choruses (". . . the gates will unlock," etc.), the sustained high note can be ornamented for emphasis, using, for example, a mordent (a quick up-and-down stepwise ornament), a rhythmic half-step trill, or even a short riff. You can also play with various articulations, textual and musical, of the word "rock." The significance of the word, and also its generality, call for graphic interpretation.

The one crack in the rock facade and in Dewey's swagger occurs on the lyric "hopefully it's comin'/I'm pretty sure it's comin' anyday." For this moment he is (pathetically) self-aware. Keep your delivery sincere, rather than deliberately comedic. The humor will arise from your honesty, and from the suddenness of your admission, and you needn't point it up in any way.

The dynamic lull at the ritardando will allow you to build back up to a bigger climax at the end of the song. Regather your resolve as the tempo resumes, and reserve your biggest outbreak of rock spirit, including any exaggerated vocalism and melodic freedom, for the final chorus, which restates earlier ideas that now demand variation. Look for a way to make the song at least temporarily dramatically conclusive—maybe something as small as finding a ten-dollar bill in your pocket, or taking an extended bow for your performance.

Coaching #4: "I Am Changing"

(*Dreamgirls*, as reprinted in the Broadway vocal selections book.)[5]

Dreamgirls was a highly innovative musical for its time (1981), and its influence on the modern musical theatre should not be underestimated. Its musical language is

---

5. Secaucus, NJ: Warner Bros. Publications, 1981.

stylistically authentic, boldly expressive, and highly effective in its dramatic context. The musical is both modernistic and traditional. At times it is quite operatic, with extensive recitative, both free and accompanied, and vocally sensational pieces such as this second act reidentification number. "I Am Changing" is one of two showstoppers sung by the principal female character of Effie. The story of *Dreamgirls* is loosely based on historical events, and any actor involved in a production should research thoroughly the factual source material of the plot, as well as the cultural and political circumstances that underlie it. Most characters in the show sing in an indigenous and somewhat intuitive musical style, so the song must be within an actor-singer's musical and vocal reach; it cannot really be "faked," or approximated, as some other less genuine, deeply felt, and vocally codified material might be. Original performances of this powerfully emotional and melodically striking piece have set a high bar; both Jennifer Holliday's Broadway and Jennifer Hudson's film interpretations of the songs are extraordinary. (Although Effie is an African American character, "I Am Changing" sung outside of its show context need not be sung by an African American, nor even by a woman, provided the stylistic requirements are met.)

The Song

The song is a very slow soul-r&b rhythm ballad, in a triple subdivision grouped mostly in 12/8 (with some 6/8 measures), in AABA form. In the show it is sung by a character who is already a polished professional singer, and whose roots are presumptively in church music and gospel. The song's grooving, deftly composed and arranged accompaniment are a perfect bed for a melody that, faithful to its stylistic origins, is sometimes rhythmic, sometimes free, and at times highly melismatic. The lyrics are highly evocative of popular songs of this nature and era, yet they are true to character. Together, the music and lyric beautifully portray the very strong-willed yet vulnerable essence of Effie, and her sincere contrition at this moment in the plot. The song builds slowly from beginning to end. The groove in the bridge is considerably more syncopated, and funkier. The bridge ends with an unexpected ritard and a stunning key change into the final chorus. There is one more ritard in the coda, and a long "money note" to cap off the singer's vocal display.

The Style

The infusion, and eventual transformation, of gospel-based melodies and triple feels into commercial pop is a seminal rock phenomenon. Early crossover hits like "Sit Down and Cry" and "It's a Man's World" inspire the vocalisms and deep grooves of "I Am Changing" (as they do the Motown stylings evident throughout the *Dreamgirls* score). The musically slick orchestral timbres are also true to style and period, and there are some quite richly jazzed-up gospel harmonies. In this musical, the historical period and the music that belonged to it are germane to the plot and treated realistically, indeed hyper-realistically, or melodramatically. The mere existence of the song, of course, is a theatrical gesture. The lyrical content does not say anything terribly specific, and the titular line recurs many times; nonetheless the lyric is specific to character and moment.

The Coaching

Context

For a rock musical to tell so much of its story in song, in other words, to set so much dialogue to music, was a bold choice. (It had been done before, in rock operas, and sung-through shows such as *Evita*.) Sung conversation has since become a staple of musical theatre, from *Les Miserables* to *Mean Girls*. There is always a certain awkwardness in sung dialogue, but "I Am Changing" is far more lyrical than most *Dreamgirls* songs, and even its dialogic sections are quite melodic. The song is at once a highly expressive musical construction and a vehicle for broad acting. Though the lyrics are sung lines of dialogue, there is great melodic intricacy, which contains a great deal of emotional content. Your work as a performer entails making the song both communicative and musical, while remaining true to style.

Characterization

Effie enters show business as an innocent, as do her friends, but she is from the start more cynical, circumspect, and arrogant than they. Throughout the play, the audience feels (or does not feel) sympathy for Effie in the same way as do the other characters in the drama. We all wish for her to do better, but over time we grow intolerant of her misguided choices. Eventually her self-centeredness and aloofness cut her off from the music and the people she once loved, and to some extent she is also treated unfairly and insensitively. She learns her lessons the hard way, but bounces back. At this point in her story, early in Act 2, Effie has realized the error of her ways, and how stubborn she has been. She has earned our sympathy because we see in her—a devoted single mother and still gifted fallen star—an identifiable and lovable underdog, one that we know has a good heart. Her intention is to rise above her transgressions and make things right with others, while also regaining her own success and self-esteem. This song is like a confessional, or a hymn to self-improvement. Her actions may include persuasion, charm, admitting guilt, and promises of restitution.

General Notes

From the song's history it might seem as if can only be undertaken by a powerhouse vocalist, but style is just as important as strength. You need not have a room-rattling sound to deliver it convincingly. You do, however, need an exhaustive understanding of the genre that generated it, a grasp of the performance practices that define it, excellent musicality, and a full commitment to the emotional life of the character.

Although gospel vocalisms often include a high chest range, the song need not be belted; a strong mix is just as convincing in this style. Do not, however, use forward or nasal resonances by themselves; the style calls for warmth and fullness to the timbre. Find a key that puts the higher end of the song's tessitura in a comfortably high place for you. You'll be spending a lot of time singing and expending a lot of emotion there. Likewise, a constantly strong dynamic is not the only way to convey the strong emotion. You might dial it down somewhat. Limit your improvisation to what you can do well.

Don't spend too much time trying to learn the music "as written." The melodies of *Dreamgirls*, and many soul, r&b, and gospel songs, are by nature not easily transcribed. Syncopations and the orientation of lyrics within a meter can be major conundrums for a copyist, and many compromises are made in notating them. Published sheet music for such songs usually loosely represents an original performance, perhaps the way the composer sang the song for demonstration purposes, or how the song developed through the production of a show. When interpretive liberties are taken in a vocal line as part of a stylistic performance practice, as they are in this song, the printed music can only be a road map. As a general rule, longer notes and vocal rhythms that are metrically oriented, as well as a good deal of a melody's pitch content, are more reliable on the page than are passages with many notes and/or many words. Listen to others' recordings, especially the originals, and work with a coach if necessary. Take the song phrase by phrase, then experiment with, and eventually decide upon how you will phrase the melody from beginning to end. Of course, this methodical learning process is also a good opportunity to explore the intention and actions of the song, and to master the music.

The lyric is quite general, and therefore your acting beats will be long, and most specifics must come from within. Think about exactly how you will be "changing," looking to your own experience for inspiration, and be specific and spontaneous in performance. Identify exactly what sort of help you are asking for, and the person you are asking for it. The generalities of the song will disappear within your own inner life and the lyricism.

Diction, stylization, and embellishment of text are in this song are acting tools as well as musical techniques. Dig into the words—even if they feel superficial, they sing beautifully—and use your sound, your vocalism, and your shaping of words and phrases to convey your personalized, specific emotions and actions.

Specifics

Begin from a place of uncertainty, as the song is a long journey and you'll need somewhere to go. The plaintive first lyric is a good starting point: "Look at me." This is a plea for help, as in "Look at me, I'm hopeless—can you help me?" The melisma/trill on the second iteration of this line is more than a musical riff; it is a gesture that begs for sympathy and support.

The first "I am changing" is a tentative claim, thus the hesitant rhythmic start, and you are still wary of the task before you in "Trying every way I can." The second two lines need not take you much further than the shaky promise of "I'll be better than I am." Melodically, these first four lines are understated, and occupy a lower tessitura than most of the song. Land the first "changing" on the beat, as notated, but use the initial consonant to widen the downbeat; it is the beginning of a resolution, and here you are just trying it out. Subsequent lines begin after the downbeat (another example of melody in counterpoint with the accompaniment), as if you are working out these new thoughts in a discussion with the establishing groove, and still approaching the subject somewhat tentatively.

The next lines, "I'm trying/To find a way to understand," break from the lower register and demonstrate the escalation of your effort. Sustain the second syllable of the first line ("try-_ing_," harmonized by a hopeful IV chord) as a means of enhancing this feeling, and also to connect the two halves of the lyric into one thought—you don't want to be merely *trying*, but trying to *understand*.

The last lines of the first A section ("But I need you/I need you/I need a hand") convey both your vulnerability and the direness of your need, rising from a lower, more soft-spoken place to a higher, more plaintive range. The slight increase in intensity carries over into the next "I am changing" and subsequent lines. In this second A section you find your footing, and become the agent of your change. Your declarations turn more proactive: "I'm gonna start right now, right here."

In the bridge, play your need for help. Use the rather aggressive, choppy, and funky accompaniment and melody to outwardly chastise yourself, review your regrets, and sound the alarm. Your actions are supported by the short, stabbing phrases and expanded pitch and harmonic content. Make sure you sing the pitches in the bridge accurately, and mark all of the rhythms pointedly.

The bridge comes to a temporary climax at "All those years of darkness/Could make a person blind." This is the highest range and most incessant rhythm yet, and the melody breaks into a brief embellishment of the value word "blind." With this musical gesture, you are at last admitting outright that you were wrong. Your intention, however, is not yet satisfied. In the next A section you retreat to a more vulnerable position, and restate your opening thoughts, now with somewhat more assurance, and somewhat louder.

From this point to the end of the song is a long crescendo of feeling, dynamic, and vocal freedom. Once you have recognized your determination as legitimate, you are free to make choices and take action. The new attitude is reflected in the sanguine "I know it's gonna work out this time."

In preparation for the key shifting up a half step into the last chorus, the melody ambiguously descends by a half step to D-flat. (Is this the leading tone to the key of D, or merely a chromatic ornament? As it turns out, it is the tonic of the new scale of D-flat.) This is not an unusual key shift for a song in this style, but its suddenness and melodic obfuscation give it extra dramatic and musical gravity, and, of course, it falls on the word "change." (Michael Jackson's "Man in the Mirror" features a similarly uplifting moment.)

Notably, in the final measures of the song, the improvisatory element and melisma retreat, and the accompaniment becomes more rigid, as well. These lines are your final decree, your setting of the new commandments in stone, and thus they are staunchly rooted to the meter. This effect is reinforced by the stop-time hits on the second and fourth beats in the accompaniment under the words ". . . stop . . . me . . ." and the gloriously long "now." Accenting "stop" and "me" is almost inevitable. If possible, sustain the final note without vibrato until the end of the orchestral activity; as the accompaniment comes to rest on the final chord, bring in the vibrato to extend the life and power of the tone. Cut off in sync with the orchestra.

Coaching #5: "Endless Night"

(*The Lion King*, original Broadway piano-conductor score, unpublished but similar to current piano-conductor *Lion King* scores.)[6]

"Endless Night" is one of several pieces of music adapted for Boradway from Lebo M's "companion" album to *The Lion King* film, entitled *Rhythm of the Pride Lands*. On that album the melody of what would become the song "Endless Night" appears in "Lala," a song of farewell. The primary motive of the melody originates in another *Lion King* theme called "Busa," which is a separate cut on the album, and recurs often in both the film score and the stage musical, as a dance, as underscoring, as part of the show's finale, and here in this song. ("Busa" translates from Zulu to an imperative form of the verb "rule.") "Endless Night," therefore, is like a well-traveled folk melody that has been given a new home in a story. For a performer, the song in the musical is a marvelously simple acting and singing moment that, by virtue of its origins and its significant place in an iconic pop story, encourages a reverential approach. (The original Broadway scene was directed and choreographed very specifically; the coaching here describes that direction, and, by association, music direction.)[7] In preparation, you might learn the chants that the background vocalists sing at the top of the song and in the extended coda, or learn to play the conga and shaker patterns that form the groove.

The Song

The song begins out of tempo, with choral vocals and windy synthesizer sounds setting the open-air scene. It turns into a very moderate rhythm ballad, with slow-moving harmonies and a subtle but constant percussive groove. The groove contains a clave rhythm in each 4/4 bar, which appears in the bridge vocal melody, as well. The song has a short form, AABAAB with a long quasi-improvised coda, or "ride-out," that in the show context is abruptly interrupted. The singer is Simba, another leading character who has been ostracized, to some extent by his own doing, and must work his way back into his own good graces, and the world's. (In *The Lion King*, he is presumed dead by his family until the end of this song.) The lyrics were written by committee, and the committee was not aiming for high art, just for a tone and connection to character similar to the other new songs in the show. It made the task much easier that there was such a short and

---

6. The Hal Leonard vocal selections book version (Milwaukee: Wonderland Music Company, Inc., 1997) provides most of the essential musical information, but none of the detail, in a song that by nature is difficult to notate effectively.

7. During my long tenure as music director/supervisor of *The Lion King*, I taught this song to many a Simba and potential Simba.

simple melody to work with, but for a long while it was undetermined where the title should go. The lyric is somewhat obvious and direct, but does not pretend to be more; thus the performer is essential in bringing the song to life.

The Style

The style reflects both pop culture and cultural authenticity. This is one of the many songs in *The Lion King* that conspicuously feature elements of South African and West African music. South African melody is customarily very diatonic and triadic, and highly rhythmic. It is also often accompanied by, or in counterpoint with, choral vocal arrangements, some of which can be quite elaborate. South and West African sounds are most apparent in the instrumental timbres of "Endless Night," some percussive and some tonal, such as wood flutes and some stringed and mallet instruments. Not so much the lead vocal, which is more pop-like, a mix of legato melody (in the A sections), rhythmic melody (in the B sections), and improvisational elements (in the ride-out). The simple harmonies and lyrical style, too, are more akin to pop. The choral chant that sets the groove in the coda is the only English-language chant in the show (the rest are in Zulu, Xhosa, and a little Swahili); still, there is an element of myth in their presence. Like other *Lion King* songs, the chants touch on the central theme of connecting to one's ancestry, and fulfilling the promise of one's ancestors. This combination of rock-based and exotic, ancient styles and themes was a novelty in the mainstream of 1997 musical theatre (the *Lion King* film premiered in 1994), and was part of a wave of "world" music popular in the 1990s. The wide appeal and influence have clearly persisted over time, in this show and throughout modern popular music.

The Coaching

Context

The Lion King, the stage musical, brings the Hamlet-like story of Simba to a worldwide audience in a musical voice that transcends national boundaries. Themes of ancestry, parenting, and growing up are certainly universal, and are heightened in the context of a tale of a royal family with a glorified ancestry. Simba not only wants to be as good a person as his father, but has been anointed as his father's successor to the throne. As a child Simba took this for granted, but as an adult who has taken what he deems to be ruinous missteps, he questions his ability to fill such a demanding role. He even questions the importance of kinghood; as an adult he has, after all, forged a functional, if solitary, life as a maverick. In these many ways Simba is a foundational rock character.

Characterization

Simba is another alienated youth, excluded from his community by his own transgressions and others'. He has grown from child to man while isolated from his former environment, and bears an ingrown burden of self-doubt, and of guilt. He has always been impulsive to a fault, and by virtue of his exile, is now more naïve than ever. He feels guilty on two counts: he believes he has caused his father's death, and he has not fulfilled his responsibility to his kingdom and his ancestors. His intention in the song is to return to his rightful place: his home. He must find his way despite his circumstances offering him no clear path. Complicating his situation is that he also a victim (of his wicked Uncle Scar), but is not fully aware of his victimization.

General Notes

The melody was notated with care, but the score for this song is by no means scripture. Over time, performances developed that strayed from the original written score. Because the music team was content with the original version even after the melody had been reinterpreted many times over, the written music was not updated to reflect subsequent interpretations. Performances that no longer reflected the writers' and creative team's original intent were reined in, but certain performers were allowed some freedom of interpretation.

The verse melody is very slow-paced and transparent, and the pitch content of the bridge melody is very static. Due to these qualities, you may become more aware than usual of the grace notes, scoops, portamentos, slurs, and glottal stops that start and end notes and connect one note to another (or disconnect them). Some of these will come naturally to you as part of phrasing the text, but you may want to plan how to use these miniature techniques as means of expression.

As in other songs that enact self-discovery in non-real time (in this song, non-real time is in the title), develop a plot for your character to follow from the beginning to the end of the imaginary time period, and the song. Simba rises from a very low state to a very high point in just a couple of (stage) minutes and with a very modest amount of musical material.

The intended vocal approach is plain and unencumbered. As director Julie Taymor would point out, the *Lion King* characters are part animal, and act on instinct more than humans might. They don't sing with panache or gospel-like embellishment unless it fits their animalistic personality. Simba's overriding concepts are leonine and large-scale: home, survival, an understanding of his place in the world, and—because this is a rock musical, about animals—sex. One of the two main threads of the story is procreation, or "The Circle of Life" (the other, of course, is death).

The ride-out section was carefully written to sound improvised and inspired by the spontaneous thought process of the character. Only slight improvisational alterations are permissible, and they must be as communicative as the existing vocal arrangement. They cannot diverge from the musical styles, nor disconnect in any way from truth of character and the dramatic moment. "Endless Night" is a delicate and purposefully simplistic song. When mishandled or overdone, it seems just primitive, rather than primitive for the right reasons.

Specifics

The opening A sections are not quite in tempo, but the melody should be sung as written. Simba begins with questions that he feels compelled to ask in reaction to being unintentionally shamed by his friends Timon and Pumbaa. In the haunting introduction and the first A section, he wanders off to seek answers, but finds instead only more obstacles, darkness where there should be light. Thus the rest between "Dark" and ". . . is the day"; Simba is surprised, and disappointed. "How can I find my way home?" is not hopeless; it is a pragmatic question. Rather than a Simba who merely pities himself, find in your Simba whatever vestiges remain of power and passion, and use them to take action.

It is in Simba's nature to feel desperation, and to be hard on himself, as his father was. "Home is an empty dream/Lost to the night," he decides. Use a glottal stop to separate and accentuate the word "empty," even though the vowel is preceded but the final "n" consonant of "an." Adding the glottal consonant is very effective in conveying the self-directed reprimand, whereas eliding the two words subdues it. Likewise, enunciate "lost" clearly and with similar emotionalism. Here, the rest between "Lost" and ". . . to the night" is an inward punch, in anger at himself for losing what he had.

Simba turns his attention at the end of the second A away from the heavens and specifically toward his father. He turns his anger outward, and rants at "the older generation" for abandoning him. This is reflected in the music. When singing the bridge, observe the written rhythms accurately and stay deeply in the groove. Individual word emphases are equally important. A rock vocalism that grabs and even "growls" the initial sounds of certain words makes specific sense of the text, and is useful in conveying Simba's angst-ridden rebelliousness: "<u>You</u> <u>pro</u>-mised you'd <u>be</u> <u>there</u>/<u>When</u>-ever I <u>need</u>-ed <u>you</u>/<u>When</u>-ever I <u>call</u> your <u>name</u>/You're <u>not</u> <u>an</u>-y-<u>where</u>," and so forth. First, rehearse the lyric without pitch and with approximated rhythms. Then add in the correct rhythms and intentional emphases.

Continue this text-based (and rock-based) melodic approach into the next two A sections (which are notated almost identically to the first two, but bear a bit of personalization), and add to it with purposeful musical gestures. Cut "break" short and bite into both the "br" and the "k" consonants. Treat the subsequent "Oh" as a rock "whoa," and using portamento, glide down off the note, and attack "<u>end</u> (-less)" with a glottal stop for re-emphasis of the title metaphor.

Connect the thought of "Sleepless I dream of the day . . ." to "When you were by my side/Guiding my path." Although there is a structural point that falls between these two lyrics, they are one sentence. You don't necessarily need to elide the phrases in one breath, just keep the thoughts together.

Observe the written crescendo on the word "way." As noted in chapter 4, if a dynamic is notated on a vocal line, it is something the songwriter or arranger considered essential to the melody. Be careful, however, not to make the crescendo showy. It's not a purely musical gesture, rather, it's a product of the character's frustration. Keep it real.

Although Simba's fury increases in the second bridge, don't give in to it entirely in your performance, and keep singing the rhythms as written. To convey the extreme emotion, intensify the rhythmic approach you took to the first bridge, and really rock the words (it is as if they want to break out of rhythm, but cannot). Again, rehearse the lyric without pitch, this time in precise rhythm with powerful diction, to summon the necessary forces from character rather than melody. Your dynamics, too, will increase accordingly. As the section ends, exasperation replaces fire, and Simba is once again despondent.

The quasi-improvisational coda is made up of five statements of a six-bar phrase.[8] It is "improvisational" only in that it is unplanned by the character in the moment; the pitches and rhythms were preplanned by the writers. The musical acting sequence of the five-part coda as originally directed was as follows: 1) Offstage vocals only; a far-off sound in the night. 2) Almost unwittingly, only subliminally aware of the encouraging, distant vocal chant, Simba begins joining in, mumbling softly at first, with indistinct words. The last bar is blank, as he becomes aware of what he is doing. 3) The first "I know" (the two pickup eighth notes to the top of the third repeat) is a quiet realization that Simba *does* know: he knows that at some point the night will end, and the sun will rise. "*Yes,*" he does know. "*Yes,*" again, more emphatically, with greater accent, and with stronger dynamic, he knows that "the clouds must clear." The alterations and melisma in the melody confirm that this is a positive upturn (the contour turns upward at the end of this phrase, as well). 4) Now singing rhythmically, Simba is getting back in the groove of his life. He reconnects with his father, represented by the relaxed triplet rhythms and the melisma of "And I'll hear your voice deep inside." Final proof of re-ownership comes in the rocked-out, forte, confident final "I know that the night must end." 5) The last phrases are a musical dance of joy, the culmination of Simba's rebirth, expressed in stylized melodic terms. (Simba's journey is not over yet, which is one dramaturgical reason for the song's being cut off, as opposed to completed.)

Coaching #6: "Will You Love Me Tomorrow"
(*Beautiful*, as printed in the *Beautiful* vocal selections book.)[9]

Carole King and Gerry Coffin's "Will You Love Me Tomorrow" was first recorded by the Shirelles in 1960, and has cracked the Billboard Hot 100 several times since that initial climb to #1. A pop song by nature, the song has a reasonably strong sense of character. It recurs often, in multiple arrangements, in the Carole King bio-musical *Beautiful*, manipulated gently to fit the scenes in which it appears. Because it is reasonably simple to sing, it is a favorite of stage performers who are inexperienced or inexpert singers. It is also a standard of musical theatre auditions, and we shall examine it here in this coaching session under those conditions. Any freestanding performance of such an

---

8. The vocal selections book does not contain Simba's exact vocal part as it appears in the unpublished piano-vocal score, but it can be heard on the *Lion King* original cast album.

9. Milwaukee: Hal Leonard Publications, 2014.

often-covered song must introduce something new, based first and foremost on the individuality and internal story line of the performer, while remaining faithful to the writers' intent. Faithfulness to rock aesthetics and truthful delivery together are the sure path to a believable performance, but for an audition, you'll need to add more. In an audition, this is a pop song, not a theatre song—unless you are auditioning for *Beautiful*—and your choices of character and intention are independent of the Carole King story. Any pop song performed in a musical theatre audition requires an extra layer of specific acting choices.

The Song

Originally aimed at a mass market, the song has endured in the repertoire for over half a century; the simplicity of its content and sincerity of its sentiment help explain its lasting appeal. The song form is best described as a large-scale, modified AABA, and within each of its A sections is a miniature verse-climb-chorus. The melody is diatonic and motivic, and very contained, spanning barely more than an octave. The harmonic content is just as uncomplicated. The sincere, natural lyric has a distinct point of view, but it is not very specific. The song can be done in tempos from moderately slow to moderately fast. King slows it down to a very contemplative pace on her breakout album *Tapestry*. For an audition, take the tempo of your choosing, according to your story. (You might also accompany yourself, as the song is relatively easy to play on the piano.) Despite its straightforwardness and restraint, the song has proven effectively communicative in many versions. Respect its modesty, and just "make the song your own."

The Style

The style lies somewhere between pop, soul, and folk. (The lead singer of the Shirelles initially resisted recording the song on the grounds that it had too much of a country flavor.) King's music, often included under the designation of "white soul," shows multiple influences of the pop, race, folk, and country records she heard from childhood on and the classical music she played as a young piano student. There is classical artfulness in this and her other songs, in the neatness and clarity of their composition and in their manageable size. Coffin's lyrical style is very much of its time: simple, carefully crafted, conversational "rock poetry," married beautifully to a tune. The melody can't bear too much variation or elaboration without crumbling. Amy Winehouse's 2011 cover goes pretty far, but even such an independent-minded interpreter as she is unable to stray far from the original melodic path.

The Coaching

Context

A combination of assertiveness and vulnerability were distinctive and contrasting traits of the emergent self-sufficient, uninhibited woman of the early 1960s (the dawn of the feminist movement), indeed of the entire young adult population of the early rock era. Women gave themselves more freely, and talked about sex and sexuality more freely, but they also demanded greater respect. They were still very much subject to sexism, and needed to speak up to be heard. Sexual "liberation" was a pathway for women into independence, into rock music, and into the less reputable rock outlaw archetype. Being a "bad girl" was becoming, in a word, cool, and women forged new, stronger, and riskier identities in the rock music scene. This song is an understated example.

Characterization

The singer is a rock era character, not a traditional character, and she is not helpless. She demands an answer to the title question so that she can make a decision on her own, not so that she can validate herself through someone else's feelings. On the surface, the lyric may seem acquiescent, but underneath is a decisive female identity, one that reflects the time when the song first became popular. The singer of this song wants to know if her lover can love her exclusively in a culture where love is shared freely. The singer's intention is not just to coax a promise from her lover, and she probably knows that his promise might be false. What she wants from him (or from her; there's no reason the song has to be exclusively heterosexual) is to be an equal in deciding how the relationship will proceed. She wants to be more than a sex object, while still exercising her sexuality.

General Notes

How does one act songs that weren't meant to be acted, at least in in the way stage actors act—pop songs with very concise, unadorned words and music that have entered the theatre through the side door, songs such as "Will You Love Me Tomorrow"? When singing at any musical theatre audition, you either tell a complete story on a microscopic scale, or you relate an excerpt of a larger story. With no larger context, this simple song, any simple pop song, has to stand on its own. You could sing it purely presentationally, but you probably wouldn't land the job. It's up to you to apply character and intention to give the lyric subtext, and turn the song into a scene. Start by devising an aesthetically and historically informed dramatic context.

Find a compelling reason to pose the crucial question of the title. Play the scene reactively, that is, act in response to obstacles that present themselves before and during your story, so that you remain active throughout in accomplishing your intention. What has just happened that makes these questions so urgent? The lyric is mostly in the second person, therefore sing it *to* someone specific. The question you ask is not an uncommon one—and it resembles a rudely familiar punch line: "Will you respect me in the morning?"—but because the song is rooted in its period and so often been re-enacted over the years, the question has implications that transcend any flippancy.

There have been many conditional love songs—love songs about the obstacles to love rather than love itself—and they are common in the theatre, which thrives on inherent dramatic conflicts and complexities. "Will You Love Me Tomorrow" is a sort of pop conditional love song, but in a modern environment in which the singer has already made love with her lover, and is still holding out for commitment. Treat the first A section as a series of conditional statements that add up to the crucial inquiry of the song.

The interaction between singer and accompaniment is especially important in this song. The melody has syncopations that require a beat for them to fall into place, and the beat lives in the accompanimental groove. There are many possible interpretations of the accompaniment, but it must be arranged rhythmically, in other words, it needs to somehow provide a groove, even when a pianist is playing solo (without benefit of bass/drums/guitar). The accompaniment as notated on most sheet music versions does not adequately represent the groove, or possible grooves, of this song. For an audition, I suggest a customized arrangement with a clearly notated piano part (as in Example 7), or perhaps bringing your own accompanist, even though many rock audition pianists will know this song well. It's an easy song to play, but a hard song to make sound good.

EXAMPLE 7

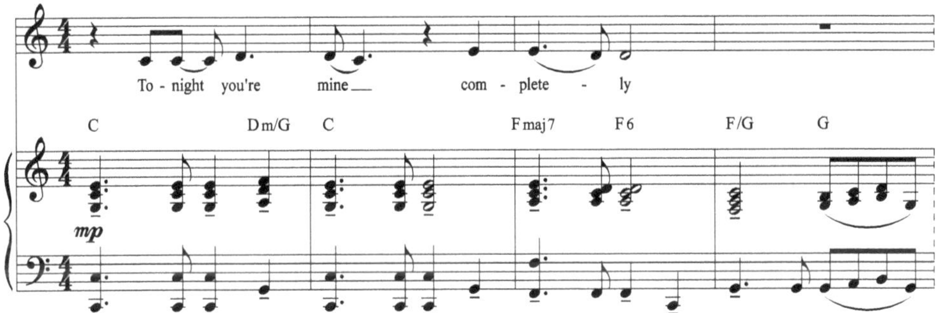

Specifics

Begin by speaking through the lyric out of rhythm, and then in rhythm, seeking ways to activate it and customize it to you. Add the pitches last, and maintain a rhythmic, text-based approach as you practice the melody. (This is a good procedure in learning any song, but especially so when handling so transparent a lyric and so simple a melody.)

Drawing on your own experience, find a situation in which knowing the truth about someone's feelings would cause you to make an important decision. As the saying goes, "raise the stakes." Counteract the modesty of the song by giving it critical importance to you at a critical moment.

Take a feminist stance, and give the female character the upper hand. If she is meek, she will be less sympathetic when singing this romantic lyric. You might even consider making your character less virtuous, which might be an interesting layer under such an amiable text (this was a very successful approach at one coaching of this song). If you find it hard to cut through the song's simplicity, your subtext could even involve something dangerous. Consider making your intention something willful, such as wheedling money from your boyfriend, or wanting to leave him for another lover. Instead of feeling sorry for you, your audience will root for you, however questionable your underlying intentions might be; your intent is couched in smoothly grooving melody.

Try the song in a very intimate setting. (This does not preclude the suggestions above.) This will make the lyric more gently affectionate, and real, rather than sentimental or overwrought. Remember that the person you are singing to might be resistant to your intention, and that he is active in the moment, and responds to you as you progress through the song.

Once you assimilate the historical context, once you fully inhabit your specific character and her intention in the song, once your story is in place, and once you are comfortable with the actions you are taking to accomplish it, sing the song like the pop-rock song it is. Don't focus too hard on the acting choices, but store them underneath the style. Use the words as rhythm and invest in them musically and emotionally, give rhythmic emphasis to words and syllables that convey your actions, sing strongly but naturally, use portamento to connect and enliven notes, and allow your own sound to come through. Avoid that which is nonnative to rock, such as nasality in your timbre, a bel canto line, or excess vibrato, and remember: groove above all, even in this ballad context.

Coaching #7: "The History of Wrong Guys"

(*Kinky Boots*, as printed in the vocal selections book.)[10]

Cyndi Lauper is an adept pop craftsperson, and the songs in *Kinky Boots* are a compendium of catchy hooks, melodies, and beats. They are inclined at times toward lyrical generalities, in keeping with their pop culture origins, but "The History of Wrong Guys" is one of the more theatrical and character-based songs in the show. The purpose behind this very entertaining solo number is to illuminate a colorful character, who sings with spicy but self-effacing and very identifiable humor. There is a good deal in the material for you to work with, and you can bring in a lot of your own personality, and even perhaps exaggerate the character somewhat. Because this is both an effective pop song and a communicative theatre song, your approach will account for the two sides equally. The sheet music is notated with great clarity by arranger Stephen Oremus, who helped Lauper extensively in creating the grooves for all the songs in the show. In this instance, the printed score is very useful in your learning process.

The Song

"The History of Wrong Guys" is a mid-first act identity/"I want" song for Lauren, one of the two female principals in the show. It's a straightforward, upbeat, 4/4 synth-pop number, typical of the late 1980s or early 1990s, very right for time, place, and character. Consistent with the style, the melody combines rhythmic, conversational phrases with more expansive lines and a bit of melisma, but never is it improvisational. The mode is entirely diatonic. The form is a verse-climb-chorus, plus a bridge (AABCABCDC). The

---

10. Van Nuys, CA: Alfred Music Publishing, 2013.

bridge briefly abandons its pop identity and fizzles into a brief, recitative-like section before breaking out once again into the final chorus. The lyrics work equally well as pop song lyrics and as a testament of character and need. There are a few awkward text settings ("Yesterday no spark/No heart aching allure" is one), but these are commonplace in pop songs of this musical genre. Although the song is in verse-chorus form, Lauren's feelings for Charlie are complex enough that they warrant multiple statements of the same lyric, and there is certainly entertainment value enough to sustain interest to the end.

The Style

In sound, the song epitomizes modern pop. A dry, staccato vamp gives the verse an agitated feel, while the climb and chorus rock out with an energetic backbeat. These qualities correspond with Lauren's nervous energy and effusiveness, while the mechanized beat evokes the factory setting. As is often the case in this genre, there are hooks everywhere: the opening instrumental vamp, the first two phrases of the climb, the third phrase of the climb, which contains the title, the top of the chorus, and the end of the chorus. Many songs like this broke into the top 40 during Lauper's heyday, and even today the style's heart beats on in EDM and other post-2000 pop genres. "The History of Wrong Guys" recalls hits by the Human League, Depeche Mode, the Spice Girls, Ellie Goulding, the Chainsmokers, and many songs from Lauper's own catalogue.

The Coaching

Context

Lauren is a factory worker who has become enamored of her boss, Charlie, despite previous conflicts between them. The song has a built-in duality; it's a droll expression of regret and distrust, and at the same time it's a love song. There's also a celebratory element, as Charlie has just unexpectedly promoted Lauren, whom he had laid off earlier in the story. Lauren's story is crucial to the plot, as well as ironic. She is the first to suggest the idea that eventually saves Charlie's struggling shoe factory. There is a glaring class difference that separates the potentially romantic pair, but naturally, they end up together. Lauren's lower-class standing embeds her in a rock aesthetic more than her Charlie, who is privileged (though on the verge of insolvency). Her East London accent makes for some enjoyable vocalism in delivering the lyric, while also securely setting the locale. If you choose to sing with the accent, research it fully as part of your character study. This regionalism should not be culturally misappropriated, especially considering how crucial its societal implications are to the story. When singing the song out of context, the accent is not essential, though still helpful.

Characterization

Lauren is an extraordinary person in an ordinary place in the world, and in this song freely admits her proneness to bad choices, but she is learning that she deserves better.

She is open about being indiscriminate in her love life, confessing in the song that she's "been here before." She is a little bit broken, but her heart seems very much in the right place. This is the reason audiences immediately sympathize with her, and also because she is charming, obviously bright, and keeps her sense of humor under duress. Her intention in the song seems to be to win Charlie over, but the lyric is ambivalent. It goes back and forth between reticence and overt feeling true to the character's situation and background. You can have, and play, conflicted feelings. It's actually in the contrast where a good deal of the song's humor lies: the same woman who swears off men because her relationships are so predisposed to failure shamelessly sings of her inclination to jump right back into a relationship.

General Notes

The multiple hooks make the song a pleasure to perform. It's as if every line is a favorite old saying that you love to repeat. Take advantage of the informality with which these phrases come out; it makes delivering the melody and lyric convincingly far easier, even when the phrases are melodically rigid or the text setting is imperfect.

You will also likely enjoy playing a character who is as outspoken and vivacious, yet flawed and vulnerable, as Lauren. Characterize her with some breadth, in voice, demeanor, and action, but underlaid with your own personality. The reason Lauren is especially animated in this song, indeed her reason for breaking into song, is that it occurs at a breakout moment in her story. You can best convey the comedic frankness of what she has to say with a colorful, spontaneous, phrase-to-phrase variety of deliveries, one that is both Lauren, and you.

The lyric is mostly interior monologue, and needs activation by having a reactive object/listener/participant with you in the scene. Having someone to sing to will also allow you to physicalize the song more. You might sing to an absent Charlie (in the original staging Charlie is visible upstage in his office, unaware of Lauren), an invisible but present Charlie, or perhaps to another man, while thinking about Charlie. You could also tell your story to a trusted friend, or perhaps to an imaginary audience of women in a similar situation. (Again, there's no reason that this song, outside of its show context, could not be sung by a man.)

Keeping the groove tight throughout the song is essential to the style. Lauren Nicole Chapman, who played the eponymous role of Lauren many times on Broadway, notes: "This song operates on a click track, with sharp, almost computer like sounds and beats that allow the singer to tune in to the orchestra and the pop sensibility. Those rhythms seem to me like the inner workings of Lauren's mind."

Specifics

Let's assume for this discussion that despite strong amorous feelings toward him, your intention in the song is to *reject* Charlie (he needn't have made an advance for you to spurn him), an imaginary version of whom is there with you. Lauren's objective as a character is to establish her independence, with or without the entanglements of romantic relationships.

Let these feelings develop as the song moves forward. Follow the predetermined rises and falls contained in the form. You can bring out the beats of your acting plot with offhanded shifts of color, vocalism, and attitude. Here is one version:

It's apparent that at the top of the song, your attraction to Charlie is already strong. Therefore your first action in rebuffing him can be educating him with a primer in sociology and female behavior. This will match well with a rigidly rhythmic melodic delivery.

The slight melisma on ". . . another one _of_ mine" reveals that you are not just lecturing, but recognizing in yourself the behavior you are cautioning against. It's a crack in your armor. The little interstitial "Uhn-ohw" is in the dialect, but is open to your own personalized rendition. It can convey any number of things, but here seems like a reaction to impending trouble. Infuse it with some whimsy or quirk to your liking to deepen its meaning on your own terms.

Next, in the second A section, bluntly tell Charlie why you don't want him. Focus on his being from "outer space" and "shy" and not on his being "cute" and "bright-eyed." (You can interpret those as undesirable qualities, as well.)

In the climb, actively resist his charms (use your physicality; walk away or otherwise expand the space). You're unable to deny your attraction, and your insults now seem more like amiable teasing, or flirting. The crack opens wider. You admit that you're on the verge of allowing history to repeat itself.

The first chorus is a chance to put on the brakes. The melody does that for you, too, by slowing to a long note. Under the extended "Charlie" can be a subtextual "no way," reinforced by "I've been hurt like this before." The remaining phrases of the chorus are highly rhythmic, and mostly syncopated. Bite into these rhythms to convey holding your ground. You know that you've now seen the best of Charlie, and that you will be able to turn him aside.

The repeated riff on "more" belies your underlying disappointment at having to let Charlie go. Musically, it's a lament, a blues lick translated to pop. The line of dialogue between the chorus and verse acknowledges that you're still imagining yourself with him.

You catch yourself in the second verse, and resume your rejection, extolling the virtues of being unattached. Find a sardonic compromise in friendship. (In the score, "friends" is in italics, and marked as an indefinite pitch.)

Self-doubt creeps in at the second climb. From here through the second chorus, you can play out a protracted encounter with Charlie. This time, use the riff on "more" to show your rising desire. Give in to your feelings, and flirt, seduce, worship from afar, any actions that feel natural. Again, physicalize. Have fun with your imaginary Charlie, and react to his reactions. There is a bit of a presentational quality here, allowable by the pop side of the song's split personality. Yet expressive improvisation does not suit this style or melody. What is left is for you to act truthfully to yourself, with a wide-ranging vocalism motivated by your passionate feelings, and appropriate physicalization. You have a strong melodic hook to sing, in a meaty register, and there's a lot of multilayered feeling charging the scene. Rock out.

Again, you come to your senses as the second chorus ends. The accompaniment halts on a whole note and the dynamic dips as you review your arguments against involvement. (There are shades of "Adelaide's Lament" from *Guys and Dolls* in this moment, and shades of Adelaide in this character.)

The bridge, with its angular harmonic parallel movement, turns from a narrative list to a childlike sing-song phrase, repeated several times. Inwardly, you are teasing yourself, belittling yourself, for thinking a relationship with Charlie is even possible. Outwardly, in our scenario, you are actively teasing Charlie in your effort to keep him at arm's length, at least until ". . . has a girlfriend named Nicola," when you can reveal your shame. Your vocalism turns from a rock singer to a childlike whine.

The last chorus comes on abruptly. You can make it your declaration of independence, powerful because you are finally admitting your attraction yet ultimately rising above it. You've "been executized," and you're proud of it; you are getting the recognition you only now began to feel you deserved. This understanding will suffuse your emotion with spontaneity and reactive joy. The lighthearted song, as it turns out, has been a significant journey of self-discovery for a modern female rock character.

Coaching #8: "Pinball Wizard" and "The Bitch of Living"

(*The Who's Tommy*, original score from the Broadway production, as licensed by MTI; *Spring Awakening*, as printed in the vocal selections book.)[11]

There are many similarities between these two songs, written thirty-seven years apart, the first for a heady rock concept album that became a stage musical, the latter for a heady original rock stage musical. Both songs are characterized by their unlikeliness. In 1969, when *Tommy* was released, the idea of a deaf, dumb, and blind kid who "sure plays a mean pinball" was outlandish, but fell within the aesthetic realm of psychedelia and youth culture. "Pinball Wizard" had a uniquely powerful, deeply rocking melody and accompaniment that drove it to hit status, twice. Audiences at *Spring Awakening* similarly came right on board when the uniformed students in an 1890s Latin class suddenly jumped up on their desks and sang about their sexual fantasies into remote hand mics, in a mildly dissonant 2000s alt-rock style. These songs both rock hard, but intelligently. Their intelligence is youth-borne, and the topics have youthful rationales. They are group

11. Milwaukee: Hal Leonard, 2006.

songs for post-adolescent males, sung in a defiant, mob psychology–backed tone of voice. (A gender-bending version of either song is not out of the question.)

The Songs

"Pinball Wizard" found its way to Broadway in 1992 nearly unchanged from the Who's original version. (It was slightly enlarged to include group singing and dancing.) In the show, it served as a climactic closing number to the first act, and in a second act reprise, featured an exploding pinball machine. The form is an extended AABA (the B is in two parts). The feel is driven by a signature acoustic guitar strumming pattern in sixteenth notes (each bar contains a clave) that composer Pete Townshend calls a "jangle." The conversational but highly descriptive lyric borders on theatricality, offering an in-depth history of its offbeat cast of characters. Pinball virtuosity is a metaphor for rock stardom, and beyond, for spiritual ascendancy. In "The Bitch of Living," the metaphor is in the style. It's not unusual that the boys are singing in response to their pent-up sexual energy (that's typical of rock 'n' roll), it's just surprising that they're singing rock in the 1890s, in a Latin class, with stylized choreography. The words they sing are again direct and conversational, and again allude to a higher concept: fatalism, another face of alienation. The song form is in a slightly varied verse-chorus. It has a mid-tempo backbeat feel that differs slightly in each section, the choruses providing the steadiest and hardest rock groove. In both songs, each solo singer in an ensemble tells a part of the story, from his own point of view.

The Styles

These two songs are each distinctive for their time, largely by virtue of their songwriters' musical personalities. Many of Townshend's guitar patterns are iconic. The jangle in "Pinball Wizard" is certainly among the most famous, as is the two-note punctuation to the groove that is a favorite of air guitarists everywhere. Daltrey's soaring rock tenor and innate flair with text and melody were a perfect match for the song, and it is hard to ignore his version when you are learning the song for yourself. Duncan Sheik's musical personality is similarly present in "The Bitch of Living." As in many of his songs, the melody is modest in range and pitch content (the near opposite of "Pinball Wizard"), yet it still has teeth. The texture is stark, sometimes arresting, but somehow always easy on the ear. Sheik's harmonic proclivities are also in full view, among them: open, fifth-based chords and pedal tones (notes that sustain through multiple harmonic changes) colored with "crunches" and "rubs" (mild half-step dissonances added to otherwise diatonic chords). Both songs might be considered hard rock, but neither is heavily electrified. This puts their vocals and lyrics in the foreground of the sonic picture, and the lyrics are worth hearing, as they are illustrative and specific. Although they tell a narrative, they are character-driven. Whereas both songs work well in a musical theatre context, it's easy to tell from their texts that one was originally a rock song and the other a theatre song.

The Coaching

Context

Rock is the unbreakable common thread, aesthetically speaking, in both the characters and the music of both songs. Each is a rock anthem that reflects its troubled society, and a younger generation's attempt to make sense of it. (A song from *American Idiot* might well have joined these two in this coaching.) The young characters in "Pinball Wizard" (other than Tommy himself) are inspired by Mods and Rockers, rival British youth subcultures of the late 1960s with sometimes violent inclinations. The boys at school in "The Bitch of Living" are stylized reconstructions of characters from an antique era, who were so profoundly repressed and misled that their actions sometimes had disastrous consequences. Yet all these characters behave in ways that belie their youth. The "Pinball Lads" and Cousin Kevin look beyond Tommy's disabilities and give in to his supremacy. They eventually come to admire him, and idolize him as an avatar. The schoolboys pose two of adult humankind's most plaguing questions: "Is that all there is?" and "Is that all I get?"

Characterization

There are multiple characters in both songs. Feelings are shared among all, but customized somewhat to each one. Each singer expresses an individualized reaction to a large-scale conflict that is coming to a head. Their singing arises in a dramatically heightened moment from frustration, angst, and self-doubt, but they know that it's not cool to admit these feelings. Singing is an outlet for their need to express themselves. Director Des McAnuff envisioned the "Pinball Lads" as junkies, as eager for a fix as they were to reclaim their pinball rankings. Cousin Kevin is humiliated and infuriated by his infirm cousin's stealing his thunder. (Their emotion is also played out in the high-energy choreography.) In *Spring Awakening*, Moritz, who begins "The Bitch of Living," is naïve, misunderstood, shy, and terrified. Melchior is his opposite, blithely self-assured and much better informed. Georg is tingling with suppressed sexual energy. Hänschen can't help but let his show a little, but he does it very quietly. Otto is already embittered, but that hasn't tamed his desires.

General Notes

The score for *Tommy* is notated quite clearly, if somewhat carelessly.[12] Although certain vocal rhythms were not revised to reflect what the singers actually sang, they're reasonably close, and the piano accompaniment is a faithful transcription of the guitar-based feel. Regardless, before trying this song, you should listen first to the original recording by the Who, followed by Elton John's highly mannered movie version, and lastly, the original

---

12. The notation of the piano-vocal score was my responsibility, so I take the blame. In retrospect, for instance, I have no idea why I notated the rhythm of the first line of "Pinball Wizard" all in eighth notes, instead of with an obvious syncopation on "ever since I was a young boy," as it has always been sung.

cast album. The *Spring Awakening* sheet music is reasonably reliable as a representative of the vocals, but the accompaniment bears little resemblance to what is played on the original cast album.

These songs epitomize rock vocalism. If one wanted to explain to a layperson the difference between rock and legit singing, you could sing these songs for them bel canto, focusing on the line and the vowels, and what was missing would be instantly evident: text-driven rhythmicism. The phrase "bitch of living" is a perfect example. Sustaining the short "ih" vowels in these words, for instance, would be unfriendly in legato singing. In rock you won't sustain them, because you wouldn't sustain them in speech. Instead, you favor the consonant sounds so that the words sound natural, and their meaning becomes clear. The notes are still connected—they are not staccato—but rather connected by consonant, phrasing, and acting.

Both songs should remain in or very near their original keys. Their keys and ranges are primary determinants of their sound. "Pinball Wizard" is a high tenor song, arranged for the stage musical to include baritones and women, while "The Bitch of Living" sits deliberately in a conversational midrange.

Your delivery in both songs is mostly "straight ahead," that is to say, without too much obvious emotion; the emotion lies largely in authentic styling. Adopt the rock characters and sing as they do, telling their stories (in "The Bitch of Living," some characters rock less than others, but in *Tommy*, everyone rocks). Deliver the narrative in character, while keeping your individual intention in mind. Rock the storytelling—these are exemplars of text-based vocalism. Sing the words in the groove, making sense of them, with immediate intent. Neither song warrants vibrato or embellishment, expressively or stylistically.

Diction is your best friend. Use enunciation as the vehicle for meaning and to enliven your vocal production. Bite the words, chew them, taste them, using your whole mouth, especially the lips, teeth, and tongue. A great deal of information about character lies in the words—unusual, highly singable words like "Bally Table king" and "the itch you can't control." The airflow propels your vocal mechanism, and your articulation of the words creates just the right amount of resistance. Adjust your placement according to the tessitura. For "Pinball Wizard," keep the diction forward, upward, and into the front teeth to raise your vocal ceiling. This will also protect your larynx from harm. In "The Bitch of Living," bring the sound downward into your lower teeth and jaw, soft palate, and tongue to enrich the lower range.

In the Who's version of "Pinball Wizard," take note of how Daltrey never forces the rhythms—in fact he seems almost rhythmically laid back. Yet his consonants explode into the vowels smack on the beat, and he is always tightly connected to the beat and to the band. Use his approach for both songs to keep your rhythms in the pocket. You needn't be rigid; some stretching of the phrase is absolutely allowable for the sake of meaning. For the most part, however, ride the driving pulsations of the accompaniment with an equally grooving vocal approach.

Specifics
"Pinball Wizard"

You can emulate Daltrey's groove by listening to and connecting with the acoustic guitar part. Listen to the jangle not just as a complete pattern, but as the components that make it operate. Identify the points where your vocal rhythm and the guitar part connect. (See Example 8.)

EXAMPLE 8

Characters in *Tommy* speak and sing in British accents because the story takes place in England. Whereas the location is specific in the original story, "Pinball Wizard" could take place anywhere. In the early 1960s, British singers borrowed American slang and dialects for their vocalism, and later in the 1960s, American pop singers would sometimes feign English accents to sound more cosmopolitan. This cross-pollination frees you from having to sing in a bygone localized accent difficult to accurately capture. A generalized lower-class British accent of the era is also acceptable.

Proper use of diction will, to a great extent, help you reach the high notes. Regardless, the high B on "<u>S</u>ure plays a mean . . ." presents a problem for many singers, who may already be exceeding their comfort zones. One solution is to alter the vowel to whatever the natural explosion of the "sh" consonant is, for you. A "sh" sound is made with the middle of the tongue raised closely to and exploding off the back of the hard palate. To prepare, open your throat as you inhale. Then, on a midrange note, let your tongue and jaw relax as you enunciate the consonant, and see what vowel comes out naturally: "shaw," "shuh," or "sheh," perhaps. Use that vowel on the high B. Open the mouth a bit wider but don't spread the jaw, which will unnecessarily engage the throat. Give the word meaning—semantically, it's an expression of emphasis, so give it specific emphasis, such as envy, wonder, or frustration—and your "sure" will be sufficiently intelligible.

Most singers, including many tenors, will confront a similar problem in reaching the high C and negotiating the subsequent descending scale on "<u>How</u> do you think he does it." To reach the high note, you can use the same method as you did for "Sure," and here the "h" consonant gives you a burst of air to propel you upward. You may need a slight spread to get you over the top, but you can release it immediately. Twang might get you there, too, but might lack the necessary accent on the word. The trickier part is coming down. The resonances you use to grab the higher notes may not work for the lower ones. Try singing "How do you (think . . .)" as "Haahdeeyah," using only the tip of your tongue as an articulator, while keeping the mouth and vowel open, and the jaw slightly tensed on the downbeat only. This will give you the best chance of keeping at least the first three notes in the same vocal register, and on "think" you can close to the "k," and use the engagement of the soft palate to move to a lower register.

"The Bitch of Living"

Admitting one's embarrassing behavior or fantasy as a dream is a common immature evasion, as is ascribing one's behavior or fantasy to someone else to gauge how people might react to it. Assuming for the moment that you are singing the role of Moritz, use an action such as this as you sing the opening verse, as opposed to trying to actively evoke the dream, as the lyric might suggest. This will keep your acting style and vocalism correctly detached, rather than expressing outwardly your feelings. As noted above, the style itself in this song carries much of the emotional meaning, as does the explicitness of the text.

Likewise, sing the choruses as rock choruses, without trying to act out or emotionalize their content. Statements of philosophy though they the chorus lyrics may be, keep the song on the ground. At this moment, the singers are seeking absolution for pleasuring themselves, not spiritual enlightenment.

Many authentic rock songs, including this one, have what appears on the page as incorrect scansion, most obviously, weak syllables placed on a strong beat. In fact, however, when you sing these words with the written rhythms—but with stresses placed according to speech rather than metrical placement—they sound correctly conversational. There are several instances of this in this song, such as "Just the bitch of living as someone you can't stand" (see Example 9). Although they fall on weak beats, "liv-," "some-," and both "can't" and "stand" should all be emphasized, because they are stressed when spoken. Their adjacent syllables on strong beats can be slightly underemphasized, but if you simply use the spoken stresses, this should happen naturally. It may take a bit of practice (other examples in other songs, especially in rap and hip-hop, can be far more complicated to unravel).[13]

EXAMPLE 9

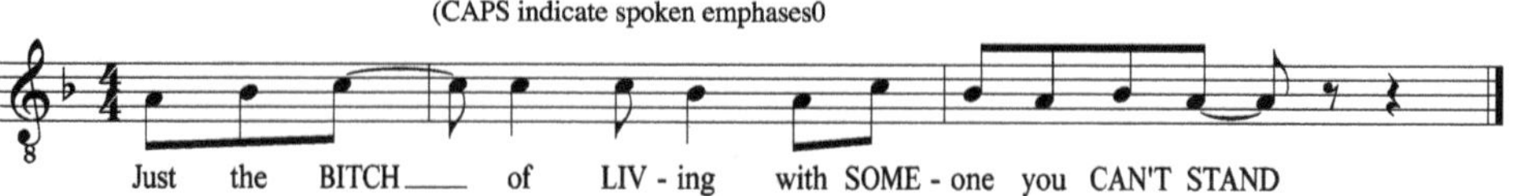

For many characters in the show, this serves as an "I want" song, and their time to state their intention is very brief. Resist the natural urge as a performer to think of your solo time as a moment to shine. It is a moment to introduce yourself, to state your version of your sexual frustration and general dissatisfaction, in the context of and consistent with the style of all the other characters, to form an aesthetically unified and musically effective whole.

Coaching #9: "Plain Jane Fat Ass" and "All Grown Up"

(*Bare: A Pop Opera*, original Conductor-Keyboard 1 score, as licensed by TRW.)

Bare: A Pop Opera is one of a handful of musicals that have gained more attention in recorded form as they have on stage. One reason for this is that they deal with subjects appealing to young adults, and young adults propel the popular music and video marketplaces. *Bare* has higher aspirations than some other shows in its niche, evident in its title (there is a good deal of dialogue in this "opera") and its serious subject matter. It's a tragedy, with vague parallels to *Romeo and Juliet*, a production of which the characters in the story are putting on. The show has had several regional theatre, international, and Off-Broadway productions, and is popular with college and repertory musical theatre groups. These two songs, for contrasting female characters, exhibit divergent approaches to theatre rock, but they also have a lot in common. I pair them because together they clearly demonstrate the apportionment of rock aesthetic and techniques according to character and situation within the same score, and because they're both excellent examples of their kind. "Plain Jane" is a proto-punk-pop rocker, and "All Grown Up" a folk-pop ballad. The harder rock belongs to the sassier, angrier character, Nadia, and the milder rhythm to an innocent in trouble, Ivy. Chances are that if you are cast in this musical, it will be according to physical and vocal "type."

The Songs

"Plain Jane Fat Ass" is a conversational piece sung by the embittered misfit Nadia to her personable, popular twin brother, Jason. She has just been cast as the Nurse in *Romeo and Juliet*

---

13.   There are, of course, other instances where the scansion is patently wrong, and it is left to you as a performer to somehow make the lyric convincing despite the awkwardness in its setting.

at their Catholic boarding school, and she (correctly) attributes her not getting the role of Juliet to her being overweight. In the song, she first sarcastically demeans herself for her obesity, then embraces it as a source of power. Her streak of confidence, though, is short-lived, as the siblings open birthday packages from their father, the contents of which make obvious his preference for Jason over Nadia. Nadia's objective is to gain acceptance, from her parents and from the world, without regard to her outward appearance. The song is a mid-tempo hard rock waltz driven by a syncopated drumbeat and guitar power chords, and by a metrically rhythmic melody. It's in a minor key, with some chromaticism, and a truncated verse-chorus form (AABAABC). "All Grown Up" is a wistful, slow pop-rock aria that evolves into a pounding power pop-rock ballad. It, too, is in a minor key, and also slightly chromatic. The form is a slightly varied verse-chorus, AABABCB. The singer, Ivy, a pretty and popular girl at school, is in love with Jason, who is gay, but has slept with Ivy to keep up appearances, and has impregnated her. (Nadia vilifies Ivy for her good looks and how easily she is able to fit in.) In this song Ivy defends herself to Nadia, admitting her anxiety over her pregnancy. Ivy's objective is to win over Jason, but it is a hopeless cause. There are musically based contours and motives in the melody, but it is the conversational text that creates the somewhat jagged phrases and rhythms, and proscribe the vocal style. As the song continues, the lyric turns from a conversation to a cry for help, supported by a rising tessitura.

The Styles

The 3/4 time hard rock groove of "Plain Jane" is unusual, as are its harmonic twists, and these musical qualities suit well the character of an offbeat outsider. The melody stays right with the groove, and helps it along. Still, it is quite melodic, in that it is very structured, almost classical, somewhat reminiscent of Richard Rodgers in its simplicity and mild eccentricity. By contrast, the lyrics are glib and barbed. The electricity of the accompanying guitar and the unsettled drum feel help to characterize Nadia's resentment, and her fortitude. When the drums go away late in the song, she is left vulnerable. The song is more prog-rock than blues-rock, though there are vestiges of the blues in the sound, and thereby in the vocalism. "All Grown Up," too, harkens back to the blues, in its subject matter, and in the freedom of its vocalism built on a melody made up of simple parallel phrases. Its harmonies are somewhat classical, but its melody is most decidedly pop (you might catch a whiff of Janis Ian's timeless "Society's Child" or "At Seventeen"). The classicism builds through the form to rock grandiosity. Most of the lyric is very direct, more like sung dialogue than song lyrics, but there is a definite hook.

The Coaching

Context

Bare: A Pop Opera belongs to what has blossomed into its own sub-genre of rock musicals, "teen angst" musicals, as some critics have dubbed them. They concern teenagers and young adults in serious crises, such as broken homes, mental illness, drug addiction, sexual discrimination, bullying and shaming, and so on. One might say that *Hair* opened the door for *Tommy, Tommy* opened the door for *Rent, Rent* for *Bare*, and *Bare* for *Spring Awakening*. Since then there have been *Next to Normal, Heathers, Fun Home*, and many more. Their scores, and *Bare's* especially, fall well within the rock continuum, and these two songs speak beautifully to their angst-ridden characters and subject matter, in their style and musical content.

Characterization

Nadia and Ivy are opposites, but they share strong feelings of alienation. Nadia is accustomed to it, but for Ivy it's new. Nadia keeps others at arm's length by being caustic, but in "Plain Jane" she clearly wants to be recognized for her talents, and not put down for her looks. Ivy's usual defenses are down when she sings "All Grown Up," an ironic title, for Ivy is clearly regressing as a result of her fear of giving birth. She's fallen for the wrong guy, she's gotten herself pregnant, and she's terrified at the consequences. Her intention is to get help, and for this moment, she sees Nadia's sympathy as the help she needs.

General Notes

Both songs play out (as the show's title promises) like opera scenes or operatically based musical theatre scenes, and include material beyond the main intention of one certain character. Only portions of these songs will work out of context, and they make much better sense in full form.

Each song moves from the conversational to the lyrical in its own way. When performing either of them, sing the conversational sections (the verses) in your own naturalistic sound that rocks only to the extent that the character is a rock character—therefore Nadia more than Ivy. In the brief chorus of "All Grown Up," rock is your means of conveyance for Ivy's utter hopelessness. Nadia, too, straddles the stylistic boundary. In the hook of "Plain Jane" the melody and harmony are at first too tonal and childlike to rock vocally any harder than they already do (by virtue of the intense groove), but the harmony goes sour in the consequent phrase to each statement of the title, and you can use that change of tone to dig in harder to those phrases.

Specifics
"Plain Jane"

The singsong quality of the melody is a reminder that Nadia is still a peevish kid, mostly because she's been mistreated. She has a good heart, and like many goodhearted but misunderstood people, rather than lashing out, she turns her anger on herself. The inward lashes are vicious, and unrelenting in the opening lines. Because of this, try to vary their actions. Use quick "internal scene changes" to provide color and humor: as an example, sing the first two lines as a rock singer fronting a band ("I know a girl full of confidence . . ."), then switch to a drinking contest ("She'll have your piece of pie . . ."), then to the bathroom stall at a club ("There's a thin girl inside . . ."). (You'll note I'm keeping these suggested mini-scenarios in rock-related contexts, but the specific choices are up to you.) Entertainment value and wit will help you overcome Nadia's abrasiveness.

Make the most of the dips in register on the lyrics ". . . there's fat, then there's Jane" and "shit them for lunch." In the first phrase you can use the low register and a darkened timbre to mock your mother's voice, and in the second, use it to pose a vocal threat to anyone standing in your way.

Take pride in "eat[ing] Jenny Craig whole," and especially in "keeping society so ill at ease." It's that antiestablishment, subversive spirit and sense of humor that motivate you to speak out in the second verse. Ramp up your vocal energy as you move through the first chorus, and stay energized through the dialogue.

As you reach the end of the second chorus, you deflate, reacting to the prospect of opening the birthday gifts, and the heartbreak you predict. The rock vocalism and attitude dissipate.

Changing from a hard rock vocalism to a folk vocalism in the coda will maintain Nadia's detached rock-based identity while conveying her very human, sympathetic disappointment. Don't let her stray from the correct aesthetic territory, and don't bow to legit musical theatre tendencies of legato and vibrato in this last, dialogic section of music.

"All Grown Up"

Direct the entire song to Nadia, and play off her reactions to each of your actions. She will be hard to get through to, as your initial standpoints are so polarized. Your continual attempts to reach her will give the song shape over time, and prevent you from conveying too much self-indulgence, a trait already built into the lyric.

Adhering precisely to written rhythms or to exact metronomic beats and subdivisions will make most lines of the song feel stilted and untruthful. Because the lyrics are so speech-like, use the text instead to shape the melodic rhythm. The notated rhythms are a good guide, but you have a good deal of freedom in how you push and pull within phrases, and how you move phrases forward or backward within the metrical phrase structure.

Your actions are relatively clear in this very direct lyric. You have no ulterior motives, and you reveal your inner conflict through the song. The biggest danger is earnestness, especially when you take liberty with the phrasing. Be careful not to over-sentimentalize the already sentimental passages of music and lyrics; they can easily turn into melodrama.

The second A section borders on a different kind of earnestness, as if a teenager had written what she thought was a profound poem. Counteract any awkwardness in these lines by continuing to deliver them actively to Nadia. You are seeking common ground with her, rather than spouting clichés. Make the lyric "Feel it, how it grows inside me" active, rather than reflective, by imploring Nadia to share in the actual physical sensations of your condition.

Ride the change in tessitura to the emotional summit, and find a vocal register that can sustain the intensity of the final two choruses without straining your voice. (Transpose the song if necessary.) Look first to the text and its enunciation for continued support in the high range, and once again, project your lines outward, focused on Nadia. Keep the airflow strong and uninterrupted. Demand answers to your questions rather than wallowing in the despondency they imply. As a rocker, always remain active.

Rock Songs for Musical Theatre Singers

The following is a chronological list of songs from the rock literature (200 songs, in keeping with the Billboard charts) that musical theatre singers might use for practice, auditions, or live performance. It includes many of the titles mentioned earlier in the book, and adds several other suggestions. (The songs analyzed in chapter 6 are not listed here.) Use these suggestions as a starting point for additional research on other songs to add to your repertoire. Songs are listed by title, with their primary recording artists, years of commercial release, and the names of the songwriters. Some of these would make excellent audition songs for rock musicals, and many can easily be cut down or rearranged to suit your needs. They range from very simple to highly complex, both in content and in learning curve.

Please review the guidelines at the beginning of Part III when choosing material. Some material may not be suitable for certain performers. Please note that certain songs may be inappropriate for younger performers, due to objectionable subject matter or explicit language. Also, by virtue of their place in history, some of these songs are also quite sexist, especially by today's standards. (Of course, the same can be said of the entire popular artistic output of the last century, including film, television, and the theatre, right up until the present day.)

1950s

"Hound Dog," Willie Mae "Big Mama" Thornton, 1952 (Jerry Leiber and Mike Stoller)
"Money Honey," the Drifters, 1953 (Jesse Stone)
"Shake, Rattle, and Roll," Big Joe Turner, 1954 (Charles E. Calhoun, aka Jesse Stone)

"Folsom Prison Blues," Johnny Cash, 1955 (Johnny Cash)

"You Send Me," Sam Cooke, 1957 (Sam Cooke)

"Jailhouse Rock," Elvis Presley, 1957 (Jerry Leiber and Mike Stoller)

"Summertime Blues," Eddie Cochran, 1958 (Eddie Cochran and Jerry Capehart)

"C'mon Everybody," Eddie Cochran, 1958 (Eddie Cochran and Jerry Capehart)

"Teenager in Love," Dion and the Belmonts, 1959 (Doc Pomus and Mort Shuman)

"Love Potion #9," the Clovers, 1959 (Jerry Leiber and Mike Stoller)

1960s

"Only the Lonely," Roy Orbison, 1960 (Roy Orbison and Joe Melson)

"Runaway," Del Shannon, 1961 (Del Shannon and Max Crook)

"Power and the Glory," Phil Ochs, 1964 (Phil Ochs)

"Downtown," Petula Clark, 1964 (Tony Hatch)

"You've Lost That Lovin' Feeling," the Righteous Brothers, 1964 (Phil Spector, Barry Mann, and Cynthia Weil)

"A Change Is Gonna Come," Sam Cooke, 1964 (Sam Cooke)

"House of the Rising Sun," the Animals, 1964 (Unknown)

"People Get Ready," the Impressions, 1965 (Curtis Mayfield)

"The Night Before," the Beatles, 1965 (John Lennon and Paul McCartney)

"My Generation," the Who, 1965 (Pete Townshend)

"I Got You (I Feel Good)," James Brown, 1965 (James Brown)

"Nowhere Man," the Beatles, 1965 (John Lennon and Paul McCartney)

"When a Man Loves a Woman," Percy Sledge, 1966 (Calvin Lewis and Andrew Wright)

"You Don't Have to Say You Love Me," Dusty Springfield, 1966 (Vicki Wickham, Simon Napier-Bell, Pino Donaggio, and Vito Pallavicini)

"Mother's Little Helper," the Rolling Stones, 1966 (Mick Jagger and Keith Richards)

"Ain't Too Proud to Beg," the Temptations, 1966 (Norman Whitfield and Eddie Holland)

"God Only Knows," the Beach Boys, 1966 (Brian Wilson and Tony Asher)

"Eleanor Rigby," the Beatles, 1966 (John Lennon and Paul McCartney)

"I'm a Believer," the Monkees, 1966 (Neil Diamond)

"I Think We're Alone Now," Tommy James and the Shondells, 1967 (Ritchie Cordell)

"Brown-Eyed Girl," Van Morrison, 1967 (Van Morrison)

"New York Mining Disaster 1941," the Bee Gees, 1967 (Barry Gibb and Robin Gibb)

"She's Leaving Home," the Beatles, 1967 (John Lennon and Paul McCartney)

"With a Little Help from My Friends," the Beatles, 1967 (John Lennon and Paul McCartney)

"Get Together," the Youngbloods, 1967 (Chet Powers)

"(Your Love Keeps Lifting Me) Higher and Higher," Jackie Wilson, 1967 (Gary Jackson and Carl Smith)

"How Can I Be Sure," the Young Rascals, 1967 (Felix Cavaliere and Eddie Brigati)

"To Sir, with Love," Lulu, 1967 (Don Black and Mark London)

"Piece of My Heart," Erma Franklin, 1967 (Jerry Ragovoy and Bert Berns)

"Nights in White Satin," the Moody Blues, 1967 (Justin Hayward)

"Chain of Fools," Aretha Franklin, 1967 (Don Covay)

"Born to Be Wild," Steppenwolf, 1968 (Mars Bonfire)

"MacArthur Park," Richard Harris, 1968 (Jimmy Webb)

"Sympathy for the Devil," the Rolling Stones, 1968 (Mick Jagger and Keith Richards)

"I Heard It Through the Grapevine," Marvin Gaye, 1968 (Norman Whitfield and Barrett Strong)

"I Started a Joke," the Bee Gees, 1968 (Barry Gibb, Robin Gibb, and Maurice Gibb)

"Both Sides, Now," Joni Mitchell, 1969 ((Joni Mitchell)

"Sensation," the Who, 1969 (Pete Townshend)

"Space Oddity," David Bowie, 1969 (David Bowie)

"Delta Lady," Joe Cocker, 1969 (Leon Russell)

"Superstar," Delaney and Bonnie, 1969 (Bonnie Bramlett and Leon Russell)

"Bridge over Troubled Water," Simon and Garfunkel, 1970 (Paul Simon)

1970s

"Maybe I'm Amazed," Paul McCartney, 1970 (Paul McCartney)

"Ohio," Crosby, Stills, Nash, and Young, 1970 (Neil Young)

"Without You," Badfinger (also Harry Nilsson, Mariah Carey), 1970 (Pete Ham and Tom Evans)

"Midnight Rider," the Allman Brothers Band, 1971 (Gregg Allman and Robert Kim Payne)

"Black Dog," Led Zeppelin, 1971 (John Paul Jones, Jimmy Page, and Robert Plant)

"Alone Again (Naturally)," Gilbert O'Sullivan, 1972 (Gilbert O'Sullivan)

"Rocket Man," Elton John, 1972 (Elton John and Bernie Taupin)

"Tumbling Dice," the Rolling Stones, 1972 (Mick Jagger and Keith Richards)

"Lean on Me," Bill Withers, 1972 (Bill Withers)

"Take It Easy," the Eagles, 1972 (Jackson Browne and Glenn Frey)

"Rocky Mountain High," John Denver, 1972 (John Denver and Mike Taylor)

"Your Mama Don't Dance," Loggins and Messina, 1972 (Kenny Loggins and Jim Messina)

"No More Mr. Nice Guy," Alice Cooper, 1973 (Alice Cooper and Michael Bruce)

"Love Me Like a Rock," Paul Simon, 1973 (Paul Simon)

"Living for the City," Stevie Wonder, 1973 (Stevie Wonder)

"Jolene," Dolly Parton, 1973 (Dolly Parton)

"Get Up, Stand Up," Bob Marley and the Wailers, 1973 (Bob Marley and Peter Tosh)

"Until You Come Back to Me (That's What I'm Gonna Do)," Aretha Franklin, 1973 (Morris Broadnax, Clarence O. Paul, and Stevie Wonder)

"Feel Like Makin' Love," Roberta Flack, 1974 (Eugene McDaniels)

"Shiver Me Timbers," Tom Waits, 1974 (Tom Waits)

"Young Americans," David Bowie, 1975 (David Bowie)

"Fight the Power," the Isley Brothers, 1975 (Rudolph Isley, O'Kelly Isley Jr., Ronald Isley, Ernie Isley, Marvin Isley, and Chris Jasper)

"Born to Run," Bruce Springsteen, 1975 (Bruce Springsteen)

"Walk This Way," Aerosmith (later with Run-D.M.C.), 1975 (Steven Tyler and Joe Perry)

"Warm Ways," Fleetwood Mac, 1975 (Christine McVie)

"Hurricane," Bob Dylan, 1975 (Bob Dylan and Jacques Levy)

"Let Your Love Flow," the Bellamy Brothers, 1976 (Larry E. Williams)

"2112," Rush, 1976 (Neil Peart, Geddy Lee, and Alex Lifeson)

"New York State of Mind," Billy Joel, 1976 (Billy Joel)

"Weekend in New England," Barry Manilow, 1976 (Randy Edelman)

"God Save the Queen," Sex Pistols, 1977 (Glen Matlock, John Lydon, Paul Thomas Cook, and Stephen Philip Jones)

"Barracuda," Heart, 1977 (Ann Wilson, Nancy Wilson, Michael Derosier, and Roger Fisher)

"(The Angels Wanna Wear My) Red Shoes," Elvis Costello, 1978 (Elvis Costello)

"So Lonely," the Police, 1978 (Sting)

"What a Fool Believes," the Doobie Brothers, 1979 (Michael McDonald and Kenny Loggins)

"Do That to Me One More Time," Captain & Tennille, 1979 (Toni Tennille)

1980s

"She's out of My Life," Michael Jackson, 1980 (Tony Bahler)

"Back in Black," AC/DC, 1980 (Angus Young, Malcolm Young, and Brian Johnson)

"That's the Joint," Funky 4+1, 1980 (Clifton "Jiggs" Chase, Sylvia Robinson, Keith Caesar, Sharon Green, Jeffrey Myree, Kevin Smith, and Rodney Stone)

"Crosseyed and Painless," Talking Heads, 1980 (David Byrne, Brian Eno, Chris Frantz, Jerry Harrison, and Tina Weymouth)

"Dancing with Myself," Billy Idol, 980 (Billy Idol and Tony James)

"Just the Two of Us," Grover Washington Jr. & Bill Withers, 1981 (Bill Withers, Ralph MacDonald, and William Salter)

"Physical," Olivia Newton-John, 1981 (Steve Kipner and Terry Shaddick)

"One of Us," ABBA, 1981 (Benny Andersson and Björn Ulvaeus)

"Juke Box Hero," Foreigner, 1982 (Lou Gramm and Mick Jones)

"Rock the Casbah," the Clash, 1982 (the Clash)

"Eye of the Tiger," Survivor, 1982 (Frankie Sullivan and Jim Peterik)

"Live Wire," Mötley Crüe, 1982 (Nikki Sixx)

"1999," Prince, 1982 (Prince)

"It's Raining Men," the Weather Girls, 1982 (Paul Jabara and Paul Shaffer)
"Here I Go Again," Whitesnake, 1982 (David Coverdale and Bernie Marsden)
"Faithfully," Journey, 1983 (Jonathan Cain)
"Hello," Lionel Richie, 1984 (Lionel Richie)
"Wake Me Up before You Go-Go," Wham!, 1984 (George Michael)
"I Want to Know What Love Is," Foreigner, 1984 (Mick Jones)
"Walking on Sunshine," Katrina and the Waves, 1985 (Kimberley Rew)
"Take on Me," A-ha, 1985 (Magne Furuholmen, Morteln Haket, and Pål Waaktaar)
"Back in the High Life Again," Stevie Winwood, 1986 (Stevie Winwood and Will Hennings)
"Papa Don't Preach," Madonna, 1986 (Brian Elliot and Madonna)
"Livin' on a Prayer," Bon Jovi, 1986 (Jon Bon Jovi, Richie Sambora, and Desmond Child)
"I Wanna Dance with Somebody (Who Loves Me)," Whitney Houston, 1987 (George Merrill and Shannon Rubicam)
"Never Tear Us Apart," INXS, 1987 (Andrew Farriss and Michael Hutchence)
"Gangsta Gangsta," N.W.A., 1988 (Ice Cube, MC Ren, the D.O.C, and Benjamin Lax)
"I'll Be There for You," Bon Jovi, 1989 (Jon Bon Jovi and Richie Sambora)
"Shotgun down the Avalanche," Shawn Colvin, 1989 (Shawn Colvin and John Leventhal)
"Roam," The B-52s, 1989 (Kate Pierson, Fred Schneider, Keith Strickland, Robert Waldrop, and Cindy Wilson)

1990s

"Poison," Bel Biv DeVoe, 1990 (Elliot Straite)
"Unbelievable," EMF, 1990 (EMF)
"Wicked Game," Chris Isaak, 1990 (Chris Isaak)
"Losing My Religion," R.E.M., 1991 (Bill Berry, Peter Buck, Mike Mills, and Michael Stipe)
"More than Words," Extreme, 1991 (Gary Cherone and Nuno Bettencourt)
"(Everything I Do) I Do It for You," Bryan Adams, 1991 (Bryan Adams, Michael Kamen, and Robert "Mutt" Lange)
"Smells Like Teen Spirit," Nirvana, 1991 (Kurt Cobain, Krist Novoselic, and Dave Grohl)
"Silent All These Years," Tori Amos, 1991 (Tori Amos)
"Under the Bridge," Red Hot Chili Peppers, 1992 (Anthony Fields, Flea, John Frusciante, and Chad Smith)
"Killing in the Name," Rage against the Machine, 1992 (Tom Commerford, Zack de la Rocha, Tom Morello, and Brad Wilk)
"Holler If Ya Hear Me," 2Pac, 1993 (Tupac Shakur)
"Walking in My Shoes," Depeche Mode, 1993 (Martin Gore)
"What's Up," 4 Non-Blondes, 1993 (Linda Perry)

"Elsewhere," Sarah McLachlan, 1993 (Sarah McLachlan)

"You Gotta Be," Des'ree, 1994 (Des'ree and Ashley Ingram)

"West End Girls," Pet Shop Boys, 1994 (Neil Tennant and Chris Lowe)

"Welcome to Paradise," Green Day, 1994 (Billie Joe Armstrong, Mike Dirnt, and Tré Cool)

"One of Us," Joan Osborne, 1995 (Eric Bazilian)

"Dreaming of You," Selena Gomez, 1995 (Franne Gold and Tom Snow)

"Roll to Me," Del Amitri, 1995 (Justin Currie)

"Fu-Gee-La," Fugees, 1996 (Wyclef Jean, Samuel Michel, Lauryn Hill, Allen McGrier, Teena Marie, and Salaam Remi)

"Salvation," the Cranberries, 1996 (Dolores O'Riordan and Noel Hogan)

"Wannabe," Spice Girls, 1996 (Spice Girls, Matt Rowe, and Richard Stannard)

"Semi-Charmed Life," Third Eye Blind, 1997 (Stephan Jenkins)

"Truly Madly Deeply," Savage Garden, 1997 (Darren Hayes and Daniel Jones)

"Get out the Map," Indigo Girls, 1997 (Emily Saliers)

"The Difference," the Wallflowers, 1997 (Jakob Dylan)

"Believe," Cher, 1998 (Brian Higgins, Stuart Mclennen, Paul Barry, Steven Torch, Matthew Gray, and Timothy Powell)

"La Vida Loca," Ricky Martin, 1999 (Robi Rosa, Desmond Child, and Luis Gomez Escolar)

"I Want It That Way," Backstreet Boys, 1999 (Andreas Carlsson and Max Martin)

"Without You I'm Nothing," Placebo, 1999 (Steve Hewitt, Brian Molko, and Stefan Olsdal)

2000s

"Lucky," Britney Spears, 2000 (Max Martin, Rami, and Alexander Kronlund)

"Superman (It's Not Easy)," Five for Fighting, 2000 (John Ondrasik)

"Drops of Jupiter," Train, 2001 (Patrick Monahan)

"Independent Women," Destiny's Child, 2001 (Beyoncé Knowles, Cory Rooney, Samuel Barnes, and Jean-Claude Olivier)

"Wherever You Will Go," the Calling, 2001 (Aaron Kamin and Alex Band)

"I'm with You," Avril Lavigne, 2002 (Avril Lavigne, Lauren Christy, Scott Spock, and Graham Edwards)

"Yeah!," Usher, 2004 (Christopher Bridges, James Phillips, Jonathan Smith, LaMarquis Jefferson, Patrick Smith, and Sean Garrett)

"Chandelier," Sia, 2004 (Sia Furler and Jesse Shatkin)

"All Lifestyles," the Beastie Boys, 2004 (Adam Horovitz, Adam Nathaniel Yauch, and Michael Louis Diamond)

"Rich Man's War," Steve Earle, 2004 (Steve Earle)

"Suddenly I See," KT Tunstall, 2005 (KT Tunstall)

"Speeding Cars," Imogen Heap, 2006 (Imogen Heap)

"Hotel Song," Regina Spektor, 2006 (Regina Spektor)

"Supermassive Black Hole," Muse, 2006 (Matt Bellamy)

"A Place in This World," Taylor Swift, 2006 (Robert Orrall and Taylor Swift)

"The Great Escape," Boys Like Girls, 2007 (Martin Johnson, Sam Hollander, and Dave Katz)

"Party Like a Rockstar," Shop Boyz, 2007 (Demetrius "Meany" Hardin, Rasheed "Sheed" Hightower, Jason Vories Stephens, Richard "Fat" Stephens, Brian D. Ward, and William Whedbee)

"Say (All I Need)," One Republic, 2008 (Ryan Tedder, Zach Filkins, Drew Brown, Eddie Fisher, and Brent Kutzle)

"Viva la Vida," Coldplay, 2008 (Guy Berryman, Jonny Buckland, Will Champion, and Chris Martin)

"Gives You Hell," the All-American Rejects, 2008 (Nick Wheeler and Tyson Ritter)

"Party in the U.S.A," Miley Cyrus, 2009 (Lukasz Gottwald, Jessica Cornish, and Claude Kelly)

2010s

"Turn on the Radio," Reba McEntire, 2010 (Cherie Oakley, Mark Oakley, and J. P Twang)

"Raise Your Glass," Pink, 2010 (Pink, Max Martin, and Johan Schuster)

"Firework," Katy Perry, 2010 (Katy Perry, Mikkel S. Eriksen, Tor Erik Hermansen, Sandy Wilhelm, and Ester Dean)

"What Doesn't Kill You (Stronger)," Kelly Clarkson, 2012 (Jörgen Elofsson, David Gamson, Greg Kurstin, and Ali Tamposi)

"She's So Mean," Matchbox Twenty, 2012 (Rob Thomas, Kyle Cook, and Paul Doucette)

"Brave," Sara Bareilles, 2013 (Sara Bareilles and Jack Antonoff)

"Bailando," Enrique Iglesias, 2014 (Enrique Iglesias, December Bueno, Alexander Delgado, Randy Malcolm Martinez, and Sean Paul)

"Give Me Back My Hometown," Eric Church, 2014 (Eric Church and Luke Laird)

"Pretty Hurts," Beyoncé, 2014 (Sia Furler, Joshua "Ammo" Coleman, Beyoncé Knowles, and Julio Ramos)

"Making the Most of the Night," Carly Rae Jepsen, 2015 (Sia Furler, Samuel Dixon, Emre Ramazanoglu, Danielle Haim, Alana Haim, Este Haim, and Carly Rae Jepsen)

"Dangerous Woman," Ariana Grande, 2016 (Johan Carlsson, Ross Golan, and Max Martin)

"Ride," Twenty One Pilots, 2016 (Tyler Joseph)

"Dance with the Devil," Katy Perry, 2017 (Katy Perry, Felix Snow, and Sarah Hudson)

"Caught in the Middle," the Temperance Movement, 2018 (Phil Campbell, Paul Sayer, Matt White, Nick Fyffe, and Simon Lea)

"Eastside," Benny Blanco, Halsey, & Khalid, 2018 (Benny Blanco, Ashley "Halsey" Frangipane, Nathan Perez, Khalid Robinson, and Ed Sheeran)

If You Play Piano

"Colour My World," Chicago, 1970 (James Panko)

"Border Song," Elton John, 1970 (Elton John and Bernie Taupin)

"Imagine," John Lennon, 1971 (John Lennon)

"She's Always a Woman," Billy Joel, 1977 (Billy Joel)

"Someone Like You," Adele, 2011 (Adele Adkins and Dan Wilson)

If You Play Guitar

"Blowin' in the Wind," Bob Dylan, 1963 (Bob Dylan)

"Jane Says," Jane's Addiction, 1988 (Eric Avery and Perry Farrell)

"Mr. Jones," Counting Crows, 1993 (David Bryson, Adam Duritz, Charlie Gillingham, Matt Malley, Ben Mize, and Dan Vickrey)

"I'm Yours," Jason Mraz, 2008 (Jason Mraz)

"Radioactive," Imagine Dragons, 2012 (Alexander Grant, Ben McKee, Josh Mosser, Daniel Platzman, Dan Reynolds, and Wayne Sermon)

Duets

"Ain't No Mountain High Enough," Marvin Gaye and Tammi Terrell, 1967 (Nickolas Ashford and Valerie Simpson)

"Stop Draggin' My Heart Around," Stevie Nicks & Tommy Petty and the Heartbreakers, 1981 (Tom Petty and Mike Campbell)

"I Knew You Were Waiting (for Me)," Aretha Franklin and George Michael, 1987 (Simon Climie and Dennis Morgan)

"Close My Eyes Forever," Lita Ford and Ozzy Osbourne, 1989 (Lita Ford and Ozzy Osbourne)

"Hate That I Love You," Rihanna featuring Ne-Yo, 2007 (S. Smith, Tor Erik Hermansen, and Mikkel S. Eriksen)

Bibliography and Suggested Additional Reading

BOOKS ABOUT SINGING

Anders, Susan, and Tom Manche. *Singing Live: The Performing Skills Guidebook for Contemporary Singers.* Nashville: Zanna Discs, 2012.

Baxter, Mark. *The Rock 'n' Roll Singer's Survival Manual.* Milwaukee: Hal Leonard, 1992.

Borch Zangger, Daniel. *Ultimate Vocal Voyage: The Definitive Method for Unleashing the Rock, Pop, or Soul Singer within You.* Milwaukee: Hal Leonard, 2008.

Danz, Teri. *Vocal Essentials for the Pop Singer: Take Your Singing from Good to Great.* Milwaukee: Hal Leonard, 2011.

Edwards, Matthew. *So You Want to Sing Rock 'n' Roll: A Guide for Professionals.* Lanham, MD: Rowman and Littlefield, 2014.

Martin, Bill. *Pro Secrets of Heavy Rock Singing.* London: Sanctuary Publishing, 2002.

Peckham, Anne. *The Contemporary Singer: Elements of Vocal Technique.* Boston: Berklee Press Publications, 2000.

Peckham, Anne. *Vocal Workouts for the Contemporary Singer.* Boston: Berklee Press Publications, 2008.

Reed, Bill. *The Last Musical Hurrah: Jazz and Pop Singing and the Onslaught of Rock.* Los Angeles: Cellar Door Books, 2016.

Sanders, Sheri. *Rock the Audition: How to Prepare for and Get Cast in Rock Musicals.* Milwaukee: Hal Leonard, 2011.

Soto-Morettini, Donna. *Popular Singing and Style.* London: Bloomsbury, 2014.

BOOKS ABOUT ROCK IN THE MUSICAL THEATRE

Miller, Scott. *Sex, Drugs, Rock & Roll, and Musicals.* Boston: Northeastern University Press, 2011.

Viertel, Jack. *The Secret Life of the American Musical.* New York: Sarah Crichton Books, 2016.

Wollman, Elizabeth Lara. *The Theater Will Rock: A History of the Rock Musical, from Hair to Hedwig.* Ann Arbor, MI: University of Michigan Press, 2006.

BOOKS ABOUT ROCK MUSIC

Buck, Kevin W. *A Concise History of Rock 'n' Roll.* Glen Rock, PA: Year of the Book, 2018.

Byrne, David. *How Music Works.* New York: Three Rivers Press, 2017.

Cateforis, Theo, ed. *The Rock History Reader*. New York: Taylor and Francis, 2013.

Covach, John and Andrew Flory. *What's That Sound?: An Introduction to Rock and Its History*. New York: Norton, 2018.

DeCurtis, Anthony, James Henke, Holly George-Warren, and Jim Miller, eds. *The Rolling Stone Illustrated History of Rock and Roll: The Definitive History of the Most Important Artists and Their Music*. New York: Straight Arrow Publishers, 1992.

Friedlander, Paul. *Rock and Roll: A Social History*. Boulder, CO: Westview Press, 1996.

Garofalo, ReeBee, and Steve Waksman. *Rockin' Out: Popular Music in the U.S.A.* New York: Pearson, 2017.

Gass, Glenn. *A History of Rock Music: The Rock 'n' Roll Era*. Bloomington: Indiana University Press, 2017.

Hall, Mitchell K. *The Emergence of Rock and Roll: Music and the Rise of American Youth Culture*. Critical Moments in American History. New York: Routledge, 2014.

Hepworth, David. *Never a Dull Moment: 1971 The Year That Rock Exploded*. New York: Henry Holt and Company, 2016.

Hepworth, David. *Uncommon People: The Rise and Fall of the Rock Stars*. New York: Henry Holt and Company, 2017.

Kallen, Stuart A. *The History of Rock and Roll*. The Music Library. Detroit: Lucent Books, 2012.

Majewski, Lori. *Mad World: An Oral History of New Wave Artists and Songs That Defined the 1980s*. New York: Abrams, 2014.

Meyers, Marc. *Anatomy of a Song: The Oral History of 45 Iconic Hits That Changed Rock, R&B, and Pop*. New York: Grove Press, 2016.

Reese, Eric. *The History of Hip Hop: "Hip Hop Truth, for the Art and Pulse of America!"* Self-published, 2017.

Shirley, David. *The History of Rock and Roll*. New York: Franklin Watts, 1997.

Starr, Larry, and Christopher Waterman. *American Popular Music: From Minstrelsy to MP3*. New York: Oxford University Press, 2017.

Steussy, Joe, and Scott D. Lipscomb. *Rock and Roll: Its History and Stylistic Development*. Upper Saddle River, NJ: Prentice Hall, 1999.

Index

CPSIA information can be obtained
at www.ICGtesting.com
Printed in the USA
BVHW091918260323
661138BV00006B/44